The Burden of Confederate Diplomacy

The Burden of
Confederate
Diplomacy

Charles M. Hubbard

The University of Tennessee Press / Knoxville

Library of Congress Cataloging-in-Publication Data

Hubbard, Charles M., 1939–
The burden of Confederate diplomacy / Charles M. Hubbard. — 1st ed.
        p.   cm.
Includes bibliographical references and index.
ISBN 1-57233-002-3 (cloth: alk. paper)
1. Confederate States of America—Foreign relations.   I. Title.
E488.H83 1998
973.7'21—dc21   97-21172

This book is lovingly dedicated to my wife, Sherry, and our children, Chuck and Caroline.

Contents

Illustrations

Preface

Writing a one-volume synthesis and reevaluation of Confederate diplomacy within a manageable number of pages imposes the burden of selectivity. Accordingly, I have chosen to focus on those major events that best relate the story of Confederate diplomacy from the point of view of the Southern operatives and policymakers involved. I concentrate on the pursuit of recognition in Europe and the negotiations between the Union and the Confederate states. Throughout the war, Southern diplomats engaged in a wide range of activities, including naval construction, blockade running, munitions purchasing, and intelligence gathering. While I discuss some of these activities, I do not give them extensive attention, preferring to focus on the major Confederate goal of creating an independent nation.

Confederate diplomacy includes the negotiations between the quasi-Confederate State Department and the old Union. While historians have not ignored these efforts, they have not been integrated into a comprehensive narrative of Confederate diplomacy. The negotiating team sent to Washington before the outbreak of hostilities, as well as the men who conducted negotiations with the Union throughout the war, should be defined as diplomats, even though they served on the North American side of the Atlantic.

Throughout this study, I have drawn liberally from the existing literature. The conclusions, based on original sources, often differ from the generally accepted consensus. My objective is to provide a narrative that emphasizes the burdens and frustrating problems that confronted Confederate diplomats, both at home and abroad. The burdensome commitment to slavery, King Cotton, and other ideological values overwhelmed an inefficient and inexperienced group of Confederate operatives. I have identified opportunities that were either misunderstood, overlooked, or mishandled. Moreover, the inconsistency between a liberal ideology that included free trade, personal liberty, and independence, while demanding the continuance of slavery in a class-conscious society committed to protecting a plantation economy, proved too much for the Southern diplomats to reconcile in the minds of the most powerful Europeans.

Examining the diplomatic objectives, strategies, and individuals selected to represent the Confederate government, enables one, I believe, to understand the objectives and values of the Southern elite and the environment it sought to maintain. The reactionary ideas that Southern Americans went to war to protect are identifiable throughout the diplomatic instructions and correspondence. A careful examination of these sources is invaluable to understanding the failed experiment to create a slaveholders republic.

No sooner had the war ended than historians and commentators began to explore Civil War diplomacy. The result is a large body of literature that includes contemporary accounts, as well as a number of monographs addressing specific subjects. Several historians have written about various aspects of the Confederate diplomatic effort while focusing on the United States foreign policy. Brian Jenkins, Norman Ferris, and Howard Jones have made important contributions to the study of Confederate diplomacy, but their interest in the Confederates remains peripheral to the main focus of their work. A number of monographs have been written on specific subjects related to Confederate diplomacy. For example, Frank Merli's *Great Britain and the Confederate Navy* is a well-researched examination of Confederate naval construction. Other important, and tightly argued works focusing on Confederate diplomatic activity include Douglas Ball's *Financial Failure and Confederate Defeat* and D. P. Crook's *The North, the South and the Powers*. However, with the exception of Frank Owsley's *King Cotton Diplomacy*, first published in 1931, there is no study that concentrates on Confederate diplomatic initiatives or attempts to synthesize the material from the Southern perspective.[1]

The clandestine activities of Confederate operatives in Europe, primarily related to Confederate naval construction and financing, were important to the Confederate cause. However, even if they had been more successful, they could not have saved the Confederacy. Beyond the battlefields of America, the only hope for Confederate victory depended on the success of Confederate diplomacy.

Recognition of the Confederacy by the powers of Europe probably would have changed the outcome of the war. It is important, therefore, to ask and answer the crucial question: Why did the Confederate diplomats fail? The answer is complex and, of course, depends on one's interpretation of historical facts. The answer, in part, is in the burdensome inconsistencies that plagued most aspects of Confederate policy and in the absence of a well-conceived diplomatic strategy. While the Confederate dream was ultimately lost on the battlefield, the failure of Southern diplomats to either negotiate separation from the Union or achieve international recognition substantially contributed to the collapse of the Confederacy.

Without the assistance and encouragement of many friends, colleagues, and teachers, this eight-year undertaking would never have been completed. I owe a special debt of gratitude to Russell Buhite, whose patient encouragement and warm friendship throughout the process was unwavering. Norman Ferris, who first introduced me to Civil War diplomacy, made the results of his many years of research available with more than a professional interest. Paul Bergeron encouraged my studies by patiently listening to my ramblings and then returning my focus to the sources. LaVerne Neal diligently typed the manuscript and faithfully made all the editorial corrections. Finally, words cannot express my appreciation to my wife, Sherry, who, for over thirty years, has supported and encouraged my interest in history.

Introduction

In 1861, after years of sectional conflict, eleven Southern states seceded from the Union and formed the Confederate States of America. Diplomatic efforts on behalf of the new Confederate government began almost immediately. Initially, Southern diplomatic initiatives sought to obtain a peaceful separation from the old Union. The failure to achieve a peaceful settlement caused both sides to resort to military force. The American Civil War that followed radically changed the United States for future generations of Americans.

Confederate diplomacy can be defined, within the broader scope of foreign relations, as the effort to identify the national interest of the emerging nation and develop policies and strategies to achieve and protect those interests. Confederate foreign relations encompassed a broad range of activities, including, but not limited to, military, financial, economic, social, and cultural affairs. Confederate diplomatic policymakers in Richmond and their representatives abroad pursued identifiable objectives. First, to negotiate for a separate nation drawn from the old Federal Union, and secondly, to obtain recognition and legitimacy for that nation from the established international community.

Historians have debated since the Civil War why the North won and the South lost. A number of commentators have suggested that the two armies were equally matched, although they possessed different advantages and disadvantages.[1] If the strengths of the respective opponents were equal on the battlefield at the outbreak of the war, then other reasons produced Confederate defeat and Union victory. Some historians say the decisions made by the civilian governments in Washington and Richmond produced the outcome, while others argue that the limited industrial resources of the South prevented Southern victory. The absence of a Confederate navy and the effectiveness of the Union blockade of Southern ports certainly affected the outcome. A number of complex arguments suggest that Confederate failure resulted from the absence of a national commitment to the cause. All of these factors contributed to Union victory and Southern defeat.[2]

The diplomacy of the American Civil War as an important element of Union success has not been ignored by historians. Secretary of State William H. Seward is often credited with conducting a remarkably successful diplomatic campaign that prevented the Confederacy from obtaining support from foreign powers or negotiating a settlement on Southern terms. This laudable praise of Seward should be tempered, however, with the political realities existing in Europe and the poorly conceived and executed Confederate diplomatic effort. It is inappropriate to suggest that the outcome of the war could have been changed had a number of diplomatic, military, economic, or political factors been different. The fact remains that the North won the war; but it is worthwhile to examine, within a historical context, the contributing elements to that victory.[3]

In 1931, Professor Frank Owsley identified the economic power of cotton as the foundation of Confederate diplomatic strategy. The result of his research, published in *King Cotton Diplomacy,* remains the standard work on Confederate diplomacy. The recent books of Howard Jones and Brian Jenkins peripherally examine Confederate diplomatic strategies, but the focus of both historians is on the relationship between Great Britain and the United States during the Civil War. D. P. Crook, again focusing on European politics and diplomacy, introduces interesting questions relating to Confederate diplomacy. In *Desperate Diplomacy,* Norman Ferris emphasizes the role of Seward and Union diplomatic efforts to prevent recognition, including references to Confederate strategies. I have drawn liberally from the scholarship of these historians and others in the following pages. By returning to the original sources, I try to build on their efforts.[4]

One question this study seeks to answer is "Why did Confederate diplomatic initiatives fail to obtain recognition?" Southern diplomats, operating both in America and Europe, were involved in a number of very different activities. The overriding objective, however, was to obtain either a peaceful separation on Southern terms from the United States or European recognition and intervention. Confederate achievement of these objectives provided the best opportunity to sustain a permanent, independent Southern nation. The efforts of a number of Confederate operatives in Europe were important to the Southern cause, but none was more important to the ultimate outcome of the war than the pursuit of European intervention on behalf of the Confederacy.

Intervention on the part of the European powers could have taken a number of forms. Formal recognition in 1861 and 1862 would have added international legitimacy and acceptance to the Confederacy, thereby pressuring the Lincoln administration to allow a peaceful separation. By the summer and fall of 1862, recognition took on the added dimension of possible military intervention. It was expected that recognition would require the protection of international commerce from the Union blockade. As the war continued in America, Southern military defeats accumulated. Southern diplomatic efforts in Europe sought to obtain mediation with the hope that the European diplomats could succeed where Confederate armies failed. By the end of 1864 and early 1865, Southern diplomats were reduced to pitiful attempts to obtain assistance in any form from their friends in Europe.

Circumstances at the beginning of the war presented Southern diplomats with apparent opportunities for early success. Europeans believed that the South could ultimately protect and sustain its independence from the Union. This belief created a natural momentum favoring Confederate recognition. To further support their position, the Confederate leadership relied on a combination of constitutional arguments that demonstrated the legality of the secession movement. The profitable commercial ties that existed between the South and its European trading partners became the cornerstone of the Southern diplomatic initiative. The Southern states that seceded from the Union in 1861, taken as a group, composed the fifth largest economy in the world. The industrializing nations of the world depended on the South's cotton to sustain an important textile industry. In addition, the southern United States also provided a large market for European manufactured goods. At the outbreak of the war, European recognition appeared possible and Confederate diplomats expected success.[5]

Jefferson Davis, president of the newly formed Confederate States of America, and his military advisers decided on a limited war based on a defensive strategy. This policy was completely consistent with the prevailing military concepts and thinking. In order for a limited defensive war to succeed, diplomatic channels to the opposing government in Washington had to remain open. If the Southern armies extracted a sufficiently high price in blood and treasure, it was expected that the moderates in the North would pressure the Lincoln administration to accept Southern independence.

In developing an overall war strategy, the Davis administration underestimated the importance of diplomacy. While the objective of separation and independence was clear, it was necessary to maintain diplomatic communications to determine an opportune time for settlement. Limited military objectives with a clear understanding of the political goals should have been combined with an active diplomatic initiative if Southern interests were to be protected. The absence of a well-conceived and implemented diplomatic initiative after the outbreak of hostilities provides the first indication of Davis's indifferent attitude toward diplomacy.

After the initial failure of Confederate diplomatic efforts to obtain a negotiated settlement from the United States, it was vital for the South to obtain European recognition and support. Great Britain and France, the two European countries most interested in the American war, were the obvious powers for the Confederates to pursue. If the interest of either of these nations, and possibly both, could be identified with the success of the Confederacy, then an alliance could be expected. The Southerners, well aware of the history of the French involvement on the side of their forefathers in the Revolutionary War, hoped to obtain the assistance of Napoleon III in both their diplomatic and military campaigns. Great Britain's dependence on Southern cotton was viewed by the Confederate leadership as an overwhelming reason for a British commitment to the South.[6]

Confederate diplomats engaged in a number of activities on behalf of the war effort, but all of these activities paled in significance to the potential of diplomatic recognition. While the success of naval construction and the acquisition of military supplies benefited the South and possibly prolonged the war, they did not alter the ultimate outcome. A successful diplomatic campaign, when combined with other Southern advantages, provided the best opportunity to secure independence for the Confederacy. The failure of diplomatic initiatives to obtain European assistance contributed as much to Confederate defeat as any aspect of the Southern effort.

The surrender of the Confederate army by Robert E. Lee and the collapse of the Confederate nation in the spring of 1865 did not eliminate the commitment of the Southern people to their fundamental values. The legal emancipation of African American slaves did not dispel the notion of white supremacy, nor did it eliminate the relationship of states' rights to racial and labor control. During and after Reconstruction, a Southern elite once again emerged to espouse the reactionary ideas of the old South. A careful look at Confederate diplomatic initiatives and the conduct of the individuals pursuing them provides an additional perspective of Southern attitudes and their view of the world. This identifiable ideology persisted in a reconstructed and reunited United States after the war.

Chapter 1

The Diplomacy of Secession

On December 20, 1860, the state of South Carolina seceded from the Union of American States and, with its secession proclamation, began the effort to create, sustain, and defend the new Confederate States of America. The Palmetto State was quickly joined in secession by Mississippi, Florida, Alabama, Georgia, and Louisiana. In the first few days of February 1861, delegates from these states gathered in the centrally located Alabama capital of Montgomery to form the new nation.[1] Confederate diplomacy began almost as soon as a provisional government was formed and well before the first shots were fired in the American Civil War.

Although the creation of a new government was the first priority of the representatives from the Southern states, they were anxious to persuade the border states to join them in secession. The direction of foreign policy, as had been the tradition in the old Union, was the responsibility of the president of the new Confederacy. Led by provisional President Jefferson Davis, the six-member Confederacy began negotiations with Virginia, Maryland, Delaware, Kentucky, Tennessee, Arkansas, and Missouri. At the same time, Davis sought to negotiate a peaceful separation of the Southern states from the Federal Union.

Jefferson Davis was a product of the New South, which included the states of Alabama, Mississippi, Louisiana, Arkansas, and Texas, where cotton was "king." This new "southernness" or, more particularly, "Southwestern southernness" distinguished Davis from his fellow Southerners from Virginia and the Carolinas. He became the sponsor for the new cotton kingdom and the spokesman for the newly formed aristocratic class in the South. Only with reluctance did the old aristocratic families in the Carolinas and Virginia accept the nouveau riche cotton planter into their class.[2]

Jefferson Davis was educated at West Point and had traveled extensively in the Deep South during his youth. The entire region influenced him as much as did his home state of Mississippi. He enjoyed the wealth and power represented by the planter class, and was particularly impressed by the constitutional interpretations of Jefferson and Madison in the Kentucky and Virginia resolutions setting forth the principles and concepts of states' rights. Study of the doctrines of interposition and nullification contributed to his ideas that states' rights and unionism could coexist. Davis was a Democrat in the Jacksonian tradition, at least to the extent of "one white man has one vote."

In the aftermath of the Mexican War, in which Davis fought with distinction, the ambitions of the cotton Southwest became more apparent. Davis, embarking on a political career, became a United States senator from Mississippi. The "cotton frontier" had, by the late 1840s, attracted not only settlers from the established Southern slave states, but many from New England, New York, and the distant countries of Europe. As the representative of these acquisitive and undisciplined men seeking to make a future from cotton and slaves, Davis articulated the position of the Southern nationalists.[3] These men believed in the sanctity of private property, and that property included slaves.

In the debates of 1850, Davis emerged as the leading spokesman for Southern rights. He was one of the organizers of the Southern convention at Nashville. The future of slavery in the ceded Mexican lands and the remaining Louisiana Territory was the topic of the hour in mid-nineteenth-century America. The acquisition of new territory by the United States once again raised the question of whether slavery could be installed in the newly acquired regions. The Nashville convention was the platform for those Southerners favoring a Western empire built on slave labor, but Henry Clay's Compromise of 1850 reduced those favoring an American stronghold for slavery to an ineffective and disorganized group. Because he had so strongly supported the Nashville convention, Davis's political popularity waned among his constituents at home; and while his convictions on states' rights and slavery remained embedded in his political philosophy, he accepted the idea that Southern ideals could coexist within the Union because the institution was tolerated by the Constitution. Undoubtedly, the new generation of slave owners could not see that revolution and secession would end slavery.

By the winter of 1860–61, Davis found himself, despite his commitment to the Union, provisional president of a confederacy of Southern states bent on the destruction of the old Union. Davis, like most of the Southern ruling class, brought a commitment to constitutional government and universal white male suffrage to his new country; but, he had little understanding of the magnitude of his task, particularly in the treacherous world of diplomacy. Even though Davis had served President Franklin Pierce as secretary of war, he had no experience in international relations and relied on King Cotton to force the European powers to recognize his new nation.[4]

Davis sought to protect Southern interest within the Union, even though he was prepared to support secession because of his strong commitments to Southern values such as slavery, independence, pri-

Jefferson Davis, president of the Confederate States of America.
Courtesy of The Abraham Lincoln Museum, Harrogate, Tennessee.

vate property, the presence of power in local governments, and support for sectionalism and Southern rights throughout the South. Since the nullification crisis of 1832, there emerged in the South a highly developed sense of Southern rights based on a strict interpretation of the Constitution. These rights included, in the final analysis, however, the values supporting the institution of slavery.[5]

For most of the planter class, including a reluctant Davis, secession was merely a Lockian withdrawal of consent by the governed that was forced upon the South by the Republicans. It was viewed by many of the Southern aristocrats as a transforming revolution that would create a fresh society, as well as a new nation. It was necessary for Davis and the new government to protect slavery by obtaining and defending Southern independence. Secession and the Civil War that followed might better be called the War for Southern Security. Historian James L. Roark suggests that the Southern revolution was "not raised for racial reasons, although race was important." It was, according to Roark, "for profit's sake." Slavery and the Southern agrarian economy cannot be separated and should be viewed as dependent on one another. The Southern elite of the mid-nineteenth century certainly understood that their prosperity depended on the continued existence of slaves as a labor force and source of wealth.[6]

When Davis arrived in Montgomery, he quickly discovered that the conflict between sections was not limited to the differences between North and South. The frustrating problems of governing created by the doctrine of states' rights persisted within the Confederacy even after secession. These problems existed despite the fact that the states meeting in caucus to write a new constitution and select leaders at this early stage did not include the border states. The problems of dissension, petty political jealousies, and the demand for geographical and local preferences quickly emphasized the problems faced by the Confederate leadership at all levels and throughout the existence of the slaveholders' republic. The need to placate the interests of the various states would hamper Davis's ability to effectively govern a nation at war.

The movement of the Southern states toward secession accelerated dramatically during the two months immediately following the election of Abraham Lincoln. The reasons for secession had been frequently articulated by Southern political leaders. The speed of the actual secession movement, however, was caused by an almost hysterical fear, particularly in the cotton frontier states of the Southwest, of forthcoming Republican injuries to the social, political, and economic structure of the South. The election of Lincoln galvanized the leaders of the Deep South in support of hurried steps to organize and secede from the American Union.[7]

The frantic pace of political activity in the South between the election of Abraham Lincoln and the firing on Fort Sumter often precludes an appreciation of the actual time that elapsed. The frenetic interlude before combat was almost half a year, far longer than Franklin Roosevelt's "hundred days" that produced most of the New Deal. The Spanish-American War was completed from declaration to armistice in less time than the new cotton republics had to organize and secede. While the rush of activity continued in the South, the administration of President James Buchanan in Washington was indecisive. The lame-duck administration was slow to appreciate the seriousness of the Southern movement and did not subscribe to the adage that action speaks louder than words.

The Southern states during this long interval had time to proceed through an elaborate process of secession. This process included the convening of state legislatures and decisions to hold elections for delegates and electors to state secession conventions in brief election campaigns. Assembling these conventions was no small task, but Southerners proceeded with rapidity and the conventions drafted ordinances of secession that eventually led to the gathering of seceded states to form a provisional government. The provisional government elected Jefferson Davis as president of the new Confederacy and installed him in Montgomery well before Lincoln could be inaugurated in Washington. The interval between the election of Lincoln and his inauguration resulted from the constitutional provision for a lame-duck session of Congress and for a span of approximately 120 days between the election and the swearing-in of the president. This period of inactivity allowed enough time for the creation of the Confederate government.[8]

This constitutional anachronism provided time for the Confederate government to select and appoint the first diplomats to travel to Washington and Europe to pursue Southern interests. Davis, acting in the traditional role of the president to guide foreign policy, sought a peaceful separation from the old Union and appointed well-respected representatives to pursue this Washington assignment. On the other hand, the men he decided to send to Europe were appointed purely for political reasons, thus began a long list of inept appointments that consistently burdened Southern diplomatic strategy abroad.

While Davis organized the Confederate government, James Buchanan struggled with the secession crisis. In a Cabinet meeting, called three days after the 1860 election, the President expressed the importance of immediate attention to the fortifications at Charleston and referred to this Cabinet meeting as the most important in his administration, but the Cabinet was no help. Howell Cobb of Georgia and Jacob Thompson of Mississippi were treading water anticipating the secession of their home states, but they did remain loyal to Buchanan until the Southern states seceded. John B. Floyd of Virginia, already under a cloud of financial improprieties, was generally weak and clearly the wrong man in the wrong place as secretary of war at this critical moment. Lewis Cass, the aging secretary of state, supported by Joseph Holt, a Kentucky Unionist, and Attorney General Jeremiah S. Black, encouraged the president to take a stronger attitude toward the secessionists. The Cabinet was divided along sectional lines and its members were hostile toward each other. The indecisiveness of his official advisers helped Buchanan decide against issuing a presidential proclamation; he decided, instead, to present his official response to the secession crisis in his annual message to Congress on December 3.[9]

Buchanan, as he stated in his presidential message, believed that the solution to the problem of secession was beyond the power of the president and could only be dealt with by Congress, and that the next Congress, with the leadership of the new Republican president, could and would address the problem more effectively.

While the Buchanan administration dithered, the president-elect of the United States in Springfield made decisions that would profoundly affect the future diplomatic efforts of the United States for years to come. Lincoln's selection of William H. Seward as the new secretary of state proved to be an excellent decision, although it was probably for his political connections and vast following in the radical wing of the Republican Party, not his diplomatic skill, that Seward was selected.[10]

Seward, although defeated by Lincoln for the Republican presidential nomination, had worked faithfully for Lincoln's election. Seward was clearly the leader of the Whig-Republican coalition that made up the backbone of the Republican Party of 1860. A senator and former governor of New York State, Seward commanded the respect of the leading Republicans within the party. His long-standing outspoken opposition to slavery, however, had led moderate Republicans to nominate Lincoln, who carried less political baggage into the election of 1860. Seward expected to receive a prominent Cabinet post, and Lincoln agreed, making Seward his first selection to the Cabinet. Seward might have expected to dominate the Cabinet and thus exercise an unusual amount of influence on the president and his domestic and foreign policies. If Seward anticipated such a dominant arrangement, neither he nor the president suggested more than the strong and influential authority normally associated with the secretary of state.[11]

While Lincoln completed the formation of his Cabinet and President Buchanan marked time, the secessionist momentum continued to build in the South. Only after the Southern states had created their national government and declared their independence could they embark upon international diplomacy, first to initiate negotiations with the Washington government, hoping thereby to win approval for a peaceful separation from the Union.

The leadership of the Confederacy now saw their new nation as a sovereign state and expected to conduct conversations and other diplomatic business on an equal basis with other nations of the world. In the view of Davis and his newly appointed Cabinet, modeled after the Cabinet of the old Union, a peaceful separation from the United States was a diplomatic effort and should be negotiated by men familiar with international law and the constitutions of the nations involved. Although no official channels of communication existed, it was not beyond Southern expectations that after a peaceful separation was accomplished, diplomats would negotiate and settle differences between the United States and the Confederacy.

Davis left foreign policy to others in the government and, rather than developing an aggressive diplomatic effort, tended to expect events to accomplish diplomatic objectives. The new president was committed to the notion that cotton would secure recognition and legitimacy from the powers of Europe. The men Davis selected as secretary of state and emissaries to Europe were chosen for political and personal reasons—not for their diplomatic potential. This was due, in part, to the belief that cotton could accomplish the Confederate objectives with little help from Confederate diplomats.

Chapter 2

The Failure of Diplomacy
Produces War

When Jefferson Davis accepted the presidency of "six nations," which quickly became seven with the admission of Texas, the Confederacy still did not fulfill the territorial expectations of its new leaders. The less impulsive states of the upper South needed to join the secessionist movement and the Confederacy to complete the union of Southern states and to deprive the United States of valuable support.[1]

The Confederate Congress sought to lure the Midwestern states, dependent on the Mississippi River, by exempting from all duty the commerce on the Mississippi from those states bordering the Mississippi or its navigable tributaries. The statutes passed in February of 1861 by the provisional Congress did not provide for duty-free commercial activities with the states of the Confederacy, but only affected shipments for export beyond the Confederate nation. Since most Midwestern commercial activity was with the Southern states, it was expected that an incentive either to join the Confederacy or create a separate western Confederacy would prove advantageous. The failure of this river diplomacy was quickly evident after the outbreak of hostilities, when the Midwestern states sent troops to suppress the rebels. By the fall of 1862, the Confederate Foreign Affairs Committee initiated an investigation to determine the reason for failure. No conclusions resulted from this shallow inquiry. It was Lincoln with his call for troops to suppress the rebellion, not the effort of Confederate agents, that forced the border states to choose sides.[2]

In preparing for these and other eventualities, Davis needed to fill out his administration as quickly as possible. The politics of states' rights required Davis to allow representation in the Cabinet from each of the seven states. The only state with two members in the original Cabinet was Georgia, represented by the sickly vice president, Alexander H. Stephens, and the large, robust, and jovial secretary of state, Robert Toombs. Alabama sent the cautious and dutiful secretary of war, Leroy P. Walker. German-born Christopher G. Memminger from South Carolina became secretary of the treasury. Louisiana provided the colorful, exotic, Jewish attorney general, Judah P. Benjamin. Florida was represented by Stephen R. Mallory, secretary of the Navy. Postmaster General John H. Reagan was a one-time plantation overseer from Texas. Finally, Mississippi was represented by the president. Unfortunately, no vacancy remained in the Cabinet for politically ambitious and capable representatives from the border states when they joined the Confederacy.[3]

Davis made three early diplomatic appointments. On February 25, 1861, he designated Andre B. Roman of Louisiana, Martin J. Crawford of Georgia, and John Forsyth of Alabama to represent Confederate interests in Washington. In his instructions to the first Confederate diplomats, Davis directed them to seek a peaceful accommodation with the incoming administration by obtaining commitments of security for all Federal forts, arsenals, and other public property located in the Confederacy. In addition, the Southerners were to make "friendly arrangements" to settle all matters of indebtedness and "other points of mutual commercial interest that might arise."[4] These instructions clearly reflect a diplomatic tone and show that Davis sought to conduct negotiations as an equally sovereign nation with the United States.

For the leaders of the Confederacy, the goal of national sovereignty required the surrender and withdrawal of Federal troops and authority. The Southern states had already occupied most Federal forts and arsenals. As early as January 3, 1861, Governor Joseph E. Brown of Georgia seized Fort Pulaski at the mouth of the Savannah River, while Florida occupied Fort Marion at St. Augustine, Fort Clinch at Fernandina, and the Chattahoochee arsenal. Alabama troops coordinated with Florida's militia to seize Fort Barrancus guarding Pensacola, causing Federal troops to move to Fort Pickens. However, Federal troops continued to occupy Fort Pickens on Santa Rosa

Island at Pensacola, as well as Fort Sumter in Charleston Harbor. The hope of the Confederate administration was a diplomatically negotiated resolution to the problem of these last two fortifications.[5]

When South Carolina seceded, requests were sent to President Buchanan to relinquish the forts within its borders. The Buchanan administration refused. Instead, Major Robert Anderson moved his command from Fort Moultrie to the more easily defended Fort Sumter on December 26, 1860. South Carolina then charged Buchanan with an overt act of aggression and claimed that Anderson's movement to Fort Sumter reflected a commitment to maintain a U.S. presence in the Charleston area. In response, South Carolina moved militia troops into the Charleston area and demanded the evacuation of Sumter.

Buchanan continued to vacillate, but sent a merchant ship, the *Star of the West,* with supplies and hidden troops to relieve Sumter. South Carolina batteries fired on the vessel and forced it to withdraw. This ugly situation was inherited from South Carolina by the Confederacy when it took charge of national defense. Davis sent Gen. Pierre G. T. Beauregard to Charleston to restrain the local militia and officials. The diplomatic effort of the Confederate ministers in Washington to negotiate the peaceful withdrawal from these military fortifications was obviously more difficult because of an openly belligerent and hostile South Carolina.[6]

The Lincoln administration assumed responsibility for the situation on March 4, 1861. If, after the withdrawal of the Southern members of Buchanan's Cabinet, President-elect Lincoln had made an unequivocal statement of his position on the Sumter crisis, some of the misunderstandings of the next several months might have been avoided— although at times these misunderstandings seemed to fit in with the diplomacy employed by both sides. Instead, Lincoln's response to frequent requests for enlightenment on his attitude toward South Carolina was to refer inquirers to his previous public statements during the presidential election campaign.[7]

It was precisely these previously stated positions that threatened the slave states. By isolating slavery in the South, where it had always existed, the slaveholders and Lincoln believed it would die a slow suffocating death. If slavery could not expand, it would cease to exist. It is doubtful that Lincoln fully realized at this stage the strength and widespread support of the secession movement. For him and other Republican leaders, secession had resulted from the actions of a few disgruntled and disappointed conspirators, and the Unionists and moderate elements would soon overcome the more radical elements in the South.[8]

Historian David Donald argues that Lincoln believed the radical secessionists wanted to change the American government to accommodate their perception of slavery. Lincoln would not compromise his previously stated position on slavery. He believed that the secessionist rhetoric was a strategy to coerce his administration and he expected reunion. The new president had previously stated his position on compromise through a number of his colleagues in the Republican Party. He admonished Senator Trumbull to "stand firm, the tug has come, and better, now than anytime hereafter."[9] Lincoln was also convinced that secession was unconstitutional and, therefore, a violation of Federal law. As such, he believed it was the responsibility of the Federal government to enforce the law—by armed intervention if necessary.[10] It is unlikely, however, that he anticipated the long and costly war that followed.

Lincoln did not believe that a compromise would prevent war, but he hoped to accommodate the border states, thus further isolating the cotton states. Anything less than capitulation on the matter of the military installations would not have satisfied the South Carolinians or the Confederacy. Decisive action by Lincoln, however, might have prevented the border states from joining the Confederacy by at least leaving the opportunity for compromise available for moderate leaders in Virginia, Kentucky, and Tennessee. It is doubtful that a peaceful separation of the already seceded states could have been accomplished regardless of the outcome of the fortifications issue, unless Lincoln was prepared to compromise his position on the fundamental nature of the Union. There is no evidence that Lincoln ever considered any policy except complete restoration of the Union.[11]

Southerners perceived Lincoln as a president likely to be dominated by the more radical elements of the Republican Party that wanted to "attempt to interfere directly and immediately with slavery in the states."[12] The Confederate envoys in Washington, seeking assurances against interference with their new nation and its peculiar institution, were frustrated by the absence of any direct response from Lincoln. Believing the Republican Party to be the dominant force in the administration, the Southerners sought assurances from the acknowledged political leader of the Republican Party, Secretary of State William H. Seward. Two Supreme Court Justices, John A. Campbell of Alabama and Samuel Nelson of New York, accepted the responsibility as intermediaries between Confederate envoys and Seward, who proceeded to engage in frequent unofficial communications with them throughout March.[13]

The presence in Washington in March of the Confederate commissioners required some action, whether unofficial or official, from the Lincoln administration. Lincoln refused to see the Confederate representatives. Seward believed that a blunt and complete rebuff of the Confederate request to abandon Forts Sumter and Pickens would result in immediate military action with an attack by the Confederates on the forts. He heard from both Sam Houston of Texas and Judah P. Benjamin that the Montgomery government was impatient and prepared to respond forcefully to any direct rebuff. Still convinced that the opportunity existed for Southern Unionists to recover their country and restore the Union, Seward allowed the commissioners to believe that the Lincoln administration would evacuate Fort Sumter and might make other concessions.[14]

Lincoln, however, insisted that Seward prepare a memorandum stating that the "so called" Confederate government was altogether unjustifiable and unconstitutional, and that the president would have no communication with the commissioners. With the knowledge of the Confederate commissioners, Seward kept the memorandum he prepared at the State Department and did not present it to the Confederates immediately. Knowing that the memorandum contained a rebuff of their request for immediate evacuation, as well as a firm denunciation of their constitutional arguments supporting secession, Crawford and Roman persuaded Forsyth to delay informing Davis of the contents of the document. Forsyth wanted to make the Lincoln administration's position clear even though he recognized the potential for immediate Confederate military action. Both Seward and the Confederate emissaries sought delay, though for different reasons. Every day that the Confederates delayed more firmly established the government in Montgomery. On the other hand, Seward wanted delay to avoid hostilities that might push the border states into the Confederacy.[15]

Two of the most important early concerns of the Confederate leaders were closely related and depended on the success of the very first Confederate diplomatic mission. Removing the Union garrisons from Confederate soil and winning the border states over to secession were vital to the success of the Confederacy. If the border states of Virginia, Kentucky, Tennessee, Arkansas, and North Carolina decided to join the Confederacy, it would more than double its white population and bring huge territorial gains.[16] The original seven states represented by the provisional government in Montgomery possessed only a fraction of the industrial and commercial facilities contained in the border states, particularly Virginia.[17] Both North and South were also anxious to obtain the support of Maryland because of its strategic naval importance and its close proximity to the capital in Washington.[18] Both sides, then, accepted the delay as advantageous; but by the end of March, the situation began to deteriorate rapidly.

On March 15, shortly after the curious arrangement between Seward and the Confederate commissioners was established, Lincoln asked his Cabinet members for their opinion on provisioning Sumter. Apparently, Lincoln had not decided whether to evacuate or reinforce Fort Sumter. The response of Lincoln's Cabinet was mixed. Postmaster General Montgomery Blair and Secretary of Treasury Salmon P. Chase argued that Fort Sumter should be reinforced, while Seward and the rest of the Cabinet argued against reinforcement. Seward stressed the importance of a nonaggressive policy so that Union sentiment in the South, particularly in South Carolina, would have an opportunity to develop. Seward and Secretary of the Navy Gideon Welles argued that the collection of custom duties should be continued, but only from a floating station outside Charleston harbor supported by naval warships.[19]

Before Seward could communicate unofficially to the Confederate representatives, the press spread the story that the administration was abandoning Fort Sumter. The Confederate emissaries quickly telegraphed Secretary of State Toombs in Montgomery that the Lincoln administration was preparing to abandon Sumter. Crawford was jubilant and believed that a great diplomatic victory had been secured. Unfortunately, this euphoric state lasted a very short time.[20]

By March 29, when Lincoln again polled his Cabinet on the question of relief for Fort Sumter, the results of public opinion had arrived in Washington and the Cabinet supported reinforcing both Fort Sumter and Fort Pickens. With the exception of Seward, every Cabinet member argued for the reprovisioning of Fort Sumter by sea. Lincoln instructed both his War Department and Navy Department to draw up plans for the relief of Fort Sumter, and Seward began modifying his assurances to Judge Campbell that the post would be evacuated.[21]

The cagey Seward communicated to the commissioners through Judge Campbell that he was confident no attempt would be made to resupply Fort Sumter without first notifying the governor of South Carolina. Seward's attitude toward the Confederacy hardened during the last weeks of March and he became less certain that war could be avoided. On March 28, he informed British correspondent William H. Russell that newspaper statements suggesting orders had been given to abandon Fort Sumter were "a plain lie." Within two weeks, Seward stated flatly that "no Federal property will be abandoned."[22] He still hoped that the Union could quickly be reunited, but it is doubtful that by the first week of April he believed there was any hope of avoiding military confrontation.

As these events unfolded in Washington, Jefferson Davis in Montgomery instructed Beauregard to reinforce his positions near Fort Sumter in preparation for an assault on the Federal stronghold. The continued lukewarm response to secession from the border states suggested the need for a prestige-enhancing resolution to the Fort Sumter question to draw them into the Confederacy. The leadership of the Confederacy certainly did not believe, nor were they prepared to be satisfied with, the territorial boundaries of the first three months of 1861. These Southern leaders entertained the imperial designs consistent with the manifest destiny concept so many of them had supported when participating in the government of the United States. Vice President Stephens proclaimed on March 21, "We are now the nucleus of a growing power, which if we are true to ourselves, our destiny, and high mission, will become the controlling power on this Continent."[23] Even the most modest of Southern expansionists envisioned the full-grown Confederacy as including the border states of the upper South. Governor Francis Pickens of South Carolina, as well as a number of Confederate leaders in Montgomery, were anxious to get on with the mission of expelling the Federals from Fort Sumter as a sign of strength directed at the border states. Much like his counterpart in Washington, Davis hoped for a peaceful resolution to the crisis. Of course, he expected the creation of a new nation, while Lincoln expected the reconstruction of the Union.[24]

The information contained in the reports to Montgomery from the three commissioners in Washington tell a confusing story. The first reports reflect Lincoln's policy communicated unofficially by Seward: if the Confederates would take no military action, the military situation would remain unchanged. The commissioners informed Montgomery that they felt Seward was stalling, but they recommended the temporary acceptance of the arrangement. Forsyth wrote Walker on March 14, "We are playing a game in which time is our best advocate, if our government could afford the time, I feel confident of winning."[25] Crawford wrote on March 16 that "two of the Republican illusions have exploded—first, that it was very easy to reinforce the forts and second, that they could collect the revenue on floating custom houses at sea."[26] This communication implied Crawford's position was that a little more time would explode other Republican illusions and bring Lincoln, at last, to the realization that he must recognize the Confederacy.

Davis and Toombs agreed with the commissioners. Toombs instructed them to maintain their present position and make no further demand for an official hearing or an official answer to their previous demands. For the time being, the Confederate leaders were content for the United States not to use military or naval force or, for that matter, to arrange peace terms that would damage Confederate prestige in the undeclared border states. As Davis put it, "It affords the Confederate states the advantages of both conditions, and enables them to make all the necessary arrangement for the public defense, and the solidifying of their government, more safely, more cheaply, and expeditiously than they would were the attitude of the United States more definite and decided."[27]

In the first week of April, it appeared that the Confederate diplomatic effort was certainly accomplishing its objective. The South was far more prepared for military action than the North—at least at Fort Sumter. Davis had more men under arms than Lincoln, and at the expected place of conflict, Charleston. The Confederates also possessed better guns and better emplacements. The stage was now set for negotiations to end and military operations to begin. Beauregard was ready to initiate military action as soon as the Confederate diplomats in Washington terminated their mission.[28]

During the next week, however, communications to the Montgomery government from Crawford, Forsyth, and Roman were filled with changing and confusing rumors. First, Lincoln was conferring with naval engineers, perhaps regarding the reinforcing of Fort Sumter. Then, a conflicting report stated that these conferences concerned the best methods of collecting revenue at New Orleans. The *Powhatan* was being put into commission to sail with supplies onboard. The destination was unsure, however, and might possibly be San Domingo. Forsyth communicated by telegram to Walker, "We have not yet been notified of movement, but the notification may come when they are ready to start. Watch all ports!" Then finally on April 8, the government in Montgomery learned from Crawford, "Our commissioners at Washington have received a flat refusal."[29] This communication was immediately transmitted to Beauregard in Charleston and Bragg at Pensacola. At last, the delaying negotiations were over and the diplomats departed. It was time for the soldiers to act.

The Southern diplomats performed a dual role. The custom of the mid-nineteenth century was for diplomats serving in various posts around the world to obtain military intelligence while acting as the official representatives of a friendly government. The Southern envoys in Washington certainly performed both functions. Although they had no official status, Crawford, Forsyth, and Roman did make every effort to accurately communicate the position of the Lincoln administration and also furnish military intelligence. The first Confederate diplomats performed the traditional role of foreign ministers, even if only for a short time, before the outbreak of hostilities. The first shots in the American Civil War were finally fired on April 12, 1861.

The initial diplomatic effort of the newly formed Confederacy was not successful in obtaining peaceful separation from the Union or in expelling Federal troops from Southern soil without military action. It was, however, successful in obtaining time for the Confederate government to establish its control over its member states. During the early months of the Confederacy, public opinion in the South had shifted away from the idea of reunification and toward support for secession and independence. With these attitudes in mind, Davis had little choice but to order Beauregard to open fire on Fort Sumter. For him to have done otherwise in the political context would have been political suicide. The use of force unified the cotton South and created an atmosphere that contributed to secession from the Union of four border states and the creation of an enlarged Confederacy.[30]

With the benefit of historical perspective, Seward's policy of appeasement, delay, and ultimate withdrawal from Fort Sumter was the best policy for the Union. Certainly, it was the policy least likely to provoke a Southern military response. The potential for a successful Confederate military effort would have been substantially reduced if the border states, particularly Virginia, had not joined the rebellion. The Seward strategy of prolonging the negotiations allowed Lincoln to appease and coerce the strategically located border state of Maryland, as well as most of Kentucky and Missouri, into remaining in the Union. However, Lincoln could not save the key states of Virginia, Kentucky, Tennessee, and, finally, North Carolina for the Union. The Southern Confederacy was now complete and the new nation was immediately at war to preserve its territorial integrity.[31]

Chapter 3

The Burden of Cotton

From the start, the Confederate leadership turned to Europe for diplomatic recognition in its struggle against the North. Southerners liked to compare their quest for independence with that of their forefathers during the American Revolution. The first American diplomats accepted French assistance that furthered French objectives during a time of continuing Anglo-French conflict. Southerners, convinced of the righteousness of their cause and comparing themselves to American Revolutionaries, lost sight of the fact that the French chose the Americans, not the other way around. This misreading of history led to the failure of Confederate officials to understand the realities of the world in which they sought to exist as a sovereign state.

One such reality was the consistent improvement in Anglo-American relations throughout the decade of the 1850s. Southerners were often directly involved in the political and diplomatic negotiations to resolve the difficult and frustrating issues concerning the Oregon territory, British involvement in Texas, and the Canadian border dispute. However, the experience gained from this leadership role did little to benefit their quest for recognition or a military alliance. The resolution of these complex and sensitive issues produced a favorable atmosphere for Anglo-American diplomacy during the 1850s. South-

erners failed to appreciate the new maturity of Anglo-American diplomacy that reflected the changing balance of power in the Western
Hemisphere and the recognition by Great Britain that outright opposition to the United States in Central America, and elsewhere in
the hemisphere, could no longer be sustained. Moreover, Britain's
commitment first to European diplomacy allowed this favorable rapprochement.[1]

Southern policymakers did understand the underlying economic
interdependence of the European powers and the United States.
During the decade of the 1850s, economic collaboration between
Great Britain and the United States reached a high point, essentially
producing a "common pool" of land, labor, technology, and capital,
reinforcing the exchange of primary and manufactured goods, including, most notably, cotton from the South. The powerful engine
of industrialization in America, with its overwhelming implications
for future generations, did not emerge, however, until after the Civil
War. The British dominated manufacturing and expected both North
and South to produce markets, as well as sources of raw commodities. The Confederate diplomatic strategy failed to take into consideration the relative merits of a diversified economy and the stable
political structure in place in Great Britain. France, on the other hand,
was under the control of Napoleon III and seemed more vulnerable
to economic pressures.[2]

Both North and South enjoyed the diplomatic advantages of cultural and linguistic ties with Great Britain. The warm reception in
October 1860 of the Prince of Wales to the United States revealed an
enormous reservoir of affection within the Atlantic community. The
comments of contemporaries consistently reflected the kinship of the
two societies based on the historical commitment of both nations to
liberty and progress.[3] Notwithstanding these improvements, traditional conflicts between U.S. and British interests still existed. For
instance, America's continued adherence to protectionism aroused
regular condemnation from the free-trade constituency in Great Britain; but while Confederate diplomats recognized this potential for
conflict, they failed to develop a successful policy to exploit it.

The Confederate leaders also failed to fully comprehend the preoccupation of Great Britain and France with problems in Europe,
although the support furnished by the European powers to anti-demo-
cratic movements in Europe in the decade preceding the American
conflict suggested early recognition of the Confederacy in its fight
for independence. The balance of power in Europe was precariously
maintained, with the French supporting the Italians against the Aus-

trians and the British supporting the Greeks and Poles in their demands for recognition and independence versus Turkey and Russia. Germany was a powder keg ready to explode in any direction. Moreover, the legacy of the Crimean War remained fresh in the minds of Europeans, with the considerable loss of life in this war creating a natural resistance, particularly in Great Britain and France, to any further military adventures. The subtleties of this European setting eluded the narrowly focused Confederate diplomatic strategy.[4]

Confederate diplomacy sought international legitimacy, as well as recognition from the European powers. The failure to create policies and strategies sufficient to obtain European recognition, protection, friendship, and intervention proved second only to military defeat in producing the destruction of the Southern dream for an independent nation. A successful diplomatic campaign would have persuaded the European powers to use naval forces to protect their economic interests in the Confederacy. If the European powers could be convinced to do this, one of the Confederacy's major military deficiencies would be overcome. The South lacked merchant vessels and even warships, which foreigners might supply if their governments could be induced to sustain and protect them.

The traditional values of the Southern elite were reflected in the diplomatic strategy of the Confederacy. It was these values of individual liberty, freedom, and local control of government that limited the ability of Southerners to develop a strategy that could realistically expect success. To obtain a military alliance with a substantial power required an appreciation of that power's vital interest. Identifying a threat or a need that could be overcome or met by an arrangement with the new Confederacy was beyond the view of the governing elite in the South. The view that cotton was king completely missed the mark and reflected a Southern appreciation of the commodity rather than its value to the Europeans. Southerners depended on cotton to sustain the virtuous agricultural plantation lifestyle that relied on slave labor. The ideology underlying the Confederacy was, in a large measure, developed to support the institution of slavery and a cotton economy. Increasingly during the war, Davis and the government of the Confederacy faced the need to balance the values of the white nonslaveholding Southerner, who was fighting the war, with those of a vastly different ruling class in the cotton South.[5]

Southerners of the 1860s—unlike the Colonials of an earlier era, with whom they likened themselves—approached independence with a strong, unified ruling class. Southern society divided itself into white and black classes. Numerous social classes and religious groups existed in eighteenth-century America. By the mid-nineteenth century, however, the Southern population was generally Protestant and Evangelical in its religious practices. The one exception to religious unity is found in the large Catholic population of Louisiana. While colonial economies varied by region, the economy of virtually the entire Old South concentrated on the production of staple agricultural commodities, particularly cotton. The majority of the Southern population in 1860 was native-born, with immigrants composing less than 1 percent.[6] The common ideology of Southern whites was anti-black, if not always pro-slavery. This was a major unifying influence that galvanized into a sense of Confederate nationalism. Southerners were prepared to go to war against the external threat to a way of life that contained an established underclass. The accompanying commitment to states' rights ultimately weakened the Confederate government, but Southerners surrendered sufficient authority to the central government to wage a bloody war for over four years.[7]

While the South entered the Civil War with deficiencies in manpower, industrial capacity, and capital resources compared with the North, it was not without military advantages. These advantages contributed to the expectation of early diplomatic success. Once secession was completed, the Southern territory was extensive and larger than any territory previously subdued by force. European military experts expected that any attempt by the North to defeat and occupy the vast territory initially under Southern control would fail and substantially weaken the North. The interior lines of supply and communication within the South were another advantage generally accepted by military leaders of the period. The most important of all the Southern military advantages was the consideration that the South did not have to win outright on the field of battle in order to achieve its independence. A defensive war was widely accepted as a major advantage for the Confederacy as long as Southerners were prepared to settle for independence without demands or concessions from the Union. The Confederacy's major deficiency was the absence of a navy and merchant marine, as well as the lack of facilities to construct and sustain such a maritime presence.[8]

Early Confederate diplomatic initiatives attempted to capitalize on the above-mentioned advantages. If war is an extension of diplomacy, and a tool in international relations, it was reasonable to expect early diplomatic success by the Confederacy. Initial military successes supported the Confederate diplomatic assessment of the situation, as did the refusal of the European powers to denounce or shun the Confederacy, thus creating the expectation of ultimate recognition and intervention. The assumption that military success, coupled with economic pressures, seemed to the Confederacy to capitalize on its strengths. This policy was flawed from the start because it focused on the inaccurate assumption that cotton was king in Europe as it was in the Southern states.

The responsibility of developing foreign-policy strategy was that of the president of the Confederacy, Jefferson Davis. Davis's preoccupation with military matters required him to consult others for guidance on foreign policy. Unfortunately for Davis and the Confederacy, these advisers, with a few exceptions, were poor choices. Lincoln, on the other hand, relied upon the brilliant and politically experienced William H. Seward to direct the Union diplomatic effort. In the early stages after Sumter, Lincoln was required to reign in Seward, who often demonstrated an excessively belligerent tone in his communications to Great Britain and France concerning the potential recognition of the Confederacy.

Seward's strategy was consistent and responded effectively to various Confederate initiatives. The American secretary of state was creative and flexible and ably supported by U.S. ministers Charles Francis Adams in London and William L. Dayton in Paris.[9] Davis, on the other hand, provided the Confederacy with a rigid and inflexible policy based on economic coercion and force. The stubborn reliance of the Confederates on a King Cotton strategy resulted in a natural resistance to coercion from the Europeans. Moreover, Davis's representatives in Europe were almost all inept diplomats and ill-equipped to deal with the problems and frustrations they encountered there. The inexperience and lack of creative flexibility of these men contributed to a failed diplomatic effort.

The use of "cotton coercion" to force the Europeans to intervene was the foundation of early Confederate diplomatic initiatives. It is logical that the Southerners would have expected cotton to force open the doors of the council chambers, treasuries, and arsenals of Europe. For years, Southerners had heard, particularly from the British, that the economy of Great Britain depended completely on cotton, while New England and France were almost as dependent on the basic commodity. Comments like the following from *Punch* contributed to this overblown value:

> Though with the North we sympathize,
> It must not be forgotten
> That with the South we've stronger ties,
> Which are composed of cotton. . . .[10]

One Southerner went so far as to express to William Howard Russell of the *London Times* in 1861 that "the British economy was a mere appendage of the cotton kingdom" and further declared, "There are four million of your people depending on us for their bread, not to speak of the many millions of dollars. No, sir, we know that England must recognize us."[11] Operating under these illusions, the Confederate leadership failed to appreciate the importance of foreign aid, recognition, and a cooperative overseas alliance based on the mutual interest of the nations entering into an alliance.

Cotton was an important and valuable international commodity and large segments of the industrialized world depended on it. As the decade of the 1860s opened, the South, even without the rest of the Union, represented a wealthy and viable economy. The hopes of the Southern economy rested on cotton production and agricultural exports.[12] Unfortunately for the Confederate diplomatic effort, the foreign-policy strategy attempting to capitalize on this economic advantage failed because it relied on economic intimidation instead of cooperation.

In the last two decades before the outbreak of the Civil War, cotton exports from America to Britain increased from £487,857,504 to £732,403,840. Southern planters took satisfaction in such figures and expected the demand for cotton to bring the greatest industrial nation of the period into its struggle for independence. Eighty percent of the British imports of cotton came from America and 20 percent of the British population earned its livelihood directly or indirectly from the manufacture of cotton products.[13] Without American cotton, Southerners believed British looms would stand idle and unemployment would eventually produce a revolution in Europe. Southerners believed that before tensions reached such a level, the British government would intervene in American affairs to secure cotton and prevent widespread insurrection in England.[14] These assumptions were flawed for two reasons. First, the South apparently relied on a British government response to a segment of the population that did not contain a large voting block that could vote officials out of office. The second miscalculation was that the economy of Great Britain was overwhelmingly dependent on Southern cotton.

The Southern economy based on the production of agricultural commodities was, of course, not restricted to cotton. The region also exported rice, tobacco, and naval stores. When formulating a foreign policy, Jefferson Davis and his Cabinet carefully considered not only the importance of cotton, but also the other cash crops. They expected the "New England Yankees," whose shipping, commercial, and insurance activities depended on Southern agricultural products, to face failing businesses. Southerners thought that, without the middleman's profits, Northern bankers would apply pressure on the Lincoln administration for a policy of peaceful coexistence. The South also provided a substantial market for European products imported by Northern businessmen. Southerners expected that the loss to the North of both a substantial producer of raw materials and a significant market for manufactured goods would create financial hardships of sufficient magnitude to require the recognition of the new independent Confederate States of America.[15]

Jefferson Davis subscribed to the philosophy espoused by leading Southern spokesmen and developed a diplomatic strategy based on cotton coercion. In fact, President Davis and his advisers were so committed to the power of cotton that they believed foreign recognition was "an assumed fact"[16] because of the insatiable European demand for cotton. Davis's friend Judah P. Benjamin remarked to British journalist William Howard Russell that when England needed cotton badly enough, "all this coyness about acknowledging a slave power will come right at last."[17] Such comments irritated Russell because they revealed the low opinion held by Southerners of British integrity. Many Southerners told Russell that the British would completely disregard their principles in pursuit of financial gain.[18] In fact, while entertaining several Southern guests at the residence of British Consul Robert Bunch, an unidentified Southern guest exclaimed, "Why, sir, we have only to shut off your supply of cotton for a few weeks and we can create a revolution in Great Britain."[19] By the time of secession, the belief in the power of cotton to force European intervention was so universal in the South as to become an article of faith.

The general acceptance of the power of cotton as a diplomatic weapon did not prevent an early debate over the best tactical method to implement the strategy. Robert Barnwell Rhett, chairman of the Confederate Congress's Committee on Foreign Affairs, recommended on February 13, 1861—even before Jefferson Davis had become provisional president of the Montgomery government—that three commissioners be immediately appointed and sent to Europe.[20] Rhett, an outspoken and radical advocate of secession, slavery, and cotton coercion, was convinced that Davis and his political cronies sought secession only to achieve favorable Reconstruction terms when rejoining the Union. The cooperatists had exposed Rhett as a radical "fire-eater" in his quest to become secretary of state or minister to Great Britain.[21] Therefore, Rhett sought to commit the Confederacy to an aggressive and irrevocable foreign policy before Davis took office. The Foreign Affairs Committee recommended that the three European commissioners be under the president's direction after his inauguration but that their first instructions be formulated by the Congress under the guidance of Rhett's committee.[22]

Through his early control of foreign affairs, Rhett hoped to establish a foreign-policy strategy based on economic coercion and mercantilist incentives. Rhett hoped thereby to achieve early foreign recognition and prevent the reconstruction of the Union. He proposed a twenty-year commercial alliance with Great Britain and France, conditional on their recognition of the Confederacy. In addition, he suggested a promise of 20 percent maximum import duty and an offensive and defensive league with the European countries to defend their existing and future possessions in North America.

To Rhett's surprise and dismay, the members of his committee, as well as the congressional leaders, rejected his political tactics as well as his proposals. Surprisingly, it was the Southern protectionist argument against the free-trade implications of the proposal that caused the most opposition. Even at this early stage, members of the Confederate Congress acknowledged the desperate need for the South to create and build an industrial base to complement its substantial agricultural foundation. The Confederate Congress rejected Rhett's initiative by amending the committee report to leave the appointments and instructions to the new president. It comes as no surprise that Davis thereafter refused, following Rhett's political intrigue, to provide him a diplomatic post.[23]

Rhett's opposition to a strategy based on threats of a cotton embargo without the olive branch of commercial treaties did not end with this initial defeat. Rhett continued to suggest that the cooperation of the European powers could only be obtained by irresistible offers of trade and commercial agreements. He made clear his intention to contest the president's reliance on King Cotton diplomacy in the next session of Congress.[24]

Rhett's final defeat came after he introduced a congressional resolution on May 13, unanimously supported by his committee, which empowered Confederate commissioners to promise a "20% maximum tariff to any nation making a satisfactory treaty with the Confederacy." The resolution received the support of Secretary of State Robert Toombs, but the protectionists again asserted themselves, claiming that continued free trade would handicap the development of Southern manufacturing. The result was to offer a five-year limited treaty, which Rhett angrily tabled because of his conviction that any treaty shorter than twenty years would not sufficiently tempt Great Britain or France to risk provoking the United States.[25] The strategy put forward by Rhett was based on sound calculations and probably had the best chance of success. Unfortunately for the Confederacy, the perception of political gamesmanship precluded Davis from taking the responsibility for foreign policy, and support was lost in the administration. It was a sign of things to come when Rhett's proposal was met by an inflexible, dogmatic President Davis, who allowed his own personal feelings about a person to cloud his judgment. A good overall diplomatic strategy using the power of cotton was lost at a time when it had some potential to benefit the Confederate cause.[26]

The defeat of Rhett's initiative committed the administration to a European diplomatic effort based on King Cotton, with little else left to offer. The Davis strategy was to hold cotton until Europeans came to get it, thus penetrating the paper blockade imposed by the North. Some members of the Cabinet, led by Secretary of the Treasury Christopher Memminger and Secretary of War Judah Benjamin, preferred to build up foreign credit by exporting and warehousing cotton in Europe before the blockade became effective. This small group within the Confederate leadership was hopelessly outnumbered and quickly overwhelmed by the external pressures from the press, merchants, planters, cotton factors, and the governors of the cotton states.[27] Benjamin H. Hill expressed the opinion of his Georgia constituency in the Confederate Congress when he compared cotton to "that little attenuated cotton thread, which a child can break, but which, nevertheless, can hang the world."[28] The widespread acceptance of a King Cotton diplomatic strategy that withheld the valuable commodity was certainly politically expedient, and Davis accepted and embraced the numerous supporting arguments.[29]

This concept of increasing the power of cotton by creating a shortage in Europe failed to take into account the large amounts of cotton already warehoused in Great Britain as a result of the large crop of 1860. British textile manufacturers already owned both a large inventory of finished cotton cloth and sufficient raw cotton to last at least a year at reduced levels of operations. Moreover, the world market was oversupplied with cotton cloth and finished textiles. Again, the better and more reasonable diplomatic strategy of Judah Benjamin and Christopher Memminger was rejected by Davis for political reasons and a failure to grasp the reality of the broad-based European economies.[30]

The Congress, too, supported the president in his commitment to the cotton strategy. Although congressmen frequently debated a national cotton embargo act, it never passed beyond the point of discussion. Davis was convinced that any such overt, coercive embargo would provoke the Europeans, as well as limit their motivation to confront the Northern blockade. In this matter, Davis did see the negative implications of such action. The subtle political sensitivity of Davis is clearly seen in his handling of the cotton embargo situation. This is an example of Davis at his political best, even though the strategy was flawed. He encouraged Congress to talk freely, but never act, and depended on other factors to keep cotton from Europe. A nationwide enthusiasm for cotton diplomacy made a de facto embargo an accomplished fact. State legislatures and extra-legal citizens committees prevented most cotton from leaving the Confederacy in 1861. So effective were these citizens movements that the British Consul in Charleston, Robert Bunch, reported to London on June 5, 1861, when referring to an embargo, "Any act of Congress would be superfluous."[31]

Another indirect Davis strategy to apply pressure on Great Britain and France was legislation passed on May 10 by the Confederate Congress to stop all trade with the Northern United States.[32] Congress passed a law on May 21 that prohibited Southern cotton to be shipped from any seaport except within the Confederate states and Mexico as long as the blockade continued. This law prevented cotton from being sent abroad through the United States and allowed the Confederacy to receive supplies through Mexico. Europeans would have to come directly to Southern ports to receive any sizable quantity of cotton.

Underneath all this legislation, the subtleties of the Davis strategy are evident. The apparent indecision regarding the cotton embargo disguised a foreign policy completely directed by Davis. It did not include a law preventing cotton export, but it did include the veiled threat of enactment of legislation prohibiting or limiting the cotton trade. The point of this effort was to create pressure without offending the Europeans. By closing all ports in the United States to transshipment, Davis hoped to force Great Britain and France to come to Southern ports through the blockade. Although Davis did conduct the two-pronged cotton strategy with a certain amount of finesse at home, the whole scheme was obvious to the Europeans and only reinforced their commitment to neutrality.

By the end of 1861, cotton diplomacy did not prove successful even though a cotton famine was acknowledged in Europe.[33] The accumulated surplus of raw cotton generated by the enormous crop of 1860 allowed time for Egypt and India to increase their cotton production. Although firmly committed to the King Cotton strategy, Davis allowed other arguments and recommendations to affect policy as long as there was no direct conflict with his fundamental strategy of economic coercion.[34]

One substantial component of the Confederate diplomatic strategy was the constitutional argument that justified and legalized the Southern withdrawal from the Union. This legal defense included the assumption that European governments would promptly accord the South recognition because they opposed the encroaching commercial policies of the North. The expectation that the British could identify with the leisurely, agrarian, aristocratic society of the South, while shunning the acquisitive, materialistic North, suggested, inconsistently, that British materialistic impulses would override the principles of antislavery and free trade in the name of anti-materialism.[35] The cultural justification for secession could provide a reason for this element to support the South.

According to a Southern spokesman, the protective Morrill Tariff passed by the U.S. Congress in February 1861 exposed the true measure of the North. The same men who condemned the protectionists in the U.S. Congress failed to see the resemblance of a cotton embargo and a cotton export duty to the Morrill Tariff. Southern protectionists led the fight to defeat Rhett's earlier diplomatic strategy and remained committed to protecting a relatively nonexistent Southern industrial base.[36]

Based on the two principles of constitutional and legal correctness and cotton coercion, the Davis administration expected speedy recognition. As early as February 19, 1861, the prominent Georgia secessionist, Thomas R. R. Cobb, wrote his wife: "Great Britain, France and Russia will acknowledge us at once in the family of nations."[37] When a blockade was suggested, Catherine Edmondson, a Southern lady wrote in her diary in April 1861: "Who cares! Mr. Lincoln's navies will be swept away like dust by the British fleet."[38]

A fundamental flaw in the King Cotton strategy of economic intimidation was the inability of Southern policymakers to understand their own vulnerability to a slowdown in the cotton trade. The Confederacy was more dependent on cotton than any of the industrialized nations it sought to coerce. The lessons of history were again lost on the Southern leadership. They failed to recall the domestic hardships that resulted from the Embargo Act passed during the second administration of their republican ideologue, Thomas Jefferson. Many of the economic hardships that handicapped Confederate diplomats were caused by the absence of profitable cotton commerce.[39]

With these expectations of recognition and intervention in mind, the Confederate government decided on a defensive military strategy. The commitment to secure and defend the borders of the Confederate states allowed Confederate envoys to demonstrate the aggressiveness and forceful nature of the Union government while also offering the certainty of military success.[40]

The South contained a large number of military and political hardliners who preferred to rely on the Confederacy's own resources rather than be dependent on the decisions of foreign powers. This group was prepared to accept arms-length support from Europeans, but pressured Davis to prosecute the war vigorously—thus, victory would require European recognition and cooperation. Davis listened carefully to these military enthusiasts, but based on his military experience, was convinced that a defensive strategy would best enable the Confederacy to meet the requirements for international recognition. Davis felt by quickly securing its sovereign territory, organizing and centralizing a government capable of carrying out its commitments, and entering the international community as a viable commercial participant capable of defending its interests, the Confederacy met the requirements for international recognition. It was against this economic and political backdrop that Davis and his secretary of state, Robert Toombs, appointed and instructed the first Confederate commissioners to Europe.[41]

Chapter 4

Poorly Chosen Diplomats
Produce Poor Diplomacy

In February, before hostilities began at Fort Sumter, the Confederate provisional Congress approved a mission to Europe to pursue Confederate interests and recognition. Davis selected William Lowndes Yancey, Ambrose Dudley Mann, and Pierre A. Rost as the first Confederate emissaries to Europe. All three sailed for Europe in March, expecting to visit the various capitals of Europe and quickly obtain recognition of the Confederacy.[1]

Secretary of State Robert Toombs anticipated the mission led by Yancey would have little difficulty in accomplishing the assigned diplomatic objective. Toombs instructed the envoys to first obtain British recognition, then proceed to the courts of Napoleon III of France, Alexander II of Russia, and Leopold of Belgium.[2] Included in Toombs's instructions was a complete treatise on states' rights, probably drafted by Judah Benjamin, the attorney general and a practicing attorney before secession.

The over reliance of Confederate leadership on the economic approach toward diplomacy and the states rights argument overlooked several important points that deserved consideration. Such problems as how to deal with the naval blockade of Southern ports, European aversion to privateering, lack of wheat and cotton in Great Britain, trade with the North, and the sensitive issue of slavery were not discussed in Toombs's instructions to the Yancey mission. The elaborate states rights argument set forth by Toombs sought to legitimize the withdrawal of the Southern states; but, it could not reasonably be expected to require recognition from an international community concerned with a wide range of interests, none of which included an appreciation of the legal reasons the South used to justify its existence.[3]

When it arrived in Europe, the Yancey mission quickly encountered a major problem that caused difficulty for the South throughout the war. An overwhelming advantage for the Lincoln administration was the existence of an established diplomatic apparatus, including ministers in European capitals, a network of consular officers, and ultimately a large aggregation of spies and intelligence operatives, all directed by a small but efficient State Department. The absence of such a network with access to official diplomatic channels and communications remained a burden for the Southern representatives.

The Washington diplomatic community included the officially recognized representatives of foreign governments with regular access to the U.S. secretary of state. The problems complicating traditionally friendly relations could easily be discussed—informally and officially. This was not possible for Confederates in Europe. The only European representatives in the South were a handful of consuls located mostly at seaports, whose exchequers were held at the pleasure of the Lincoln administration.

Seward only needed to maintain the status quo and stay in contact with his representatives overseas to occupy the diplomatic high ground. His Confederate counterpart, on the other hand, needed to develop a strategy that would allow the safe and speedy flow of diplomatic communications between the new Confederate State Department and the ministries of Europe. The official diplomatic doors were locked securely by the events of the spring and summer of 1861. The arguments of the Yancey mission could only be presented on an unofficial and infrequent basis to the foreign ministers of Great Britain and France. Meanwhile, Seward, aware of the nature of the Confederate arguments, pursued official diplomatic initiatives that contributed to the Confederate lockout from official European diplomatic circles.[4]

The failure of Davis and Toombs to appreciate the problem of diplomatic access is evidenced in Davis's selection of envoys. It is difficult to understand how Davis could have selected three less qualified Southern leaders for the task of obtaining an initial positive response from Great Britain and France.

Yancey, a vehement defender of the institution of slavery, while an

excellent political choice because of his popularity with radical secessionist elements, was a poor choice to represent the slaveholding South
in antislavery Europe. Another reason why Yancey was selected was
the nineteenth-century tradition of diplomatic exile of opposition
political leaders. Yancey, Davis's leading opponent for the Confederate presidency, had contributed, in no small measure, to the splinter-
ing of the Democratic Party during the nationwide election of 1860.
His flamboyant, exaggerated, pro-slavery oratory endorsing the return of the slave trade and the constitutional protection of slavery
placed him at odds with Lord Palmerston, the British prime minister,
and his foreign minister, Lord John Russell. Robert Bunch, British
Consul in Charleston, reported to his superiors that Yancey was able,
but "impulsive, erratic, and hotheaded; a rabid Secessionist, a favourer
of revival of the Slave-Trade, and a 'filibusterer' of the extremist type
of 'manifest destiny.'"[5] The preexisting perception of Yancey by British leaders proved consistent with his behavior throughout his tenure
in Europe. He was consistently impulsive, arrogant, unreasonably
demanding, and inspired little desire on the part of Russell for any
official audience.[6]

William Lowndes Yancey, Confederate envoy and leader
of the first diplomatic mission to Europe.
Courtesy of The Abraham Lincoln Museum, Harrogate, Tennessee.

Lord Palmerston (Henry John Temple, viscount),
British prime minister during the American Civil War, ca. 1860.
Courtesy of The Abraham Lincoln Museum, Harrogate, Tennessee.

Pierre Rost, selected by Davis because of his French birth, was a successful planter and Supreme Court Judge in Louisiana before secession. Rost, like his superiors in Montgomery, overestimated the influence of his language skills and French origin. His Creole-French appeared crude to the French Court, who showed scant enthusiasm for the Southern slaveholder. A French nobleman asked Paul DuBellet, a New Orleans lawyer and self-appointed Confederate agent living in Paris, "Has the South no sons capable of representing your country?"[7] Rost's activities can be characterized as inept and ineffective. His clumsy and crude overtures to the French embarrassed Southern expatriates like DuBellet, whose commercial and professional interests required their residence in France. The large community of Southern Americans, generally sympathetic to the Confederacy, contributed to the limited success of the Confederate diplomatic effort in France. The Southern expatriate community invested in Confederate securities and was eager to use their business and social contacts to provide both information and access for Confederate agents to the French government. But Rost made little contribution to winning support from the French or soliciting the Southern Americans residing in France.[8]

Yancey and Rost traveled together to London by way of New Orleans and the Danish island of St. Thomas, while their colleague, Dudley Mann, decided to sail from New York. Against Davis's advice, Mann determined to pass through Washington and secretly confer with Senators James M. Mason, John C. Breckinridge, and the former U.S. attorney general, Caleb Cushing. Mann's presence in the capital, conducting the business of the seceded states, raised serious diplomatic and legal questions for the newly inaugurated Lincoln administration. Should the administration instruct Federal agents to arrest or detain Mann and confiscate the alleged treasonous papers in Mann's possession, or simply allow him to have his say with several moderate Democrats residing in Washington? The Lincoln administration's decision to allow Mann to proceed on this trip was influenced by the desire to placate the border states and prevent any claim by Southerners that Mann's civil rights were being violated. The policy of the Union would change immediately after the outbreak of hostilities with regard to Confederate agents and their documents.[9]

When questioned about the possibility of his arrest by the State Department before his steamer left the dock in New York, Mann stated, "Until I do something under my commission, I have done nothing that can be construed into treason . . . if it arrested me, the administration would be forced to release me, and it would be damaged even in the North by its having committed so arbitrary an act."[10] For the time being, Seward accepted Mann's argument and allowed him to proceed. Mann's self-assurance reflected a lack of appreciation of the administration's commitment to uniting the nation using whatever power necessary, including the suppression of civil rights.

According to Mann, the opportunity to present the Confederate constitution and supporting arguments for secession to leaders of the border states more than justified the risk of capture. Seward's decision to allow Mann to proceed was correct because of the sensitive and unofficial negotiations in process. Seward hoped for the return of the Southern states and, at least, wanted to prevent the border states from joining their Southern brethren. Any aggressive move could be viewed as forceful coercion, requiring a sympathetic response from the border states and a possible premature outbreak of hostilities in the Deep South.[11]

Mann presented his arguments to the sympathetic Democrats in Washington. When shown the new constitution, Cushing remarked, "There is brains there, gentlemen, brains!."[12] The Confederate constitution praised and encouraged a limited budget, allowed Cabinet members to sit in Congress to discuss departmental affairs, and granted the president a six-year term, while denying reelection. In addition, the African slave trade was prohibited, but slavery was explicitly guaranteed. Mann was naively convinced that the world would recognize the political sophistication contained in the constitution endorsed by the new republic. He sailed for London on March 30 aboard the *Europa* surrounded by sympathetic British cotton brokers and bankers, who contributed to his overconfident attitude. Mann's success in presenting the Confederate arguments in Washington and New York was arguably his only diplomatic success, even though he remained in Europe throughout the Civil War.[13]

Mann arrived in London on April 15, two weeks before his colleagues.[14] The Confederate commissioners quickly made contact with Southern sympathizers, both in and out of government. One of the most enthusiastic members of Parliament championing the Southern cause was William H. Gregory, who arranged an informal interview with Lord Russell for May 3, just four days after the arrival of Yancey and Rost.[15] Since Charles Francis Adams, the U.S. minister, did not arrive in London until May 13, the Confederates had the advantage of arriving first on the field of diplomatic battle.

When the Confederate commissioners met with Russell, news had just arrived of the outbreak of hostilities at Fort Sumter. Yancey, supported by his two colleagues, presented the Confederate position to Russell based on their original instructions of March 16, without comment on the outbreak of armed rebellion. According to the Confederate envoys, Russell opened the meeting by saying, "While it would give pleasure to hear what we had to communicate, he should, under present circumstances, have little to say."[16] Yancey then proceeded to assert that "secession was legal and justified by the steady encroachment of the federal government upon the reserved rights of the states."[17] Yancey emphasized the peaceful nature of Southern secession and the desire of Southerners to remain at peace with the world. These comments, in the light of the recent bombardment of Fort Sumter, must have seemed strange indeed to Russell.

The Confederates saved what they perceived to be their strongest argument to conclude the interview. As Toombs had suggested, they made a "delicate allusion" to the difficulties for Great Britain if the supply of cotton was cut off. The commissioners then concluded their presentation with a request that Great Britain recognize the Confederate states and an expressed hope that "the government of Great Britain would find it to be not only for the benefit of industrial interest generally, but as tending to subserve the interest of peace."[18]

Lord John Russell, British foreign minister, ca. 1863.
Courtesy of The Abraham Lincoln Museum, Harrogate, Tennessee.

In response, Russell asked Yancey to confirm or deny the rumor that the slave trade would be reopened. Yancey promptly denied that the Confederacy had any intention to engage in the international slave trade.[19] Russell then explained that he was not prepared to express any opinion immediately, but assured them he would take the matters discussed to a Cabinet meeting as soon as possible. The Southerners reported to Toombs that the interview suggested a profound hostility toward the Confederacy on the slavery issue, but that the prevailing desire in Parliament and the Cabinet was to recognize the Confederacy in the near future, despite Great Britain's opposition to slavery.[20]

Meanwhile, the news that Americans were engaged in armed conflict created an urgent need in Great Britain to develop a policy position toward the developing "American question." The outbreak of civil war in America had come as no surprise to the Europeans. For several months preceding the fall of Fort Sumter, an active correspondence discussing the potential problems of armed insurrection had been conducted between the British and French ministers in Washington and their home governments.[21]

The result of the correspondence from British Minister Lord

Richard Lyons and French Minister Henri Merciér in Washington was to create impressions and preconceived notions in the minds of British and French officials charged with the responsibility of contriving a policy toward the American crisis. It was, of course, the responsibility of diplomats serving in a foreign nation to provide the home government with thoughtful and accurate impressions of the situation, particularly as a crisis evolves. Lyons and Merciér met the requirements of this responsibility with frequent reports throughout January, February, and March. As early as January, Merciér communicated his concerns to Paris of a northern blockade of southern ports and advised Paris that such an action would certainly provoke the southern states to arms.[22]

The Morrill Tariff passed by Congress on February 20, 1861, provoked Lyons to remark to Merciér, "We, therefore, are threatened with finding ourselves stopped by a northern blockade—in the south by ships, in the north by the tariff—and we must, therefore, take precautions."[23] Concerned over trade restrictions and the protection of neutral citizens should hostilities occur, Lyons and Merciér recommended to their home governments that a unified policy of cooperation toward America be adopted. The ministers believed a consistent and uniform policy would prevent the cagey Seward from playing one nation against the other.

The ensuing policy of cooperation and unified action by Britain and France with regard to the "American question" contributed substantially throughout the conflict to the Confederate diplomatic failure. The Anglo-French entente was made official after negotiations between the foreign ministries of the respective governments in Europe. The initial suggestion of this policy, however, apparently came from Lyons and Merciér.[24]

Most members of the foreign diplomatic community in Washington in the winter of 1861 believed the secessionists would succeed in partitioning the United States into two nations. Baron Edouard de Stoeckl, the Russian minister in Washington and a close friend of Lyons and Merciér, advised his government that the expected success of the Confederacy would create a disruption in the existing balance of power. The Russians never joined with the British and French in any attempt to act jointly on the "American question." Although Stoeckl compared Southern slaves to Russian serfs and the emerging Southern aristocracy to Russian aristocrats, the official Russian policy was to support the Union position throughout the war. Social similarities notwithstanding, the Russians opposed any further Anglo-French expansion into the Western Hemisphere and remem-

British Minister Lord Richard Lyons. Courtesy of
The Abraham Lincoln Museum, Harrogate, Tennessee.

French Minister Henri Merciér. Courtesy of
The Abraham Lincoln Museum, Harrogate, Tennessee.

bered who their enemies were during the Crimean War. A strong United States, in the Russian view, encumbered French and British ambitions.[25]

Seward, however, through Lyons, threatened British trade and even suggested that war against a European power might unite the divided Americans against an external threat. While Seward's strategy worked to counter any receptivity to the Confederate recognition strategy in Europe, his policy also encouraged Anglo-French cooperation and contributed to the neutrality the British and French ultimately adopted. Any possibility that the British, in particular, would cooperate with the recognized government of the United States in suppressing a rebellion was precluded by Seward's bellicose rhetoric.[26] Seward had every reason to believe early recognition of the Confederacy was probable. He sought first to prevent the Southern envoys from conducting an effective policy to obtain legitimacy and recognition. His style and techniques appeared to be desperate, but the strategy succeeded in the face of what looked like long odds.[27]

Yancey and his colleagues failed to seize the early opportunities for the success of their mission. Instead of assiduously following the instructions of Toombs, they could have asked Russell and the British leadership how Southerners could assist them in confronting the frustrating problems that would result from the outbreak of hostilities in America. Yancey made no attempt to address British concerns. He and the other Confederates remained both insensitive and inflexible.

On May 3, the day of his first interview with the Confederate emissaries, Russell received a memorandum from the attorney general advocating recognition of the South as a belligerent. On the next day, May 4, he informed Lyons in Washington that the South would be thus recognized.[28] On May 7, Lord Henry Cowley, the British ambassador in Paris, wrote that the French government would act in concert with the British in issuing a proclamation of neutrality that would automatically carry a recognition of belligerency.[29] The British foreign office issued a formal proclamation on May 13, recognizing Confederate belligerent status and taking a neutral position toward the American conflict. The proclamation was published in the *London Gazette* on May 14. The Anglo-French position appeared to both the Confederates and the Lincoln administration as the first step toward recognition.[30]

Newly arrived in London, U. S. Minister Charles Francis Adams quickly sought a meeting with Russell to protest recognition of belligerent states; and in an interview on May 18, told Russell that the British government, acting in haste, had showed its bias in favor of the Confederacy. Adams claimed that the British had recognized the South as a belligerent state "before they had ever showed their capacity to maintain any kind of warfare whatever, except within one of their own harbors under every possible advantage . . . it considered them a maritime power before they had ever exhibited a single privateer upon the ocean."[31] The first objective of Adams was to forestall any further formal recognition and stop the momentum that was building toward Confederate recognition. Remarkably, this decision to cooperate with the French, adopt a neutral position, and recognize Confederate belligerency was completed without the aid, advice, counsel, and, apparently, the knowledge of the Confederate diplomatic agents sent to coordinate the Confederate effort.

While the British and French foreign ministries were completing the details of this important policy position, the Confederates asked for and received another interview on May 9 to present instructions and information they had received since their first interview with Russell. The British foreign minister kept the Confederates in the dark about the imminence of his government's forthcoming neutrality proclamation and agreed once again to take up the matter of recognition with the Cabinet at a convenient time in the future. In this extraordinary diplomatic atmosphere, Yancey wrote Toombs that the British government would "postpone recognition of the independence of those states as long as possible, at least until some decided advantage is obtained by them or the necessity of having cotton becomes pressing."[32] It is amazing that the Confederates did not immediately recognize the implications of the neutrality proclamation and seek to exploit the opportunities presented by British recognition of their belligerent status.

It should have been clear to the Southerners that the Palmerston ministry was preparing for the possibility of dealing with two American nations. Russell was confronted with the task of maintaining communications with the North and South, while at the same time solidifying British relations with France to prevent Napoleon from exploiting any Anglo-American troubles for French interests. Instead of offering cooperation and protection for British citizens and interests in the South, Yancey stubbornly continued to expect cotton to bring the most powerful nation in the world over to the side of the Confederacy.[33]

The Union's response to the Queen's neutrality proclamation was quick and verbally ferocious. Charles Sumner, chairman of the Senate Foreign Relations Committee, called it "the most hateful act of English history since the time of Charles II." When Seward received

the information that France would take a similar position, he warned
both nations of the possibility of war.[34]

Both North and South failed to appreciate the state of emergency
felt by the Europeans in the aftermath of the outbreak of hostilities.
Lincoln's blockade announcement required interpretation within the
established framework of international law. Davis's authorization of
letters of marque to legitimize privateering required the maritime
powers to take action to protect their commerce. The failure to appreciate the potential diplomatic implications of their actions suggests that both Lincoln and Davis were ignorant of international law,
or at best, its practical application by neutrals.

Americans on both sides suddenly found their interests better served
by the traditional arguments of the maritime powers of past wars.
The North, in particular, was now involved in a blockade similar to
the blockade of Europe during the Napoleonic Wars that contributed to the War of 1812. The experienced Palmerston, who was almost as old as the United States, understood international law. He
appreciated the need to prevent the establishment of precedents that
would encumber future British maritime policy. Both American administrations were attempting to force and coerce Europeans into
accepting positions favorable to their respective governments. The
rhetoric from Washington was harsh and threatening, and the South
continued to depend on the "righteousness of their cause" and cotton extortion to achieve their goals.[35]

In 1861, the conditions of the Treaty of Paris seemed advantageous to the United States. Seward instructed Adams in London and
Dayton in Paris to sign the treaty. American adherence would require
the British and French fleets to pursue and capture privateers and
prosecute them as pirates, holding the government responsible that
issued the letters of marque. But one of the conditions of the Treaty
of Paris was to require the unanimous consent of all previous signees
to the addition of any future signees. After extended negotiations,
both the British and French refused to allow the United States to
join with the other nations agreeing to the treaty. They believed the
United States' participation would interfere with their commitment
to neutrality. The British did request that both North and South adhere to the conditions of the treaty and agree, in general, to its terms,
even though they would not allow either side to formalize their commitment to the treaty.[36]

Soon after the issuance of the British neutrality proclamation,
Pierre Rost hastened to Paris for an interview with Count de Morny,
a close advisor and half-brother to the emperor. Rost hoped to gain

a commitment to recognize the Confederacy and assumed that belligerent status was the first step in that direction. The Neutrality Proclamation notwithstanding, de Morny seemed friendly but explained to Rost that the French expected to treat the South with "perfect neutrality for the present." He went on to say that neither France nor England wanted the United States reunited, but at the present, nothing beyond belligerent recognition could be accomplished. He added that "the French government would always be ready to receive unofficially and to give due consideration to any suggestions" offered by the Confederate agents. Telling Rost that "in his opinion, recognition was a mere question of time," he advised the Southerner to maintain strict secrecy concerning their unofficial communications. In the same interview, de Morny apparently pledged to Rost that France would not recognize the Northern blockade. The count assured Rost, according to the Southerner's report, that "[s]o long as we produce cotton for sale, France and England would see that their vessels reached the ports where it was to be had." The Confederate envoys were encouraged by the unofficial comments of such a highly placed French official, but failed to appreciate the implications of his unofficial status.[37]

In their June reports to the Confederate State Department, Yancey and Mann emphasized the European reluctance to recognize the Confederacy beyond its belligerent status until there was evidence of the new republic's ability to protect and sustain itself. As soon as news of a substantial military victory reached Britain and France, recognition might reasonably be expected.[38]

The Commissioners also reported that slavery remained a stumbling block to recognition. Yancey noted that he expected the demand for cotton, along with guarantees not to engage in the international slave trade, to overcome this obstacle. He had declared to the British government that the Lincoln administration was no more abolitionist than was the South. In fact, Lincoln, like Davis, was prepared to guarantee slavery where it already existed, while outlawing the slave trade. Yancey expected these arguments to place both North and South in similar positions as far as the Europeans were concerned with regard to slavery. Yancey did not report to his home government the persuasive arguments being offered by Adams to the Palmerston government regarding slavery. Adams was arguing that any accommodation of the South would be to give support to slavery in opposition to popular opinion in Great Britain.[39]

Yancey decided to join Rost in Paris three weeks after the favorable interview Rost had with de Morny. After examination of the

political and diplomatic atmosphere in Paris, Yancey and Rost concluded that France and Britain were only waiting for a decisive victory before recognizing the South. When the French government
was satisfied that the North and South were irreconcilable, the two
commissioners reported to Toombs, "They will be easily satisfied as
to our ability to maintain our position, and . . . when the cotton crop
is ready for market, their necessities will force them to conclusions
favorable to the South."[40] The two men successfully obtained an interview with the French Foreign Minister Antoine Edouard
Thouvenel, who confirmed the French position of neutrality and suggested that it would be unwise to press for immediate recognition.
Yancey concluded correctly that Thouvenel was pro-Union and reported that Napoleon was primarily concerned with European affairs
and would, therefore, allow England to make the initial decisions
regarding the recognition question.[41]

Yancey failed to report that Napoleon was preparing to expand
the French empire into Mexico. In addition, Napoleon had earlier
instructed Merciér to recommend Anglo-French mediation to the
United States. Although the Confederate commissioners did not always have access to complete and timely information from home,
they should have gauged more accurately the realities in Europe.
Apparently, the only accurate observation contained in the Yancey-
Rost report of July 15 was the expression of need for a decisive military victory to expedite recognition. Even this assessment was
downplayed while the cotton solution was emphasized. Yancey reported that "the question of recognition must be determined by the
cotton situation." Yancey expected recognition to come in the fall
after the cotton was gathered and "the supply of that article here is
exhausted and no other means of replenishing it can be found than
through treaties with the Confederate States."[42] Even though Yancey
and Rost misunderstood his motives, Napoleon did favor the separation of the United States and joint Anglo-French intervention both
to obtain cotton and improve his chances of a successful Mexican
adventure.[43]

Movement toward Confederate recognition continued in Paris
despite the miscalculations of the Confederate commissioners. One
of the recognizable realities of mid-nineteenth-century international
relations was military power. If the Confederates could demonstrate
decisively their ability to overcome their enemies on the battlefield,
they could overcome their diplomatic failures.

Most European military experts expected the South to prevail
militarily, if for no other reason than the sheer magnitude of the ter-

ritory to be occupied and controlled by their enemies. A widely accepted military axiom of the day was the overwhelming advantage of the defense engaged in battle. The Confederacy expected to defend its borders and, therefore, conduct an essentially defensive war. Unfortunately for the Confederacy, the expectation that its army would prove its military ability in the long run suggested that European countries could remain unengaged while awaiting the fulfillment of their objective of a divided America. Nevertheless, the Confederates persisted in their expectation that recognition would be forthcoming in the fall following the expected early Confederate victories.[44]

On July 21, at Bull Run, Virginia, the Confederate army under the command of Gen. Pierre G. T. Beauregard routed the Federal army under the command of Gen. Irvin McDowell. Now the Confederate commissioners had their victory. On July 22, Lyons wrote his superiors of the stunning defeat of the North. Palmerston remarked that Bull Run should be known as "Yankees Run,"[45] and went on to report to his colleagues that the Northern defeat demonstrated a "lack of resolution attributable to its fighting for an idea chiefly entertained by professional politicians, whereas the Confederates were fighting for what they considered, rightly or wrongly, vital interests."[46] Charles Adams now feared that diplomatic recognition of the South hinged on the Union's "trial by fire." He would not have been surprised had Confederate recognition been forthcoming,[47] confiding to his diary that the British press unanimously acknowledged the Union's humiliation and spoke favorably of Southern independence.[48] Meanwhile, the Confederate commissions received the news of the Confederate victory from the new secretary of state, R. M. T. Hunter. They believed the European newspapers to be correct in their conclusion that this proved the South was invincible. Yancey and Mann in London hastily wired Rost to return from Paris immediately so that they might submit a demand for recognition.[49]

The Confederate commissioners dispatched a note to Russell requesting an informal interview as a preliminary to a formal presentation and request for recognition. The British foreign ministry previously had snubbed both Yancey and Mann, particularly offending Yancey. Despite the previous rejection of their social and official presentments, the commissioners expected, in light of the Confederate victory at Bull Run, to be received unofficially by Lord Russell. Instead, the British minister sidestepped their request and requested they communicate only in writing. Although offended by Russell's response, the commissioners were already preparing their formal communication, so the preparation of their response was not delayed by the need to reduce it to writing.[50]

On August 14, within a week after Russell's initial request, the written Confederate argument went forward. Again, the arguments previously presented to Russell on May 3 and May 9 were advanced, backed by an elaborate dissertation on Confederate military power. The commissioners pointed out that the Confederacy now included four more states: Tennessee, Arkansas, North Carolina, and Virginia. They explained the "impregnable military position" resulting from the vast territory included in the Confederacy and pointed out the complete failure, thus far, of all efforts at conquest by the North. The Union army had failed to penetrate any distance into the Confederacy and had been overwhelmed in the one great battle fought so far. Finally, the commission included an attempt to overcome the antislavery sentiment in Britain by pointing out that "the very party in power has proposed to guarantee slavery forever if the states of the South would but remain in the Union."[51] Unable to pass up an opportunity to suggest the British need for cotton, the commissioners suggested the Lincoln administration might cause a servile revolt that would forever prevent the production of cotton at a reasonable price.[52]

The commission had acted without the knowledge that Toombs had resigned and been replaced by Robert Hunter as secretary of state, and without formal instructions from their superiors. In fact, Hunter had communicated little more than the news of Bull Run to his emissaries in his July 29 dispatch. If Hunter had appreciated the importance of a military victory to the Confederate diplomatic effort, he would not have waited nine days to communicate such important good news.[53]

On August 24, Russell replied to the Confederate request. He reaffirmed British neutrality by stating that Her Majesty's government would wait until "the fortune of arms or the more peaceful mode of negotiation shall have more clearly determined the respective positions of the two belligerents."[54] In communicating to their government, the Confederate commissioners expressed little surprise at the British reserve action and suggested that recognition would be forthcoming before Christmas. If the Confederate cause needed a victory to obtain recognition, Bull Run was certainly an overwhelming victory. The Confederates were content to play a waiting game because of their confidence in the power of cotton and the success of a defensive military strategy.

As events in America and major policy decisions in Europe continued to build toward recognition, threatening to involve European powers in the American Civil War, a number of diplomatic issues in America contributed to the confusing malaise. The initial defense of British neutrality was solidly grounded in international law, but the Lincoln/Seward administration threatened in the spring of 1861 to close Southern ports instead of declaring a blockade. By closing Southern ports, the Federal government was exercising its right to control and suppress an internal insurrection. The Southern states could be declared in a state of rebellion. A blockade of international trade, however, suggested the existence of a belligerent state and tended to legitimize the Southern government. Seward exploited the port closure maneuver to prevent British recognition of the Confederacy. The simplicity of the maneuver enabled Britain, if they so desired, to avoid confrontation over the definition of a paper blockade while affording the Union navy an opportunity to interdict commerce in Southern ports.[55]

The issue raised constitutional questions for the Union because the Constitution prohibited favoritism of one section or state over another, including its ports. Ports could be closed under the Constitution only if they were not a part of the United States and municipal laws did not apply. The issue was not resolved because by midsummer, the British decision to accept the blockade made the port closure issue irrelevant. Nevertheless, the Confederates failed to recognize any opportunity to exploit the fiery rhetoric from Washington and the potential for a breach of international law and an unconstitutional interpretation. Although they argued that the blockade was illegal later in the diplomatic campaign, it was necessary first to acquire evidence that international commerce with the South remained heavy before the Union could be accused of an ineffective blockade.[56]

A successful diplomatic effort closer to home involved a less sophisticated diplomatic community than existed in Britain and France. On August 12, 1861, Albert Pike, a Confederate commissioner, concluded several treaties between his government and the elements of the "five civilized tribes" living in the Indian territories (Oklahoma). The treaty contained several ambiguous clauses with references to horse stealing and the Indians' commitment not to "go on the warpath." The Indians did pledge, however, to support the government of the Confederacy in exchange for protection from "any power or people, state or person whatever."[57] Pike was resourceful and knowledgeable and made sound suggestions to President Davis on Indian policy. The treaty accomplished several things. It protected the western door of the Confederacy from an Indian uprising and it created a loyal ally. The Indians contributed a fighting force to the Confederacy at Pea Ridge in March 1862 and in earlier campaigns.

With the Confederate defeat at Pea Ridge, the Southern armies were unable to protect the Indian territory from Northern invasion. As the Union army pressed its advantage, the Indian tribes lost their enthusiasm for the Confederacy.[58] The Confederates could have used Pike's treaty as evidence of their stature as a nation, but no evidence exists that it was ever cited in any diplomatic argument. The agreement itself is a credit to Pike, given the fact that only a generation earlier, the tribes had been expelled from the South. The Confederate leadership could have benefited from the Indian situation by recognizing that military power, or the absence of it, often creates an ally or an enemy. The Indians had little concern for King Cotton, nor did they understand the nature of states rights, free trade, or constitutional government. They did understand and appreciate, however, the need to protect and sustain their own best interests—with force of arms if necessary.[59]

Another opportunity was presented to the Confederates as the result of the political disruption in Mexico. The Richmond government expected to secure an alliance with Mexico against the "land-grabbing Yankees." The establishment of friendly relations guaranteed access to the outside world from Mexican seaports and the opportunity for lucrative trade and land transportation across the Rio Grande into Texas. These opportunities were obvious to the Southerners, but the Mexicans remembered the "land-grabbing Yankees" were generally supported and led by Southerners, particularly in the Mexican War and the Texas revolution.

The Confederate State Department remained consistent in its poor selection of commissioners and appointed John T. Pickett, a former Cuban filibusterer and first-class conniver, to Mexico City. Pickett quickly assessed the liberal Juarez government as sympathetic to the Union, particularly in light of current negotiations with the United States for an eleven-million-dollar loan. He, therefore, decided to support the conservative Church Party, offending the liberal government in power. Pickett reasoned that Juarez only controlled part of Mexico and the conservatives were likely to strengthen their position.[60]

Throughout the summer of 1861, Pickett was involved in numerous unsavory incidents culminating in a barroom brawl with another U.S. citizen sympathetic to the Juarez cause. The fight resulted in Pickett spending thirty days in jail, only to be released after bribing a local judge. Fortunately for Confederate/Mexican relations, Pickett beat a hasty retreat to Richmond to await the triumphant return of the Church Party to Mexico City. While Pickett was engaged in these activities in late 1861, he forwarded a number of dispatches to Richmond by way of a New Orleans postmaster. Embarrassingly for Pickett, the postmaster was a Union spy and turned over the incriminating dispatches to the Union authorities for publication. Neither the Church Party nor Pickett returned to Mexico City.[61]

Juan A. Quintero, a Confederate agent sent to operate along the Mexican border, performed far better and more effectively than any of the Southern agents operating in northern Mexico. After visiting the governor of Monterey, Santiago Vidaurri, Quintero returned to Richmond and reported to Hunter that Vidaurri was prepared to enter into a permanent alliance against Juarez in northeastern Mexico. Hunter and Davis, although aware of the importance of the area to the Confederate border, were reluctant to embroil the nation in Mexican politics. Despite the rejection of a firm alliance, Quintero returned to Monterey and engaged in extensive commercial activity across the Rio Grande. Southern cotton was exchanged for arms, ammunition, powder, metals, coffee, sugar, and other goods from the outside world. Matamoras flourished and was protected, remaining a port of entry supporting the Southern war effort west of the Mississippi throughout the war. In spite of Pickett's failure in Mexico City, Confederate activities along the border secured a solid base for future diplomatic and commercial activity.[62]

Chapter 5

Interrupted Momentum and Disrupted Strategy

In the fall of 1861, England and France ventured to the brink of formal recognition of the Confederate states. Yancey and Rost reported to Hunter that Napoleon had been discussing the possibility of official recognition within his Cabinet since his return from a Vichy vacation in late September.[1] Thouvenel instructed Merciér again to approach Lyons in Washington about recognition.[2] Meanwhile, several frustrating problems brought the British to grudgingly consider formal recognition.

One nagging problem for both European nations involved the status of their citizens within the Confederacy. Both nations expected to continue to use their consuls in important trade centers throughout the South to communicate with the appropriate officials. Unfortunately, foreign consuls residing in both sections of the country received their accreditation from the U.S. State Department in Washington. Immediately after the outbreak of hostilities, Seward declared that the United States expected foreign consuls in the areas of insurrection to transact official business only through their ministers in Washington. According to Seward, any direct communication with Confederate officials would jeopardize their diplomatic status.[3] Therefore, it became extremely difficult for the consuls residing in the South to conduct their routine business, which included the need to contact government officials on behalf of foreign citizens.[4] It was not consular routine, however, that concerned Seward, but the possibility that the representatives of foreign governments would engage in official diplomatic communications with the de facto Confederate government, thus acknowledging its existence as a sovereign independent government. Seward, at least to this point, was remarkably successful in excluding Confederate representatives from official diplomatic circles at home and abroad, causing great frustration for the Southerners.[5]

In mid-August, Seward learned that Robert Mure, a businessman from Charleston, was en route to New York on his way to England. Seward's informants charged that Mure was carrying official dispatches from Richmond to the British foreign office in London. Mure was traveling on a British passport issued by Robert Bunch, the British consul in Charleston, thus placing the issue of the limits of consular activity squarely in front of Seward.[6]

Seward decided to order the New York police to seize Mure, a Colonel in the South Carolina militia and a cousin of the British consul in New Orleans, along with his papers. After Mure's arrest, a search of his luggage produced a sealed consular mailbag, a huge batch of private letters, a letter of introduction written by Bunch, and several unsealed copies of an inflammatory pamphlet praising the South's victory at Bull Run.[7] These documents implicated Bunch in a British initiative to obtain Confederate adherence to the Declaration of Paris. The use of Bunch's official consular position to safeguard Confederate dispatches infuriated Seward. Many of the letters from sympathetic British expatriates were treasonous in Seward's opinion. After examining the unsealed letters, but not the contents of Bunch's sealed consular pouch, Seward decided to act.[8]

Seward sent the unopened consular dispatch bag to Adams in London by courier, with instructions to deliver it directly to Russell. He pointed out to Adams that the seals remained unbroken because of his faith in the traditionally friendly relations with Great Britain and his commitment to diplomatic propriety. Seward instructed Adams to point out that British consuls did not have the authority to issue passports and to remind Russell that diplomatic communications should be conducted through official channels.[9]

By sending the bag through Adams to Russell, Seward left the British an exit from the awkward situation. Russell could disavow any knowledge of the documents, refuse to accept them, and declare them illegal, or instruct Adams to leave the matter to the discretion of the American secretary of state. Adams was convinced that British and French consuls in the South were working closely with the Confederates. After a cursory examination of the unsealed documents, Adams declared the papers were treasonable and that Bunch should be recalled immediately. In fact, one of the letters addressed to a Confederate agent in Europe contained the statement that "this is the first step of direct treaty with our government," suggesting that foreign recognition was endorsed by Bunch and other British citizens sympathetic to the Confederacy.[10]

Russell denied the allegations of Seward and Adams that the consular activities of Bunch were treasonous. Although he acknowledged that Bunch had acted under "secret instructions which were only now acknowledged because they have come to light,"[11] he affirmed that nothing in the bag supported a charge of conspiracy. Reminding Adams of the difficult communication problems imposed on British citizens as the result of the Union's suspension of normal postal service, Russell refused to recall his consul and denied that Great Britain had taken the first step toward recognition. "The British," he declared, "have not recognized, and are not prepared to recognize, the so-called Confederate States as a separate and independent state."[12] The Bunch affair emphasized the frustrating problems caused by the lack of access by official representatives of the British government to the Confederate State Department. The Mure documents showed that the British were interested in negotiating with the Confederate government on a quasi-diplomatic basis.

As early as May 18, Russell had instructed Lyons to take steps to secure the assent of the Confederate officials to the rules of the 1856 Paris Declaration. Robert Bunch was to undertake this mission. On July 5, therefore, Lyons wrote Bunch, including a copy of Russell's May 18 instructions. About the same time, orders from Thouvenel were forwarded by Merciér to the French consul at Charleston, Belligny de Saint-Croix. Both consuls, who resided in Charleston, were advised not to go to Richmond to negotiate directly with the Confederate government, and, above all, to avoid any implication of recognition. Lyons was determined to remain as distant from the negotiations as possible and warned that any disclosure of his involvement might lead to an "inconvenient outbreak."[13] The communication from Lyons leaves no doubt that Bunch was to engage in unofficial diplomatic negotiations with the as-yet-unrecognized Confederate government to secure its adherence to the Paris accord. Lyons's expectation that Seward would demand Bunch's recall or withdraw his exequatur if the purpose of his mission was exposed is unmistakable. Even though the British and French continued to deny any anticipated recognition throughout the summer and early fall, the instructions to open diplomatic communications to protect British commercial and neutral interests suggested at least another step toward recognition.[14]

After receiving their instructions, Bunch and Belligny met and decided to approach William Trescot, a former assistant U.S. secretary of state residing in South Carolina, with the idea of carrying their unofficial message to Richmond. On July 19, the Europeans— joined by Durant St. Andre, Belligny's designated replacement—met with their intermediary. During the evening meeting, the emphasis was on secrecy. When Trescot asked for their recommendation on how to maintain a "secret announcement," the Europeans suggested that a "spontaneous announcement" of acceptance of Articles 2 and 3 of the Declaration of Paris would not reveal the clandestine negotiations that preceded it. The consuls emphasized to Trescot that the mission did not imply recognition but stated, "The consequences would be most agreeable and beneficial to the Confederate government."[15] Excited by the opportunity, Trescot agreed to go to Richmond, meet with his old acquaintance Jefferson Davis, and advise that he bore an important communication from Bunch and Belligny which could only be revealed in the strictest confidence. Trescot promised the consuls that he would not open negotiations unless Davis agreed to accept the condition of secrecy.[16]

Trescot, a veteran diplomat, realized the potential for recognition. The South Carolinian set out from Charleston by train for Richmond on July 20, carrying copies of Bunch's instructions. Upon arriving in Richmond on July 22, he learned of the Confederate victory at Bull Run and decided to continue his journey the next morning to Manassas Junction to locate Davis, who had gone to meet with his generals and victorious troops. While traveling toward Manassas, Trescot learned that Davis was aboard a train carrying wounded soldiers to Richmond and decided to get off and await the train en route to Richmond. Trescot managed to board the train and rode with President Davis to Richmond, arranging a formal interview for the next day.[17] In the subsequent interview with Davis, Trescot presented the papers entrusted to him and reported on his meeting with the three European representatives. The President readily appreciated the significance of the proposal and agreed to call a Cabinet meeting to discuss it, telling Trescot that the government's decision would be communicated to him by the secretary of state.[18]

Trescot was well qualified to carry the Anglo-French proposal. He had served as under-secretary of state during the Buchanan administration, holding the position of acting secretary of state at one point.

His diplomatic career had begun in November 1822, when at the age of thirty, he had been appointed secretary of legation at London. Thereafter, he combined intermittent diplomatic service with the practice of law until his return to Charleston in early 1861. Throughout his final days in Washington before the war, he had assisted Jefferson Davis and prominent Southern representatives in their negotiations with the Buchanan administration. Within his chosen field of diplomacy, Trescot was one of America's earliest historians, and published *The Diplomatic History of the Administrations of Washington and Adams* in 1857. He counted among his acquaintances high-ranking British officials and continental diplomats, as well as a host of prominent Americans.[19] Jefferson Davis's failure to appreciate the value and experience of Trescot, while appointing the likes of Yancey, Mann, and Rost to key diplomatic positions is inexplicable. After the summer of 1861, Trescot joined the staff of Gen. Roswell S. Ripley, but his diplomatic skills were never requested by Jefferson Davis. After the war, Trescot returned to diplomatic service to continue a distinguished career.[20]

On the morning of July 26, Davis met with the members of his Cabinet who agreed to introduce a resolution to Congress to accept Articles 2, 3, and 4 of the Declaration of Paris, omitting the article outlawing privateering. The Congress passed the initial resolution on August 8, but quickly amended it on August 13, emphasizing the Confederacy's determination to exercise its right to issue letters of marque and continue privateering "as established practice and recognized by the law of nations."[21]

While Trescot continued attempts to impress on the president and his new Secretary of State Robert M. T. Hunter the urgency of the opportunity presented for recognition, confusion and indecisiveness prevailed within the administration. The responsibility of presenting and passing the resolution was Hunter's, who clearly underestimated the potential of the resolution as a weapon in the diplomatic war for recognition.[22] Instead, he sought to use the important moment to enhance his political ambitions and demonstrate his authority and prestige within the administration. Hunter was an experienced politician, having served previously in the U.S. House of Representatives. Like his predecessor Robert Toombs, he feared that service as Confederate secretary of state might relegate him to political obscurity. While Toombs and others basked in military glory, Hunter believed it was his fate to introduce dry and insignificant resolutions such as the one proposed by Trescot. The success of the Confederate army at Bull Run sealed the resignation of Toombs and immediately created political anxieties for his successor. Like Toombs, Hunter was miscast as secretary of state, more because of his motives and ambition than lack of skill.[23]

Although Davis received encouraging communications from the Confederates in Europe following the glorious news from Bull Run, he failed to recognize the opportunity to seize the diplomatic initiative. The failure of the Confederate State Department to aggressively pursue the diplomatic opportunity presented by Bunch and Trescot demonstrated a lack of understanding of current realities. Davis could have appointed the experienced Trescot as a special envoy to communicate directly to Russell the Confederacy's acceptance of the Paris Declaration, thereby establishing an additional semi-official line of communication. The parameters of the recognition debate would certainly have been expanded, creating an opportunity for a Confederate breakthrough. Instead, the Confederate government remained unshaken in its commitment to the power of cotton.[24]

Under pressure from Adams and Seward and worried about diplomatic complications emanating from the commissioning of Confederate privateers, Great Britain closed her ports to Confederate prizes. This made it difficult for the Confederates to successfully engage in privateering. Davis instructed Trescot to communicate to the European consuls his grave concern over the "spontaneous acknowledgment" of the anti-privateering clause of the Declaration of Paris and the closing of British ports to Confederate privateers. The result was to reduce the positive impact of adherence to the remaining articles of the treaty. Instead of showing resentment, the Confederates could have seized the opportunity to demonstrate a spirit of cooperativeness and concern for European interests within the territories under the control of the Confederate government. The Confederates might have pointed out that problems created by the lack of official diplomatic channels could be alleviated through recognition.

Seward, continuing to seize the initiative at every opportunity, escalated the Bunch affair to crisis level. He demanded the recall of Bunch and ultimately withdrew his exequatur. The result was to keep the British policymakers on the defensive by requiring Russell to defend the actions of Bunch and accept responsibility for the negotiations. There is little doubt that both the British and French consuls were conducting diplomacy on behalf of their home governments without the proper credentials to the Confederate government. An opportunity was lost by the Confederate State Department to offer some form of unofficial status to the consuls. This would have left options for Russell to combat Seward's one-sided demands.[25]

Russell told Adams, while denying any wrongdoing, that if the Confederacy was not a foreign state, Bunch did not deserve to have his exequatur revoked. Bunch was not an American and had no instructions to help a foreign government at odds with the United States because the Richmond people were not a recognized government.[26] No assistance was rendered to Americans to attempt to circumvent the established government.[27] Moreover, Russell could not evade the plain fact that Bunch had gone far beyond normal consular functions to make diplomatic overtures to an unrecognized rebel government. The issue of Bunch's credentials gave Seward an opportunity to maintain his aggressive diplomatic posture throughout most of 1861. The Confederates, on the other hand, remained relatively passive and chose not to engage in any diplomatic strategy that might interrupt the momentum moving toward recognition by the Europeans.

Contributing to the momentum in the summer of 1861 was Napoleon's decision to aggressively pursue an imperialistic policy in Mexico. He joined with Great Britain and Spain in an allied military operation to collect debts owed the three countries by the Mexicans. After initial cooperation and a demonstration of force, the British and Spanish abandoned Mexico to Napoleon, who continued military action aimed at the creation of a French puppet state in Mexico. The French ambitions in Mexico, coupled with the economic distress within France caused by the disruption of normal commerce with the United States, influenced Napoleon to consider normalizing relations with the South. He was prepared to join the British in recognizing the Confederacy by October of 1861. Indeed, Thouvenel informed Merciér that unless Southern ports could be reopened and neutral commerce reinstated, France would be compelled to recognize the Confederacy.[28]

Seemingly, there were compelling reasons for European governments to recognize the Confederacy. The previously flourishing commercial activity between the two continents had been badly disrupted by the Northern blockade and might be interrupted further by Southern privateers. The absence of normal communications created friction over minor issues. European citizens residing in the South needed protection from the ravages of war. The United States, blockading the Southern seacoast and searching for Confederate warships off foreign shores, might cause an international maritime incident sufficient to cause a military response. The French adventure in Mexico, as well as a smaller Spanish incursion into San Domingo were provocations which the United States government was bound to resist sooner or later. Although these issues seemed to overshadow Northern opposition to recognition, Confederate diplomats failed to incorporate them into a comprehensive strategy to attain that goal.

For the Confederacy to gain recognition in the fall of 1861, the South's leaders needed to demonstrate to the Europeans that such a step was not likely to embroil them in a war with the United States. By controlling the diplomatic high ground throughout the summer and fall of 1861, Seward made the British and French feel that the risk and cost of war was too high a price to pay to normalize relations with the Confederacy. If the Davis administration had capitalized on Palmerston's belief that the United States would not "draw its sword" against the power of Europe and persuasively outlined the advantages of recognition to the Europeans, the initial Confederate diplomatic effort might have succeeded. The recognition momentum seemed to be moving toward a favorable decision for the Confederates by October 1861. Despite the lack of able envoys in Europe and the apathy of the Confederate State Department, the assumption remained firmly in the minds of Confederate policymakers that recognition would come as a result of its own initiative and required no positive action from Southern diplomats.

In November, the issue shifted away from recognition toward direct military confrontation because of the seizure of two Confederate envoys, James Mason and John Slidell from the British packet ship *Trent*. The diplomatic explosion caused by the *Trent* affair brought the question of sovereign rights on the high seas to a point of potential confrontation. The issue of an Atlantic war, which would reasonably include all members of the Atlantic community, was defined by the *Trent* incident. British demands for an apology and the return of the Southerners gave Lincoln and Seward a chance for the European war they had discussed in March of 1861. The British, on the other hand, sought the support of the French and examined the consequences of military action against the United States. The capture of the Confederate commissioners caused excitement and raised the hopes of Southerners that the British would declare war on the United States, thus becoming the de facto ally of the Confederacy.[29]

The seriousness of the *Trent* issue deflected the recognition momentum and excluded the Confederates from the negotiation process. Trans-Atlantic diplomacy was dominated during the *Trent* crisis by Washington and London. Lincoln and Seward ultimately controlled the outcome of the imbroglio while Southerners passively petitioned the British government from the fringe of the diplomatic circle. The Confederates made an impassioned plea, but were unable to back up their demands with any significant display of power or offers of mutual assistance.[30]

The incident over the *Trent,* at least indirectly, resulted from the failure of the Yancey-Mann-Rost mission to achieve recognition. When Davis saw the need for more able envoys to replace Yancey, he appointed James Mason as his commissioner in London and John Slidell in a similar capacity at Paris.[31] Davis and Secretary of State Hunter believed that the atmosphere in Europe was favorable for recognition and expected the newly appointed envoys to pursue Confederate aims more aggressively than their predecessors. Their general instructions, however, still did not contain any new diplomatic ammunition, except that they were instructed to shift their emphasis to what Hunter described as the illegal Federal blockade.[32] As Mason and Slidell prepared to depart for Europe, they collected information on ships that had successfully run the blockade. Armed with this information, Mason and Slidell expected to demonstrate to the British and French that the blockade was ineffectual and, therefore, illegal under the Paris Declaration. Mason and Slidell were widely respected political figures in the South before and after secession.

John Slidell, the Democratic "boss" of Louisiana[33] was, according to the London *Times,* "an excellent judge of mankind, adroit, perceptive, and subtle, full of device and fond of intrigue."[34] He had been appointed by Democratic President James K. Polk to negotiate with the Mexican government for a settlement as part of the preliminaries to the end of the Mexican War. Although he did not locate an established government with which to negotiate, the diplomatic experience had been valuable. Slidell was an avid Democrat and supported Bell in the 1860 election. He apparently expected his appointment to Paris to be of long duration because he took his entire family, as well as the family of his secretary, former Louisiana Congressman George Eustis.[35] Slidell was, indeed, a powerful politician within his home state of Louisiana and the national Democratic Party. Unlike Rost, his predecessor, Slidell's French was excellent and his wife's and daughters' Creole French and charm proved invaluable during his tenure in Paris.[36]

James Mason differed considerably from his Louisiana colleague. Mason was a "Virginia aristocrat" and traced his ancestry back to a grandfather who was a Revolutionary War hero. Confederate leaders expected Mason to get along very well with the British because he was "so manly, so straight-forward, so truthful and bold."[37] Like Slidell, Mason was a lawyer by training and a politician by vocation. As a member of the U.S. Senate from 1847 to 1861, he had served

James Mason, Confederate representative in London, ca. 1859.
Courtesy of The Abraham Lincoln Museum, Harrogate, Tennessee.

John Slidell, Confederate representative in Paris, ca. 1860.
Courtesy of The Abraham Lincoln Museum, Harrogate, Tennessee.

that body as chairman of the Foreign Relations Committee and claimed greater knowledge of foreign affairs than most of his Southern colleagues. Throughout his tenure in the Senate, Mason had been outspoken on states' rights and committed to the preservation of slavery. He was popular with his fellow Southerners in the Senate and for a time was expected to be the heir apparent to John C. Calhoun's nullification legacy. Indeed, it was Mason that Calhoun selected to read his address to the Senate during the 1850 Compromise debate. Mason never grasped the baton passed on to him by Calhoun, but he had, nevertheless, continued to play a prominent role in Southern politics, ultimately supporting secession.[38]

By all appearances, Mason, like Slidell, was well qualified to pursue the Confederate diplomatic initiatives in Europe. Robert Barnwell Rhett's *Charleston Mercury,* for example, declared that "Mr. Mason and Mr. Slidell possess character, ability, and what is no less important, imminent social fitness for their respective posts; and whatever be their instructions, we wish them prompt and perfect success."[39] Appearances are not always what they seem, however, and Mason, at least, carried with him to London a number of handicaps. For all his engaging charms, according to Mary Chestnut his dress was slovenly, his pronunciation of the English language terribly accented, and she despised his habit of chewing tobacco.[40] His appearance and demeanor apparently offended others as well. Richard Cobden, on his visit to the United States in 1859, found Mason's reference to "English demagogues of the Revolutionary period" offensive.[41]

The instructions the two envoys received from R. M. T. Hunter were not known to Robert Rhett at the time, but he certainly would have approved. Rhett had already argued in the Confederate Congress that the earlier Yancey mission was premature and could only confuse the issues confronting the powers, and delay or prevent recognition. The secretary of state emphasized to the new appointees the stronger position of the Confederacy with the addition of the border states. He also told Mason to point out the high probability that Maryland, Missouri, and Kentucky would eventually be able to join the Confederacy and that Richmond would "become the seat of an immense power." Hunter's instructions also directed Mason and Slidell to point out to the Europeans that the division in the United States would curtail the ambitions of a manufacturing and maritime North and force a commercial alliance with the South that would benefit both Great Britain and France.[42]

A balance of power, according to Hunter, could be restored in the Western Hemisphere and the "overwhelming desire for the annexation of contiguous territory on the part of the vast and overshadowing political and military organization in the North will be dissipated."[43] Mason was further authorized to quote, chapter and verse, Russell's Italian correspondence to illustrate that the Confederate argument resembled the principles on which the British government had acted toward the Italians. Finally, Mason was promised adequate information to continue a forceful argument against the legality of the Northern blockade. Carrying these instructions with supporting documents, and accompanied by a sizable entourage of family, staff, and baggage, Mason and Slidell were ready to depart for Europe.[44]

The highly publicized departure could hardly be kept secret. Seward and Lincoln were furnished day-by-day information on the progress of the Confederate diplomatic mission, from its beginning with a Senate resolution until their departure from Cuba aboard the *Trent*. The Navy Department notified the ships enforcing the blockade to expect the attempted breakout. The Confederates made little attempt to keep the mission or its objectives secret, but did take care to run the blockade under optimum conditions for success. Once aboard a neutral ship on the high seas, the envoys believed they would be safe and protected under international law.[45]

Mason and Slidell may have recognized that if they were removed from a neutral British ship as contraband, the Union government would have recognized the belligerent status of the Confederacy. If they were removed merely as private American citizens charged with treason, while under the protection of the British flag, the sovereign status of the neutral ship would be violated, thus breaking international law. In either case, the removal of Mason and Slidell would create a serious dispute between Great Britain and the United States.

On October 12, 1861, Secretary of State Hunter received a telegram from Trescot in Charleston stating, "Our friends left here last night at one o'clock, their escape favored by having a fast steamer with good officers, and by the darkness and rain. The boat will be back in about a week and nothing should be said of it in the meantime."[46] The original plan of the Confederates had been to charter the steamer *Nashville*, because it was fast enough to run the blockade and large enough to cross the Atlantic without too much difficulty or inconvenience to the passengers. Another benefit of the *Nashville* was its ability to return to Charleston laden with munitions. But it was difficult to keep secrets from union spies in Charleston, and the proposed use of the *Nashville* to run the blockade was common knowledge on the waterfront.[47] Mason and Slidell, therefore, decided to abandon the *Nashville* in favor of a smaller ship with less draught in order to permit a safe passage out of the harbor in bad weather, the best way of avoiding Northern blockaders who had recently been strengthened by several "trim looking steamers."[48]

The Confederates had considered traveling overland to Mexico and then boarding a British ship to Europe. This idea was discarded because of the extended time required to complete the voyage. Keeping the urgency of their mission in mind, Mason and Slidell decided to charter the *Gordon,* a small, fast steamer.[49] The *Gordon* was known to have successfully run the blockade several times. In fact, the *Gordon* was so successful at outdistancing the blockading ships that Union captains frequently gave up the chase as soon as the *Gordon* was identified. Mason and Slidell made arrangements with the captain of the *Gordon* to carry them to Havana, where they expected to transfer to a British vessel. On the night of October 12, the *Gordon* changed its name to *Theodora* and the Mason-Slidell entourage boarded and departed.[50]

The night was black, and the rain pelted the sails of the blockade runner, which had no running lights. Its passengers were huddled in silence, and the vessel easily eluded the Federal blockade, making for Nassau. Unfortunately, it missed connections with the British steamer and discovering a three-week delay before the next large British vessel, decided to press on to Havana. The *Theodora,* after discovering a shortage of coal, was forced to land its passengers 100 miles up the Cuban coast from Havana. Having traveled overland to Havana, Mason and Slidell awaited passage aboard a British vessel. After successfully reaching Cuba, Mason wrote his wife of his security: "because under any foreign flag, we are safe from molestation."[51]

News reached Seward, through Secretary of the Navy Gideon Welles, that Slidell and Mason had successfully eluded the naval blockade at Charleston. The report, however, suggested the envoys were aboard the *Nashville.* Seward and Welles quickly discussed the situation, and Welles dispatched the *James Adger* and several other warships to pursue the *Nashville.*[52] The *James Adger* continued all the way across the Atlantic and caused the British foreign office some agitation by anchoring at Southampton to await the arrival of the *Nashville* and the two special envoys expected to be aboard. A preliminary opinion by the Crown law officers ruled that an American warship would be justified under international law in waylaying the *Nashville,* a Confederate ship, and removing any contraband aboard, including Mason and Slidell. The ruling applied to the Confederate ship and did not include British vessels.[53]

Captain Charles Wilkes of the USS *San Jacinto,* was cruising the waters around Cuba, as the *James Adger* crossed the Atlantic. Although he had not been ordered to look for the Confederates, he decided after receiving information that the two envoys were in Havana, to intercept the *Theodora*. After refueling at Cienfuegos, Wilkes steamed to Havana, only to discover that the two commissioners were patiently waiting to depart Havana aboard the British mail packet *Trent*, scheduled to sail on November 7.[54]

Wilkes was an ambitious and aging navy professional, hungry for fame and promotion. He expected to become a hero as the man who captured the Confederates, "stopping their diabolical scheme."[55] Wilkes left Havana on November 2 for Key West, where he hoped to secure support vessels to pursue the *Trent* in the Bahama Channel. No U.S. ships were available, so Wilkes set out alone to intercept the *Trent* and take it as a "prize." During the voyage, Wilkes consulted all the available books on international maritime law and believed he would be correct in seizing "the captain, officers, and engineer of the *Trent*, as well as the Confederates."[56] On the morning of November 8, Wilkes stationed the *San Jacinto* in the middle of the Bahama Channel and waited. Shortly before noon, the smoke of the *Trent* was sighted. Within a few minutes, the *San Jacinto* fired a shot across the bow of the *Trent*, requiring it to heave-to. After a second shot, the *Trent* reduced speed and shut down the engines. Two boatloads of seamen from the *San Jacinto* boarded the *Trent*, but Wilkes had decided not to take the mail steamer as a prize. He explained his change of mind in a report to Welles that "the small number of officers and crew, combined with a large number of civilian passengers destined for a long trip to Europe" would have created too much inconvenience.[57]

The passengers aboard the *Trent* not only included the Confederate group, but a large British and European contingent. Many of the passengers voiced their indignation, while the ship's captain and the British naval officer responsible for the mail made no pretense of disguising their fury.[58] Slidell demanded from the American lieutenant a show of force greater than could be reasonably resisted by those onboard. The result was a show of arms by the American boarding party, and Slidell and Mason ceased to resist. During this encounter, however, Mason had the presence to place the diplomatic instructions of the Southern envoys in the hands of Commander Williams, the British mail agent, for safekeeping. The Confederate commissioners were then removed, along with their secretaries, and transported, after a brief stop at Fort Monroe in New York, to Fort Warren in Boston to await their fate.

The tidal wave of public exhilaration that swept the North is not surprising. For a few days, the course of the war appeared dramatically to have changed. In addition to Wilkes's success, the U.S. Navy had captured the custom port of Port Royal in South Carolina, a victory that gave the Federals an opportunity to offer cotton to Europe. From a Northern perspective, two dangerous men feared able to exploit the Confederate strategy of King Cotton had been captured, while a major Southern port of call had fallen. Among the cautious leadership, concerns remained about the British response to the removal of Mason and Slidell from a British vessel. Americans had, after all, "fired a shot across the bows of the ship that bore the British lion at its head."[59] If the British wanted an excuse to justify intervening in the American Civil War, with probable support from France, the *Trent* affair provided the opportunity. The illegal capture of Mason and Slidell secured French support for the British if they intended to pursue the breakup of the United States. Within the Confederacy, particularly in the Confederate capital of Richmond, there was hope that the British would "resent and punish the act" of Captain Wilkes.[60] The British were now required to live up to their long-standing commitment to maintain the "right of asylum" within their jurisdiction. These men "were as much under the jurisdiction of the British government upon that ship and beneath its flag as if they had been on its soil."[61]

The Confederates had high expectations that a hostile British response to the *Trent* affair would receive support from British Canada as well as from the French. In anticipation of the outbreak of naval conflict, the British began to strengthen their West Indian fleet and sent troops to the maritime provinces of Eastern Canada.[62] Lyons was determined to maintain "entire resolve on the question"[63] and worked to obtain a ruling from U.S. Attorney General Bates pronouncing the removal of the Confederates from the *Trent* as unlawful, but he was unsuccessful. As he waited for formal instructions from London, Lyons was shocked when the U.S. newspapers published a letter of congratulation and commendation to Captain Wilkes from Secretary of the Navy Gideon Welles. The Confederates in Richmond had every reason to believe that popular opinion in both Washington and London favored armed conflict between the two Atlantic naval powers.

When news of the capture of the Confederate commissioners reached London on November 27, 1861, Russell immediately called for a Cabinet meeting. The gravity of the situation was apparent to Palmerston and he postponed the Cabinet meeting until November 29 in order to obtain a legal opinion from the law offices. On November 28, Russell met with Adams at the foreign office, but the American minister could provide little additional information because he had not yet received instructions from Washington. The British Cabinet met in the early afternoon of November 29 to hear the law officers affirm that the seizure "was illegal and unjustifiable under international law."[64] It was evident to the somber gathering that the government must demand reparation and redress. A decision was made to send an ultimatum through Lyons for the Lincoln administration, demanding a disavowal of the action and requiring the Americans to restore the prisoners to British protection. The dispatch would further instruct Lyons to "retire from the United States if these demands are not met exactly and promptly."[65]

The responsibility of the actual draft was left to Russell, and the Cabinet agreed to reconvene the next day to discuss what he proposed to send Lyons. Palmerston then forwarded the document, over Russell's objection, to the Queen and Prince Consort. Before the Queen approved the dispatch, the Prince softened its tone but left unchanged the basic demands, which included a specific timetable requiring the United States to respond within seven days after presentation of the British demands.[66] In addition, Russell provided Lyons with detailed suggestions on how to conduct his meeting with Seward and listed legal points he should make supporting the British case.

Lyons's instructions allowed no discretion, with one exception. The Cabinet was willing "to be rather easy about the apology," said Russell, provided the Confederates were released.[67] Finally, Russell informed Lyons that the French had already promised moral support. He told Lyons that he should delay his formal presentation to Seward of the British demands for a few days in expectation of receiving a statement from the French supporting the British position.[68]

In Washington, Seward had begun to receive pressure to release the Confederate commissioners from Adams in London and U.S. Consul John Bigelow in Paris. Adams argued that the United States should remain true to "its honorable record" of defending neutral rights at sea and use the *Trent* crisis to obtain "a great concession of principle from Great Britain."[69] Both these U.S. representatives believed that because of the indignant support throughout England and France for the British in this crisis, war could only be prevented by releasing the Confederates. Both men hoped to gain a clearer definition of international law as it applied to search and seizure on the high seas while preventing armed conflict.[70]

Eventually, the British demands were presented to Seward, although informally, and he delivered them to the president. Finding support within the Cabinet, Lincoln appeared reluctant to comply with the ultimatum. He directed Seward to draft a compliance response, while he would draft a declination for discussion by the Cabinet on Christmas Day. At that December 25 meeting, Lincoln accepted Seward's draft and the decision was made to release the Confederates. The decision of the United States to accede to the British demands prevented the possibility of war over this issue.[71]

The *Trent* affair caught the Confederates unprepared to respond. No instructions were forthcoming from Richmond to the Yancey Commission in London and the commissioners were forced to take action on their own, without the benefit of advice from their State Department. Their feeble attempts only served to further demonstrate Confederate diplomatic ineptness.

The resolution of the *Trent* affair dealt a serious blow to Confederate diplomatic efforts. First, it deflected the recognition momentum developed during the summer and fall of 1861. It created a feeling in Great Britain that the United States was prepared to defend itself when necessary, but recognized its responsibility to comply with international law. Moreover, it produced a feeling in Great Britain and France that peace could be preserved as long as the Europeans maintained strict neutrality in regard to the American belligerents.

The delayed arrival of Mason and Slidell in Europe prevented the timely presentation of the Confederate government's argument that the blockade was ineffective and illegal. By the time they reached London in January, the atmosphere was less receptive to their presentations. The British government quickly took action to strengthen its neutrality laws under the old Enlistment Act. Overall, the peaceful resolution of the *Trent* affair improved relations between the United States and Great Britain. It proved devastating, however, to Confederate attempts to obtain recognition, by completely destroying the favorable momentum that had built up prior to November 1861.

Some historians have suggested the possibility of a Confederate conspiracy to create a diplomatic incident with the potential to produce war between Great Britain and the United States. This argument is supported by the publicity in Southern newspapers before the departure of Mason and Slidell, combined with their statements after their capture.[72] There is no evidence contained in the Confederate diplomatic papers and archives that supports the idea of intrigue. Indeed, the theory of conspiracy is easily refuted by the actual course of events. The decisions to change from a Confederate ship to a blockade runner, and subsequently to a British ship, were made spontaneously well after the Confederates arrived in Charleston. In addition, it is clear from his communications to his wife that Mason felt secure aboard the British ship *Trent*.[73] Moreover, it is unlikely that Slidell would have put his family in harms way to carry out such an intrigue. The idea of a Confederate conspiracy, while interesting and certainly supportable by reasonable circumstantial evidence, must remain, at best, a speculation.

Chapter 6

A New Initiative in Europe: The Blockade

With the arrival of Mason and Slidell in London on January 29, 1862, the direction of Confederate strategy shifted away from the arrogant demands of Yancey toward a legalistic attack on the blockade. President Davis and Secretary of State Hunter charged the new Confederate emissaries with persuading the British that the Union blockade of Southern ports was illegal under the Declaration of Paris. Yancey's letter to Lord Russell demanding recognition of the Confederacy in the aftermath of the capture of Slidell and Mason embarrassed Southern sympathizers in Parliament. Moreover, Yancey's demand, based on arguments already presented, emphasized economic and constitutional issues within the United States without capitalizing on the *Trent* advantage. Yancey also failed to emphasize the ineffectiveness of the blockade. His dispatch was published by Russell and provided Union supporters with rebuttal opportunities in the forthcoming debate on the blockade.[1]

Mason and Slidell quickly recognized the inadequacy of Yancey's simplistic approach. Despite the cool atmosphere in London when they arrived, they immediately sought the cooperation of prominent British citizens sympathetic to their cause. After a brief stay in London, Slidell left for Paris, expecting Mason to coordinate and pursue Southern objectives in London while he took charge in Paris. The two Confederates expected to maintain a coordinated effort and were generally optimistic about their chances of success.[2]

Unlike their predecessors, the new Southern envoys recognized the need to stress European self-interest in seeking recognition. The hardships of the blockade were being felt in Europe. If the British or French could be persuaded to challenge its efficiency and legality, the potential for maritime conflict between the European and American navies was enormous. A denouncement of the blockade was considerably less than the goal of recognition; but if another naval incident similar to the *Trent* affair could be prompted, it would certainly increase the chances of naval intervention by one of the European powers.

A number of other options favorable to the Confederacy were open to the Europeans should they decide to intervene. They might, for example, decide to offer mediation, suggest an armistice, or demand special exemptions or access to certain blockaded ports in the South. Any of these options might result eventually in armed intervention by one or more European powers.

The Davis administration, while anxious for assistance, was reluctant during 1861 to allow concessions to the British because they feared future exploitation by Great Britain.[3] When Mason and Slidell received their instructions and departed for Europe, the military defense of the new nation was going well and the Confederate State Department could afford the luxury of such diplomatic restraint. But Union victories at Forts Donelson and Henry in 1862, the subsequent loss of Nashville in Tennessee, and the Port Royal naval campaign on the Atlantic coast quickly demonstrated the power of the North and emphasized the need to obtain intervention by the naval powers of Europe.

The first opportunity to employ a more realistic and aggressive diplomatic strategy was presented to the Confederates immediately upon the arrival of Mason and Slidell in London.[4] Simultaneously with the news of the North's release of Mason and Slidell, news reached London and Paris that the Federal navy had attempted to close Charleston Harbor by sinking twenty old whaling vessels loaded with stones in the approach channels. The old ships were sunk on December 20 at the height of the excitement over the *Trent* affair. Both the French and British protested through Merciér and Lyons, who earlier in November had reported the departure of the "stone fleet" from Northern ports. The permanent damage of a natural port was a violation of accepted international law.[5] Russell characterized the event as an admission of the North's defeat and desperation and condemned the action "as a plot against the commerce of nations" and "a project worthy only of the times of barbarism."[6]

In Paris, French newspapers praised the release of Mason and Slidell, while denouncing the closing of Charleston Harbor. On January 22, the French newspaper *Moniteur* reproduced a London *Times* article claiming that a natural harbor, such as that of Charleston, was a place of refuge for international shipping. It claimed that a maritime power had a right to remonstrate or go even further to prevent "an act of inhuman and barbarous revenge." The *Pays* denounced the stone fleet as "an act of vandalism and barbary only worthy of the dark ages." Moreover, the *Patrie* went so far as to hint at official French recognition of the South.[7] Unfortunately for the Southern cause, Confederate diplomats in Europe failed to vigorously pursue the stone fleet incident for its maximum benefit.

Mason and Slidell arrived in Europe in this highly charged atmosphere, but they, too, failed to appreciate or capitalize on the anti-Union sentiment produced by the stone fleet episode. Instead, Mason lamented the British coolness in high places toward his presence. The failure of Confederate agents to provide their well-placed allies in London and Paris with quick encouragement to exploit this opportunity allowed Adams and Dayton to present official U.S. responses to the British and French foreign ministries. This began the process of neutralizing the threat of European indignation at the stone fleet blockade.[8] Slidell did not arrive in Paris until Dayton had already placated Thouvenel. Seward's emissary, Thurlow Weed, and the U.S. consul at Paris, John Bigelow, sought out other influential French officials on the same mission.[9]

Dayton saw Thouvenel on January 25. During a meeting that lasted over an hour and a half, Dayton explained the implications of Seward's response to the *Trent* affair. Thouvenel demanded an explanation for the "outlawry demonstrated in the stone fleet incident." Dayton explained that only two channels were closed and that the sunken vessels could quickly be refloated and removed from the channel at a later date. The American minister expressed his appreciation of French concerns about permanent damage to an international waterway and reassured Thouvenel that the obstructions were only temporary. He further expressed the expectation that Southern ports would soon be available for French commerce again because of expected Union capture of Southern ports. These explanations seemed to satisfy Thouvenel, who basically favored nonintervention.[10] In London, Adams quickly responded to Lord Russell with similar explanations while Seward reassured Lyons in Washington. These explanations cleared up "misunderstandings" in the minds of British authorities regarding the stone fleet.[11]

It was unfortunate, indeed, for the Confederate cause that the absence of leadership in Europe prevented an appropriate Confederate diplomatic initiative. The Yancey-Mann-Rost mission effectively ended with the release of Mason and Slidell. Moreover, the Confederate leadership in Richmond failed to appreciate the potential to exploit the *Trent* affair by contributing information that might have made the explanations of Dayton and Adams more difficult.

Anticipating the shift in Confederate diplomatic strategy and appreciating the economic impact of the blockade on the European economies, Seward once again decided to seize the diplomatic initiative. The French, in particular, were concerned over the economic hardships caused by the cotton shortage, and Merciér had repeatedly asked throughout the fall of 1861 for exceptions to the blockade.[12] Dayton, warned from Paris of a severe cotton shortage in the French textile regions, feared intervention by the French to obtain cotton from the South. Seward feared a united Anglo-French intervention to force open Confederate ports.

On January 20, Seward instructed Dayton to present to Thouvenel the idea that the French and Americans had traditionally supported a liberal interpretation of neutral rights on the high seas. Seward suggested that the *Trent* affair presented an opportunity for further defining the law. Dayton was to urge a Franco-American stand that would compel Great Britain to accept the principles set out in the *Trent* case.[13] Obviously, any Franco-American approach on the question of neutral rights would arouse suspicion in Great Britain. Seward hoped the British would then become defensive and concern themselves more with British security in Europe, thus leaving the American question to the Americans. Seward hoped that the French would fall into his diplomatic trap; but if not, he could again control the parameters of the continuing diplomatic debate until a successful military campaign in the spring of 1862 could demonstrate that the Union would prevail. The rigors of the blockade would diminish as Union military successes along the Confederate coast opened ports once again to French commerce.

Perhaps Seward underestimated the diplomatic expertise of both the French and the British, particularly the French. Thouvenel was completely sympathetic to the Union cause and was determined to prevent an overambitious Napoleon III from expanding his commitments in the Western Hemisphere.[14] Thouvenel easily sidestepped Seward's trap. Nevertheless, a wedge was driven into the Anglo-French entente. Napoleon often referred thereafter to the failure of the British to appreciate French support in the *Trent* affair and demonstrated a new coolness and suspicion toward Great Britain concerning the entire American question.[15] As for Palmerston and Russell, they recognized Seward's diplomatic initiative and felt that Seward had entrapped Napoleon in an ill-conceived policy. From their viewpoint, a policy of expanded neutral shipping rights would not serve the British empire.[16]

When Mason and Slidell arrived in Europe to implement a Confederate strategy focusing on an illegal blockade, they completely failed to recognize or appreciate the subtleties of the new Seward strategy or its potential vulnerability to a Confederate initiative. The Southern diplomats overlooked the potential weakness within Seward's strategy and failed to exploit the opportunity to identify Seward as a manipulative intriguer attempting to further divide the British and the French. Again, a lack of timely information on the stone fleet incident and the absence of any diplomatic advice from Richmond contributed to Confederate failure. The diplomatic controversy surrounding the *Trent* placed Confederate diplomacy on the sidelines as it focused on U.S.–British relations.

About this time, R. M. T. Hunter concluded his tenure as Confederate secretary of state. The office did not have the glamour and high public profile that he wanted to further his political career. While Hunter was articulate, as his instructions to Mason and Slidell clearly demonstrate, he was not prepared to engage in diplomatic battles with the likes of Seward, Thouvenel, and Russell. Davis, well aware of the high esteem held for the Virginian throughout the South, appointed Hunter to replace Toombs for political reasons—not because of his diplomatic experience. There is no evidence to suggest that any of the Confederates sensed a shift in U.S. policy until after Seward accomplished his objective to use the blockade debate to postpone any aggressive joint intervention on the part of the Europeans. Unfortunately, the Southerners cooperated with Seward's plan by engaging in an extended debate over the blockade, which postponed action while reconfirming the European commitment to neutrality. Seward feared a joint Anglo-French naval action that would bring a preponderance of naval power into the conflict. He sought to avoid such a move by creating doubts about the stability of the Anglo-French alliance.[17]

Confederate hopes recovered in the aftermath of the *Trent* disappointments when rumors reached Pierre Rost that Napoleon would attack the illegal blockade in his speech opening the French legisla-

ture on January 27.[18] This exhilarating expectation for the Confederates produced mild panic within the Unionist community in Paris.
Dayton provided information through Thouvenel that he hoped the
French minister would use to prevent the emperor from denouncing
the Union blockade. In the same interview with Thouvenel in which
he explained the "misunderstandings" of the stone fleet, Dayton presented arguments in favor of the legality of the blockade. Thurlow
Weed, in the meantime, obtained an interview with Prince Napoleon, and the prince offered to intervene with the emperor on behalf
of the Northern position. Amidst this diplomatic activity, Confederate agents remained remarkably placid and did not seek opportunities to present the Southern case.[19]

In all fairness to the Confederate agents operating in Paris, they
had little current information about shipping activities through the
blockade. The legal arguments had already been presented and the
blockade issue resurfaced suddenly in the atmosphere produced by
the *Trent* settlement. The absence of instructions from Richmond,
combined with the lack of experienced leadership, prevented an aggressive Southern initiative at the most opportune time.

The French Cabinet met at the Tuileries two days before the emperor was to deliver his speech to the legislature. In the meeting,
Thouvenel, and probably Morny, presented the arguments and information they had received from Dayton and Prince Napoleon.
Thouvenel's position, particularly in light of other foreign policy considerations, prevailed on the blockade question. It was decided, although Napoleon remained convinced that the blockade was ineffective and illegal, that strict neutrality should be maintained with regard
to the American troubles.[20] The emperor put the finishing touches
on his address and decided not to mention the blockade. However, it
was not until Napoleon delivered his speech that the opposing fac-
tions in the American Civil War knew his precise position. The emperor recognized the kingdom of Italy, but stopped short of recognizing the new American Confederacy. "The Civil War now ravaging
America," he stated, "has come to compromise seriously our commercial interest. However, . . . as long as the rights of neutrals are
respected, we ought to limit ourselves to praying ardently that these
dissensions may soon come to an end."[21]

After the emperor's speech, Unionists rejoiced while Confederate
representatives were obviously disappointed. John Bigelow reported
to Seward that "the paragraph about the United States was received
by the Assembly with audible expressions of satisfaction."[22] The
Unionists, under the leadership of Dayton, succeeded in winning the

first round of the debate on the blockade. The Confederates failed to persuade a sympathetic Napoleon to override the advice of his foreign minister. Napoleon's speech fell far short of supporting the Confederate position and was a victory for the Unionists. The emperor, however, did not denounce the rebellious states of the South or raise the issue of slavery. The phrase "as long as the rights of neutrals are respected" seemed to leave the door open for further Confederate initiatives on the blockade.

The usual practice of the French government was to publish a detailed report on the state of the empire, expanding on the emperor's speech, within a few days after its delivery. In this document, published three days later on January 30, the official position of neutrality was restated. No mention was made of the stone fleet or the legal status of the blockade. Although the document contains a lengthy comment on the economic effects on France of the American conflict, it concludes by stating that "the government of the Emperor . . . had . . . only one line of conduct to follow: adherence to strict neutrality."[23] A number of other factors influenced Napoleon to adopt the official position of neutrality. The situation in Italy, as well as concerns over political uncertainties in Central Europe, contributed to the emperor's decision. The French decision not to condemn the Union blockade as ineffective concluded the first round of the blockade debate, and ushered in the beginning of round two in London.[24]

Mason and Slidell concluded at the same time that the emperor was defining French neutrality. Both men were disappointed, of course, by the failure of Napoleon to denounce the blockade as illegal. But, they were optimistic that both Great Britain and France were prepared to entertain and debate a move to denounce the blockade and recognize the Confederacy. The position of the Palmerston ministry within the House of Commons had not, as yet, been forced to withstand a prolonged and forceful attack from the opposition on the American question. Mason, based on his instructions from Hunter, prepared to encourage Southern sympathizers to engage in an official debate. In general, the Tories were sympathetic to the Confederate position and, Mason believed, would support a resolution denouncing the blockade as ineffective and illegal. The only issue preventing unqualified support from a number of Tories was slavery. Mason and Slidell decided temporarily to sidestep the slavery issue and focus their efforts on the blockade.[25]

The Confederates enjoyed backing from powerful friends in the commercial and shipping community and hoped for support within Parliament. Moreover, they expected support from the political opposition led by Benjamin Disraeli. Shipping interests represented by William Lindsay and John Roebuck were to some extent motivated by economic considerations. However, their concerns extended far beyond the need to obtain cotton. Lindsay was committed to unrestricted free trade and believed that the Confederacy represented a potential ally in the international community. The Southern commitment to King Cotton underestimated the potential contained within a broader economy that included interests beyond the cotton manufacturers. Nevertheless, the Confederates proceeded to encourage and support the members of Parliament who were prepared to introduce resolutions denouncing the blockade.[26]

The British had anxiously awaited Napoleon's speech and followed its implications, both for the European and American situations, with great interest. The emperor's failure to denounce the blockade validated to the British leadership their policy of strict neutrality, recognition of Confederate belligerent status, and respect for the Union blockade. The Anglo-French policy of united action on the American question remained acceptable to the French. Napoleon continued to insist for the remainder of the war that Great Britain join him in recognizing the Confederate states. In February, he renewed his proposal, through Flahault in London, that Great Britain join him in breaking the blockade. Russell and Palmerston repeatedly denied knowledge of any formal proposal from the French minister, and Thouvenel denied that the proposal was made. Although Napoleon insisted that the proposal was made and that Seward was apprised of the offer, there is no correspondence to indicate a formal proposal was made.[27]

Further, there is no evidence of a Confederate reaction to an informal proposal at this time. It is reasonable, since both Russell and Seward often refused to take official responsibility for informal communications, that they were denying "official knowledge." Thouvenel followed the same practice of denying the existence of anything inconsistent with his objectives that did not require an official communication or response. Napoleon's claim is probably consistent with an informal proposal that he could recall at his convenience in the future.[28] If, in fact, the French made overtures to the Palmerston ministry, they were informal. The emperor's speech on January 27 contributed to a favorable environment for Palmerston and Russell to engage in a parliamentary debate on the blockade.

Consistent with his instructions from Richmond and advice from the Confederate lobby, Mason prepared to attack the blockade in a parliamentary debate. He was delighted with the support and cooperation he received from Confederate sympathizers like James Spence, William Lindsay, William H. Gregory, Alexander Beresford-Hope, and Lord Campbell, who were prepared to press the attack by introducing appropriate resolutions in Parliament. These men also encouraged Mason to meet with Lord John Russell, and Gregory volunteered to arrange the interview.[29]

Mason suggested to Gregory that he help to obtain an official interview with Lord Russell in which the Confederate envoy could present his credentials and read his instructions. Gregory advised against requesting an official interview, explaining that "I should state that you are here as an envoy from the Southern Confederacy, but that as the Confederacy is not yet recognized, you apply for an unofficial interview. This is, I think, the most dignified course to pursue."[30] The two men agreed on this course of action and Gregory then wrote Russell requesting the interview. Russell's immediate reply granted an unofficial interview to Mason at the residence of the foreign minister on February 10.[31]

During the meeting with Russell, Mason offered to read his credentials. Russell pointed out that it was unnecessary, since no official relations existed between the Confederacy and Great Britain and Mason was there only as a private citizen, being received as one gentleman to another. Russell did agree to hear "unofficial expressions of opinion" and Mason was cautious in selecting the portions of his instructions to read to the British minister.

Several British sympathizers advised against mentioning British dependence on the cotton South. Mason therefore omitted any reference to that topic and focused instead on the recognition and blockade arguments. Mason pointed out that the Confederacy was not prepared to insist on recognition, even though the Southern union of states was a legitimate nation that met all the requirements of recognition. He did, however, insist on the inefficiency of the blockade and presented Russell with the warmed-over statistics previously presented by the Yancey mission.[32] Mason left the interview convinced that the foreign minister's sympathies were with the North, and that the British government would not support a pro-Southern position in parliamentary debate regarding the sufficiency of the blockade. In fact, Russell refused to engage in any discussion of a position that the government might take in the future. Even though Mason followed up the interview with an extended list of blockade violations to support his argument, Russell only acknowledged receipt of the statistics and offered no further comment.[33]

As part of the Confederate strategy, it was agreed before Mason's meeting with Russell that William Lindsay would take the initiative to force Russell to make a commitment on the blockade issue. Lindsay, the largest ship owner in Britain, had a vested interest in reopening trade and forcing the blockade.[34] Therefore, it was decided that Lindsay would ask Russell for a legal opinion from the government to protect his shipping interests. On February 5, Lindsay wrote Russell explaining that "being desirous of dispatching one of my vessels with an assorted cargo of British goods, not contraband of war, to the Southern states . . . with which I have carried on commerce at various ports, I shall be greatly obliged by your Lordship's informing me, before I undertake the enterprise, what port or ports of the coast are now in such a state of blockade as to render it imperative on one to avoid them in order to be protected against lawful capture?"[35]

Lindsay's specific request would require an answer that would apply to other British shipping interests and furnish a precedent for further debate and action. If, for example, Russell's response suggested that Savannah and Jacksonville were not securely blockaded, while other ports remained securely closed by the Union blockade, an ineffective blockade under the Declaration of Paris existed. If, on the other hand, Russell's response claimed all Southern ports were adequately and securely blockaded, Mason, Lindsay, and their colleagues could argue by using shipping manifests that the blockade was ineffective and, therefore, a paper blockade. In either case, the response would define the parameters of the forthcoming debate.

After Russell met with Mason on February 10th, and after he received Lindsay's request, Russell and Palmerston decided to attempt to postpone an official response to both men, at least for the time being. Palmerston summoned James Spence from Liverpool to try to persuade him to tell Lindsay to back off, but Spence supported the effort to force Russell and Palmerston to commit the government on the blockade issue. Meeting with Russell, Spence reinforced Lindsay's request for a decision.[36] At about the same time Spence was meeting with Russell, Mason received word from Slidell in Paris that his February 7 meeting with Thouvenel was very discouraging because the French firmly supported the *entente cordiale*.[37] Mason accurately assumed that the British would feel more secure in supporting the blockade now that Napoleon, in his January 27 speech, refused to commit France and confirmed his support of a unified response.

Mason, although frustrated, decided to pursue a British decision on the blockade. Slidell, having just arrived in Paris, would continue to encourage independent French initiatives. Mason expressed doubt that "the English mind seems adverse to so strong a step as breaking the blockade and I doubt very much, from what I can learn, whether the House of Commons will take the initiative."[38] The best the Confederate envoy hoped for was that the House of Commons would press the government for a firm expression of policy with regard to the blockade. Once the ministry's position was clear, public opinion could be aroused and pressure applied for breaking the blockade.

Lindsay's letter to Russell, Mason's interview with Russell, and Spence's summons to London prepared the way for a public airing of the question in Parliament. The Confederates were forcing the British to take a stand and establish a firm position in an attempt to separate the French and British positions. Ironically, Seward was prepared to accept a break in the entente to prevent any united action to break the blockade if the debate favored the Southerners.[39]

In anticipation of the forthcoming debate, Russell made an official commitment on February 15 in his communication to Lyons on the issue of the blockade.[40] Russell had consulted his legal and naval advisers and decided to resist the Southern lobby, not only to protect British neutrality, but to safeguard future British maritime policy. In order to protect future British interests, it was necessary to remain committed to the expanded concept of blockade. In his dispatch to Lyons, which soon attained public attention, he explained that "assuming the blockade is duly notified and a number of ships is stationed and remains at the entrance of a port, sufficient really to prevent access to it or to create an evident danger of entering it or leaving it, and that these ships do not voluntarily permit ingress or egress, the fact that various ships may have successfully escaped through it . . . will not, of itself, prevent the blockade from being an effective one by international law."[41]

With his instructions to Lyons, Russell established the doctrine of "evident danger." This concept, originally contained in the Anglo-Russian convention of 1801, was considerably more liberal in its interpretation than the Declaration of Paris formula. The British position not only alarmed Southerners, but other traditional neutrals. The subtleties of the "evident danger" doctrine contributed to the success of Seward's tactics. In Paris, Dayton, Bigelow, and Weed added the new British interpretation to other European precedents to defend the Unionist position.[42] Mason was obviously disappointed in Russell's position and wrote Slidell, "It would seem to be an official exposition on the part of government of what is to be considered an effective blockade, and I think that you will agree with us—is little better than the old doctrine of paper blockade revived."[43] Mason decided, along with the Southern lobby, to direct the anticipated parliamentary discussions along party lines to arouse public opinion and, possibly, achieve his objectives if the Palmerston government fell.[44]

The debate that the Southern lobby and Confederate representatives in Europe hoped would define the blockade as illegal began on March 7 in Parliament. In February, both Gregory and Bentinck gave short speeches announcing their intention to demonstrate the ineffectiveness of the blockade. Unfortunately, Mason did not understand the inside politics of British government, nor was he familiar with the rules of the debate. It was up to Gregory to lead the attack and direct the political campaign.[45]

Initially, Gregory wanted to introduce a motion proposing Southern recognition; but, after consulting Disraeli, he decided to direct his attention to an attack on the blockade. If successful, and the House failed to confirm Russell's position on the blockade, future opportunities would be available to obtain recognition.[46] Mason furnished Gregory with twenty-six pages of information on the blockade. Included was a written response from Henry Hotze, editor of the Confederate-financed London newspaper, the *Index*, refuting the doctrine of "evident danger."

In airing the South's protest, Gregory accused Great Britain of selfishly conniving an illegal blockade to justify future arrogant pretensions, possibly against France. He further argued that Great Britain was risking a continental response of armed neutrality in the distant Western Hemisphere, and that "Englishmen in Lancashire are suffering unduly because of an illegal blockade." Gregory's speech was concise and to the point. Presenting the statistics furnished by his Confederate allies, he concluded that "secession was a right, that separation is a fact, and that reconstruction is an impossibility."[47]

Unfortunately for Southern hopes, Gregory's articulate and persuasive speech produced an unpatriotic impression by attacking long-established British blockade precedents. Moreover, the idea that secession was a right did not meet with the approval of British leadership committed to a far-flung British empire. Another mistake was made by Bentinck, whose speech followed Gregory's. Bentinck urged that the blockade be repudiated and asked that Great Britain recognize the South, thus introducing issues that Mason and Gregory had agreed not to introduce. The suggestion that breaking the blockade would lead to recognition and intervention was a point the Confederate lobby hoped to avoid.[48]

William E. Forster and John Bright quickly seized Bentinck's tactical error as an opportunity to reconnect all three issues. Forster suggested that to repudiate the blockade "would be an act of war which would ally the South with England."[49] Bright and Forster ridiculed the statistics presented to support the ineffectiveness of the blockade and pointed out, once again, that the absence of cotton in the Lancashire District was sufficient proof that the blockade was effective. Of course, Bright, more than anyone, understood that the voluntary cotton embargo in the South contributed substantially to the shortages. However, for Southern sympathizers to suggest the shortages were caused to a large measure by Confederate attempts to coerce Great Britain would be fatal to any Southern hope of recognition.

An impressive array of British leaders spoke in support of Gregory's motion. Sir James Fergussen believed that the consular reports printed in the papers demonstrated the ineffectiveness of the blockade, while William Lindsay added more figures, pointing out that 600 vessels had run the blockade until early November. Lord Robert Cecil also spoke eloquently in support of the Confederate position.[50]

Roundell Palmer, the solicitor general, delivered a powerful and eloquent response in opposition to Gregory's motion. Palmer denied that the British government could be an advocate of recognition and at the same time adhere to strict impartiality. If the question of recognition "were permanently and precipitately decided before the course of events has justified such a policy, it would be an act wholly inconsistent with the neutrality which we profess to observe." He further went on to hint at Gregory's unpatriotic acceptance of anti-British writers on the continent. Palmer emphasized that Great Britain should not do anything inconsistent with her previous practices and principles and went on to say that it was Britain's responsibility to resist "newfangled notions and interpretations of international law which might make it impossible for us effectively at some future date to institute any blockade."[51]

Blockades, as the British well knew from previous experience, were never entirely airtight and probably never would be. Palmer asserted that the introduction of steam and other naval technologies made it increasingly impractical to maintain an exact technical definition of blockades. He concluded by stating that the British's view and the law officers' position ought to be that "the blockade was effective at major ports, and it was not willing to maintain that an efficient blockade must cut off access to small coasters using shallow interwater channels to evade capture."[52] Palmer's arguments were so persuasive that even James Spence, who previously condemned the blockade, decided to support the government's position out of concern for national security. Spence said, "We have maintained the right of blockade when in our favor; it becomes us to uphold it as rigidly when against us."[53]

In his final remarks, Palmer concluded that any challenge to the legality of the blockade would ally the British with one of the world's last strongholds of slavery. The subtle inclusion of such statements in Palmer's concluding remarks should not be interpreted as an antislavery statement, but rather as a political ploy to prevent Gregory's motion from turning along party lines. He knew well that neither the conservative nor liberal parties were willing to appear supportive of slavery.[54]

Gregory decided to withdraw his motion in the face of possible defeat. The Southern lobby could not afford to suffer a loss on the blockade issue. After consultations with his colleagues, Gregory decided to postpone any further debate until he was assured of successful passage. Sympathy for the Confederate cause remained strong in the House of Commons, but the expected support from the conservative opposition that would make the difference in a vote appears to have vanished because of Palmer's crafty political maneuver of introducing slavery into the debate.[55]

On March 10, Russell confirmed the government's position in the House of Lords. After restating the government's position, Russell claimed that British interference with the blockade would mean war, and war would only provoke an emancipation proclamation from the North, causing "the horrors, murders, and pillage" of a slave insurrection by four million blacks. He further suggested that the war would end within months by mutual consent and peaceful separation.[56]

The Southern position was stated in the House of Lords by Lord Campbell, one of the staunchest members of the Southern lobby. Campbell's attack on the blockade focused on Palmerston's letter to Lyons of February 15. Like Foster in the House of Commons, Campbell's speech presented a formidable list of blockade violations. The Confederate lobby, by this time, realized that the government was not going to change its position. Therefore, the debate in Parliament on March 7 and March 10 did not produce a vote. The best the Confederates could expect was to direct public opinion by means of parliamentary debates to the economic hardships, which the Federal blockade was inflicting on British citizens, and force the Palmerston ministry to make its position clear.[57]

The close and very open relationship between active Confederate agents in London and members of Parliament sympathetic to the Southern cause is clearly illustrated in the preparation and delivery of the attack on the blockade in Parliament. For example, Lord Campbell in preparing his speech to the House of Lords, sought the assistance of Henry Hotze, a newly arrived Confederate agent. Mason felt Hotze, having just arrived from America, would have update information. So, at Mason's suggestion, Campbell requested Hotze's assistance. Hotze reported to Hunter that "this being properly within the providence of my commission and also my private instructions, I prepared for him, in the shape of a letter under my official signature, the strongest argument against the efficiency of the blockade that I was able to base upon the facts."[58] Hotze spent ten days actually writing Campbell's speech after preparing the introductory letter. While Campbell's speech was prepared by a Confederate agent, the speeches of Gregory, Bentinck, and Lindsay to the Commons were strongly influenced by Mason, Hotze, and other Confederates operating in London.[59] The failure to obtain a favorable vote was reported by Hotze when he wrote to Hunter that "there was no intention in either House to push the question to a vote, nor to initiate open hostility against the present government. It was simply a demonstration intended for our benefit, and has fulfilled that expectation."[60] Mason added that any expectation of action against the blockade was premature, for the cotton manufacturers in England remained overstocked with goods and therefore, for the time being, remained comfortable with the status quo.[61] Hotze and Mason obviously benefited from hindsight in the communication to Hunter. Before and during the parliamentary debates, there is no indication that the Confederate effort was solely for the purpose of providing a forum for the blockade issue.

Mason's first diplomatic exercise actually had disastrous implications for future Confederate efforts—both in Britain and France. By forcing the Palmerston ministry to endorse the legality of the Federal blockade, the Southern lobby had reinforced the government's commitment to neutrality. A stricter interpretation of the neutrality laws by the British government followed, which severely encumbered clandestine Confederate activities in Great Britain—particularly those of James Bulloch and the Confederate naval agents.[62]

The firm stance taken by the British eventually limited Slidell's freedom of action in Paris, although Slidell took more time than Mason to acquaint himself with the diplomatic environment before acting. Still, both men acted impulsively. A more deliberate and thoughtful approach would probably have led to a strategy supporting joint intervention or mediation, leaving the legality of the blockade for continued open discussion.

The third and final episode in the spring diplomatic campaign on the blockade issue occurred in both Paris and London. The clear stance taken by the British following Napoleon's speech at the end of January seemed to confirm, at least for the immediate future, the nonintervention policy of both countries. Despite the Southern discouragement over their two previous defeats, William S. Lindsay decided to make a bold effort in April to obtain recognition for the Confederacy. Lindsay was anxious to end the Civil War and completely sympathetic to the Southern cause. He despised the Morrill Tariff imposed by the Union, and as a British ship owner, suffered severe losses from the imposition of the blockade and the disruption in trade. As a member of Parliament, Lindsay contributed to the preparation and negotiation of the Cobden Trade Treaty with France in 1860 and enjoyed influential contacts in both commercial and government circles on both sides of the Channel. As a leading member of the Confederate lobby, he presented a formidable adversary to the Union diplomatic effort.

Lindsay was convinced that something must be done to restore peace and normal commercial activity in America. He determined to go to France and urge Napoleon to force England into joint action to break the "illegal" blockade or, without British support, recognize the legitimacy of the South. He believed that Napoleon could be persuaded that the benefit to France might be sufficient justification for independent action. He was convinced that if France took the initiative, Great Britain would cooperate to protect British interests.[63]

The Confederate agents, along with their Southern sympathizers, suffering in the depths of despair, quickly seized the opportunity to pursue the Lindsay initiative. On April 8, Lindsay arrived in Paris. He immediately visited British Ambassador Lord Henry Richard Charles Cowley to arrange an audience with the emperor. His purpose was to discuss anticipated changes in the navigation laws prompted by the recent blockade debates. Cowley, aware of Lindsay's earlier role in negotiating the commercial treaty, made the request and received an appointment for Lindsay at 1:00 p.m. on April 11.[64] While Cowley was making the requested arrangements, Lindsay met with Minister of Commerce Eugene Rouher. Rouher was distressed over the decrease in cotton imports and other trade disruptions and blamed Great Britain for preventing any appropriate action to remedy the problem. Rouher further pointed out to Lindsay that, in the summer of 1861 and again in March 1862, France had made proposals to England for a joint action without any response from the British.[65]

The emperor received Lindsay cordially on April 11, but somewhat to Lindsay's surprise, told the self-appointed British diplomat that he was aware of the Rouher conversation and was generally sympathetic.[66] After the two men discussed the possibility of creating a steamship line between Bordeaux and New Orleans, Lindsay discussed the ineffectiveness of the blockade and furnished statistics on the blockade-runners. Napoleon pointed out that he had previously proposed to Cowley that a joint Anglo-French action should be taken against the blockade, but the British had not responded. In due course, Lindsay suggested joint recognition of the Confederacy as an alternative and told the emperor that he believed the South could not be reconquered and reconstructed into the Union, and that the American conflict should be stopped for humanitarian reasons. Lindsay interrupted the continuity of his presentation at this point to explain that the North could receive all the war supplies it wanted, while the South was "effectively cut off." After this digression, Lindsay returned to the original line of pursuit and attempted to explain to the emperor that the North was not trying to abolish slavery and, therefore, the emphasis should not be on the slavery issue.[67]

Napoleon replied that he was in full agreement with Lindsay's position and that, although he favored the preservation of the Union, he was prepared to send a fleet to open New Orleans if England would join him in the venture. He asked Lindsay to discuss the matter with Cowley and return to the palace on Sunday morning, April 13.[68]

Excited over the emperor's response, Lindsay went straight to Slidell's residence to discuss the matter. Slidell was, of course, excited and hopeful that Lindsay had accomplished a breakthrough in the stalled effort toward recognition. Slidell recommended that Lindsay suggest to Cowley that Great Britain respond immediately to the emperor's initiative. Lindsay asked Slidell's opinion whether to raise the issue of a European cotton shortage, and the two men decided that Lindsay would suggest to Cowley that the Northern interruption in the cotton trade actually represented an interference in the internal affairs of both France and Great Britain. In this manner, they felt, the cotton issue could be tactfully introduced.[69] This preposterous suggestion to reintroduce a sensitive issue had little chance of success and could only irritate the British.

Lindsay then went to see Cowley at the British embassy and reported on his interview with the emperor. He asked Cowley's advice on intervention to obtain cotton, based on the "internal affairs" approach. Denying that France had approached Great Britain on ending the blockade, Cowley said that he was not aware of any approach made through the French representative in London. Moreover, he told Lindsay, the blockade was becoming more effective with every passing day. It was his opinion that Great Britain had made the right decision to acquiesce in the blockade, and he expected the policy to continue. Lindsay was obviously disappointed in Cowley's response but returned to meet the emperor as scheduled, determined to pursue his objective.[70]

On Sunday, April 13, Lindsay reported to the emperor on his conversation with Cowley. The emperor also appeared undaunted and determined to proceed. He suggested that Lindsay return to England and tell Russell and Palmerston his views. The emperor also suggested that Lindsay convey the same information to Disraeli and Derby. He then asked that Lindsay not disclose that the information came directly from him, because he did not want to appear to be communicating with the opposition while his duly-appointed ministers were communicating in an official capacity. After meeting with Disraeli and Russell, Napoleon said Lindsay should return to Paris to report their response, for he did "not want to be embarrassed by the forms and delays of diplomacy, as I feel the necessity for immediate action."[71]

Cowley was irritated by the unofficial encroachment of his authority by Lindsay and felt duty bound to report the conversations to Thouvenel. He proceeded on April 14 to call upon the French foreign minister and, after briefly discussing the situation, asked the minister to confirm or deny knowledge of the alleged notes sent to England. Thouvenel emphatically denied any knowledge of any such notes and assured Cowley that he would discuss the matter with the emperor immediately. Thouvenel proceeded in a more thoughtful manner to explain that "he had endeavored to show both the emperor and Rouher that to have recognized the independence of the South would not have brought cotton into the markets, while any interference with the blockade would probably have produced a collision."[72] Thouvenel did confess, however, that he, like the emperor, continued to be concerned over the cotton shortage and hoped the North would open Southern ports shortly.[73]

Napoleon recognized Thouvenel's irritation when he met with his foreign minister to discuss the Lindsay affair. He told Thouvenel he had no intention of acting independently of Great Britain, but was concerned, particularly after Rouher's remarks, about the cotton shortage. He went on to explain that he hoped Lindsay would communicate the commercial concerns informally with the British government, because Lindsay was affected and was particularly concerned with disrupted trade. When the informal, self-appointed British represen-

tative returned to Paris, the emperor hoped to gain an informal understanding and appreciation of the British position. He asked that
Thouvenel communicate this information to Flahault, the French
ambassador in London.[74]

When Lindsay, having returned to England, sought a meeting with
Russell, he was quickly rebuffed. Russell pointed out to Lindsay that
the British government had an ambassador in Paris and the emperor
had an ambassador in London. He thought it best that the two governments communicate through their respective representatives and
embassies. He told Lindsay he was always ready and willing to listen
to any message from the emperor and his representatives in London,
and upon request, would provide a response to questions through
official channels from the Cabinet.[75]

Lindsay was obviously discouraged when he returned to Paris on
April 17. To bolster his spirits and provide Confederate acceptance of
the outcome, he took along James Mason. Lindsay confided to Mason on the trip that he had also seen Disraeli. When the two unofficial diplomats arrived in Paris, they sought out Slidell right away.
Slidell asked Lindsay about Disraeli's reaction. At this point, Lindsay
reported that Disraeli believed Russell and Seward had made a secret
arrangement in which the British were committed to nonrecognition
and nonintervention.[76]

Lindsay met with the emperor on April 18. Reporting the rebuff
in London, he expressed the hope that Napoleon could pursue French
objectives independently. Napoleon appeared disappointed and told
Lindsay that, in spite of French support of Great Britain during the
Trent affair, Russell remained indisposed to cooperate with him. He
also thought Disraeli's opinion on the "secret arrangement" probably explained the British government's lack of response to his previous request.[77] The emperor further suggested that the U.S. government should be approached concurrently by France and Great Britain
with a request to open ports. If they refused, the proper force should
be employed on the Southern coast and a declaration issued not to
respect the blockade. The Union's taking of New Orleans, however,
might change the situation, he pointed out.[78] Napoleon's request for
confidentiality met with Lindsay's disdain, and he immediately conferred with Mason and Slidell.

Cowley and Thouvenel, and even Flahault, were irritated by
Lindsay's unauthorized pursuit of objectives inconsistent with recognized British and French policy. Flahault responded strongly in a letter, which Thouvenel shared with the emperor. "I cannot conceal
from you," wrote Flahault, "that these kinds of relations are helpful

to no-one's position, not to the Emperor's or to mine. I should pre-
fer a thousand times to cease to be His Majesty's representative in
London than to continue to occupy this post after I no longer possess his entire confidence."[79] After hearing of Flahault's indignation,
Napoleon told Cowley, "I have not been at all shocked that Lord
Russell did not receive Mr. Lindsay."[80] Clearly, Napoleon had learned
a lesson and was backing away from the situation.

When Slidell and Mason learned of Russell's inflexibility and
Napoleon's retreat from the Lindsay initiative, their recently revived
hopes again gave way to depression. The rebuff of the Lindsay mission was accompanied by other bad news from home: on April 23,
the Confederates were thrown back at Corinth; on April 24, Island
No. 10 in the Mississippi fell to the Union; and on May 6, Fort Pulaski
near Savannah was captured. Hotze, writing from London, despaired,
"I have little hope of the initiative either in raising the blockade or in
recognition, being taken by the Emperor."[81] The emperor apparently
expected a different outcome in the fighting around New Orleans.
He continued to distance himself from the Lindsay affair, particularly
after New Orleans fell and news reached Paris on May 11 from Merciér
in Washington that Seward was restoring postal service and opening
the city, relaxing the blockade of the port.[82]

Before Adams and Dayton could request withdrawal of belligerent recognition, Russell and Thouvenel quickly issued a statement of
their intentions to remain strictly neutral and "maintain their position relative to the two parties."[83] Meeting with Thouvenel on May
14, Slidell was unable to downplay the consequences of the fall of
New Orleans. The Confederate commissioner admitted that "it was a
heavy blow for us and we would give the enemy command of the
Mississippi and its tributaries, and enable him to harass and annoy
our citizens living on navigable streams or in the immediate neigh-
borhood."[84] Slidell's obvious depression demonstrates the failure of
the third Confederate initiative in 1862 to obtain support for breaking the blockade or recognizing the Confederacy. The failure of the
Lindsay mission, coupled with the earlier loss in the British Parliament, sustained Napoleon's initial January 27 neutrality statement.
With his demand for the withdrawal of belligerent rights, Seward
quickly drew attention away from intervention as the Europeans
sought access to captured Southern ports. Napoleon confessed to
Cowley on May 13, "I quite agree that nothing is to be done for the
moment but to watch events."[85]

The diplomatic events of the summer of 1862 significantly affected
the diplomatic engagements during the Civil War. First, the parlia-

mentary debate on the blockade galvanized and identified the Confederate lobby. The failure of the lobby to obtain a denunciation of the blockade eliminated the issue from consideration during the subsequent debate in the British Cabinet in the fall of 1862. Moreover, it identified and focused attention on the slavery issue that Southern envoys had desperately tried to camouflage. Finally, from the British perspective, the debate articulated a policy of self-interest by defining the need for future blockades to be less dependent on overwhelming naval force. The doctrine of "evident danger" became a cornerstone of future British naval policy. These implications further burdened future Confederate diplomatic efforts.

Chapter 7

Benjamin Takes Control of
the State Department

W hile Mason, Slidell, and the Confederate lobby opened the blockade debate in Europe, Jefferson Davis took the oath of office as the first president of the permanent Confederacy on February 22, 1862. The mood in Richmond was reserved and concerned because of recent military reverses. The early defensive success of the Southern armies in the field began to fade in the face of a large and rapidly mobilizing Union army. As the list of defeats grew longer, Davis found himself facing both a Cabinet crisis and a loss of public confidence in the new government.[1] The Confederate Congress demanded that Davis change both strategy and personnel before it was too late. Much of the criticism focused on Secretary of War Judah P. Benjamin, a long time friend and confidante of the president from their early days of public service in Washington. Davis had first appointed Benjamin attorney general, but in September 1861, Benjamin became the secretary of war.[2]

As the Cabinet member responsible for the prosecution of the war, Benjamin was blamed by the public for the military reverses during the winter of 1862, especially the loss of Roanoke Island in February. The assaults on Benjamin were not limited directly to his competence, but also included vicious and vulgar attacks against him personally. He was referred to as "Judas Benjamin" and "Mr. Davis's pet Jew."[3] Gen. Howell Cobb wrote his wife, "The clamor compelled him to change his Cabinet, and you know him well enough to know that he must have winced awfully under the inflection."[4] While Davis recognized the need to make changes within the Cabinet, he was not prepared to lose the advice and administrative skill provided by his close confidante and friend.

Davis confronted a full-blown Cabinet crisis in late February and early March. The resignation of Thomas Bragg as attorney general enabled Davis to appoint Thomas Watts of Alabama to that position, satisfying the demands of old Union Whigs for Cabinet representation. He recalled Gen. George Randolph from the field to serve as secretary of war, temporarily satisfying criticisms from the army. The State Department was conspicuously vacant with the absence of R. M. T. Hunter, who resigned to avoid any responsibility for the administration's frustrating failures. Hunter could now join the opposition and pursue his presidential ambitions. Hunter's withdrawal enabled Davis to appoint Benjamin, who took office on March 18, 1862, after Senate confirmation.[5]

Davis was not insensitive to public opinion but tended to operate within a closed circle of confidants. Much like the nation he led, Davis rejected the advice of outsiders when it did not confirm and support

Judah Benjamin, Confederate secretary of state and advisor to
President Jefferson Davis. Courtesy of The Abraham
Lincoln Museum, Harrogate, Tennessee.

his policies. The appointment of Benjamin illustrates in many ways the president's stubborn refusal to accommodate his political opponents or public opinion.

As secretary of war, Benjamin made a number of enemies among the army generals, including Stonewall Jackson and Joseph Johnson. Nevertheless, the newly appointed secretary of state characteristically charged the State Department with a commitment to reorganize and implement a more consistent diplomatic strategy. More than any other member of the Confederate government, Benjamin was a committed internationalist with an appreciation of the European press on public opinion, especially in Great Britain. He realized the major role European recognition would play in the success of the Confederate effort.[6]

Benjamin initiated a new policy to entice or purchase European intervention. He decided, after consultation with the president, to offer Southern cotton at remarkably low prices to the French. He outlined his new idea in a dispatch to Slidell on May 11, 1862.[7] Benjamin hoped to secure French intervention by providing lucrative commercial concessions while actively soliciting European financing for Confederate naval construction in Europe. He hoped the emergence of France as the leading trading partner with the Confederacy would induce French involvement. It is doubtful the newly developed strategy would have helped the debate on the blockade, but it was clearly an aggressive change from the previous passive reliance on cotton.[8]

Stephen Mallory, secretary of the Navy, agreed with Benjamin that the best hope for Confederate success was in Europe. The defeat of the ironclad *Virginia* and the loss of "impregnable New Orleans" led Mallory to observe privately that "he looked now only for divine assistance or European intervention."[9] Next to Judah Benjamin, Mallory was the most criticized member of the Cabinet. The failure of the British and French to recognize the Confederacy, even though the new nation had existed for over a year and had sustained and protected itself, continued to frustrate Southerners. Mallory understood the desperate need for foreign naval support to assist the Confederacy against the Union navy. Despite the creativity and engineering genius of Matthew Fontaine Maury, demonstrated in the creation of innovative naval weapons, the Confederate navy was being overwhelmed.[10]

Naval operations in Europe conducted by Confederate operatives began early in the Civil War and continued to burden Confederate diplomacy. The clandestine activity of Confederate agents in Europe posed definite problems for diplomats seeking to create a navy. One of the functions of nineteenth-century diplomats included the supervision and financing of secret operations in neutral countries. This was certainly true of Confederate diplomats, and the demand for discretion and secrecy often burdened and encumbered the open diplomatic effort to obtain recognition.

With the arrival of James Bulloch in 1861 to supervise Confederate naval construction and purchases in England, the problem of circumventing the British and French neutrality laws was quickly presented. The demands of Bulloch for both funds and legal opinions contained the potential to embarrass the Confederate diplomats. Should Bulloch's attempts to purchase and construct a Confederate navy in Europe be exposed and connected in some way to those operatives pursuing recognition, a diplomatic disaster would result. Those members of Parliament and the Palmerston government sympathetic to the Union could well demand the expulsion or arrest of Mason and others connected to a plot that violated British neutrality laws. If the Confederates had any hope of achieving recognition, a reasonable distance would have to be maintained between the two operations.[11]

The escape of the surface raiders *Florida* and *Alabama* just before a writ could be served for their detention provided the U.S. minister, Charles Francis Adams, the potential for a diplomatic incident sufficient to end any hope of recognition for the Confederates. Bulloch and his colleagues managed to contain the threat of disaster and continued their activities in Great Britain until the last days of the war. Mason and Slidell, the unrecognized diplomatic representatives of the Confederacy, managed to provide funds to purchasing agents at critical times for the purchase of munitions and supplies, without being directly connected to the illegal operations. The confusion that resulted from a large number of men operating under various Confederate departmental authorities often threatened to expose the involvement of the senior Confederate representatives.[12]

The success of the Confederate surface raiders was highly publicized in the British press, due to the efforts of Adams and others sympathetic to the Union cause. The persistent efforts of Adams and Thomas Dudley, U.S. consul in Liverpool, to expose the continued illegal construction of ships destined for the Confederacy consistently handicapped the recognition initiatives. The distractions and demands for support that naval construction required from Mason, Hotze, and others burdened the Confederate effort. Moreover, the problem of supervision was complicated by the absence of timely information and instructions from the Richmond government. The agents often operated under instructions from various departments without any coordination from the State Department. The War Department, Navy Department, State Department, and Treasury Department all sent agents to Europe to accomplish various tasks. Each department often carried vague or conflicting instructions to Mason. The ever-present danger of exposure, should any of these men mishandle their assignment, contributed to the heavy burden of Confederate diplomats.[13]

During the winter and spring of 1862, while Confederate diplomatic agents in Europe pursued the blockade issue, the French minister in Washington, Henri Merciér, decided on a different initiative. Merciér decided to expand his instructions from Paris to include a trip to Richmond. French Foreign Minister Edouard Thouvenel had previously issued standing instructions for Merciér to offer the French good offices to mediate the American crisis and bring about peace. At no time, however, did Thouvenel instruct Merciér to pursue independent negotiations with the Confederate government. In spite of Napoleon's recent overtures to the British suggesting intervention or mediation, the Emperor remained committed to Anglo-French cooperation with regard to the American Civil War. Merciér believed the best hope for peace was a negotiated separation of the Southern states from the Union, but he was certainly prepared to pursue any opportunity to restore peace by the reconstruction of the United States. When an opportunity to visit Richmond resulted from a casual comment during an interview with Seward, Merciér decided to seize the opportunity to evaluate the situation in the Confederate capital.[14]

During January and early February, Thouvenel repeatedly pointed out in his dispatches to Merciér the distressing economic situation in France. He further asked Merciér to discuss the possibility of reopening Southern ports to commercial activity. In several meetings in Paris with William Dayton, Thouvenel repeated the French hope for the restoration of commercial activity between French and Southern ports. Merciér dutifully communicated these requests to Seward, enabling the perceptive Seward to reverse the King Cotton strategy on his Confederate adversaries. Promising the French access to captured Southern ports in exchange for the withdrawal of belligerent status for the Confederacy, Seward hoped to separate France from England and thereby prevent joint intervention by the two European powers.[15] Seward obviously knew he could not deliver cotton in any large amount, even after capturing Southern ports, because of Southern dependency on cotton to finance the war. At this point, the best hope of diplomatic success for the Confederacy rested on the European demand for cotton.

The recent military reverses suffered by the Confederacy suggested to Merciér that many of his old friends in Richmond might be prepared to accept favorable terms and rejoin the Union. Seward certainly wanted to pursue the issue, and encouraged Merciér to travel to Richmond. He insisted, however, that the French minister not communicate anything less than the Lincoln administration's commitment to reunion. Seward made the statement to Merciér that he, "for one, was prepared to take a seat alongside any of the former rebel Senators in the United States Senate should they choose to return."[16] This remark was clearly an expression of a conciliatory attitude the Southerners might expect on rejoining the Union. Unfortunately for the reunion cause, Merciér would return from his Richmond trip with a new appreciation for the determination of the rebel leadership to achieve independence and separation.[17]

By encouraging Merciér's trip to Richmond, Seward pursued several different diplomatic objectives simultaneously. First, he demonstrated a willingness to cooperate with the French to obtain cotton and ease the economic depression caused by the disruption in their Atlantic trade. Secondly, the trip would contribute to speculations already encouraged by Lyons that the French were pursuing their interest independently of Britain. The suspicion that Merciér was acting on instructions from Paris received additional credibility when Russian Minister Stoeckl was invited to accompany the Frenchman on his visit. The speculation that the Russian and the Frenchman were pursuing negotiations with the Confederacy, to the exclusion of the British, was a welcome catalyst to the Seward strategy. A third reason why Seward encouraged the visit was that he hoped it would not only produce informal intelligence about the state of the Confederate government and its determination to continue resistance, but also allow Merciér to communicate to his Southern friends the power of the U.S. Army and Navy and the hopelessness of the Southern situation.[18]

Merciér was warmly received in Richmond by his old friend Judah Benjamin late in the evening of April 16. Benjamin, aware of Merciér's reputation as a gourmet, apologized for the absence of fine wine and food. He told Merciér that he hoped to entertain him more hospitably after the war. The next day, Merciér began a round of visits in hopes of determining how the South felt after its recent defeats. His interviews included Senators L. T. Wigfall of Texas, James L. Orr of South Carolina, and Clement C. Clay of Alabama, all of whom he had known in Washington prior to the rebellion. He also met with Gen. Benjamin Huger and Gen. Robert E. Lee in an attempt to as-sess the military situation.[19] Merciér was impressed with the commitment of all these men—regardless of their professions, business interests, or the regions they represented—to maintain independence from the Union no matter what the cost. He reported to Thouvenel that "the South was determined to gain its independence at any price of blood and treasure."[20]

The most important interview was with Benjamin. Merciér began the interview by explaining that the purpose of his journey was "only to assure myself of the true state of things, and I came to ask you to help me to attain this."[21] Benjamin responded graciously and said he would be glad to assist Merciér in determining the accurate state of things because it appeared that the "truth seemed so little known abroad." Referring to the North's preponderance of naval power, Merciér asserted "frankly, that he considered the capture of all our cities within reach of the water as a matter of certainty, that it was purely a question of weight of metal, ... that . . . he did not deem it possible for us to save any of our cities, and he asked me to say frankly what I thought would be the course of our government in such an event."[22] Benjamin replied to Merciér that it was "quite possible that all the seaports and main cities would be captured, but that the enemy would find in those cities only women, children, and old men, for the fighting population would retreat to the mountains and wage ceaseless warfare until the Northern armies had withdrawn from the South."[23] The forcefulness of Benjamin's reply was not lost on Merciér. It contributed to his conviction, lasting throughout the war, that the South would fight and sacrifice everything for the cause.[24]

Merciér next approached the subject of reunion, as Seward had expected he would. He suggested to Benjamin that such sacrifice would not be necessary if reunion was considered. Benjamin responded by explaining that any such opportunity had long since passed. The reality of two distinct peoples prevented any reunion and each should exist under its separate government.

According to Merciér's report, Benjamin said, "Our population have today more hatred for the Yankees than the French have ever had for the English. Nothing but independence could possibly be considered."[25] Apparently, Merciér accepted Benjamin's logic. He continued to argue for separation as a solution to the hostilities long after his return to Washington. When he returned to Washington, Merciér reported to his colleagues, as well as to Seward and Thouvenel, that the South was determined to resist. The best hope for immediate peace was through mediation. The sacrifice in blood and treasure, he argued, would ultimately destroy the Union in any case.[26]

It was now Benjamin's turn to inquire of the French minister why the European powers continued to withhold recognition of the Confederacy and accept the effectiveness of the Union blockade. Merciér responded with the usual argument, and Benjamin apparently understood the reasons for nonrecognition, but pressed his old friend on the blockade issue. Benjamin asked why the French did not protest the ineffective blockade when the Federal government first announced it. Merciér was embarrassed, for he knew that his government did not really consider the blockade effective, but had acquiesced because of the British position. His feeble response to Benjamin was that blockade recognition was a matter of international law and multilateral consideration.[27]

The only remaining issue for discussion was French access to Southern cotton. Merciér asked, "Are you really determined to burn your cotton and tobacco? If your ports are open to commerce, do you believe your planters can resist the temptation of selling their crops to the brokers?"[28] Benjamin responded by pointing out that very little cotton was in the cities and most of the recent crop remained on the plantations and in warehouses in the interior.

There is a discrepancy between Benjamin's account to Slidell and Merciér's communication to Thouvenel. According to Benjamin, he pointedly explained that Southerners would not hesitate to burn their crops before allowing the Yankees to take advantage of Southern produce to reopen Southern ports to European commercial activity. Merciér, on the other hand, wrote Thouvenel that "any planter who tried to sell would be exposed to the retaliation of his compatriots." Benjamin may have expressed to Slidell a firmer commitment to the destruction of cotton than he actually told Merciér. Undoubtedly, Benjamin was both diplomatic and gracious to his guest and hoped to make a favorable impression on the French minister by not aggravating the sensitive issue of the cotton embargo.[29]

Four days before Merciér arrived, Benjamin had written Slidell asking him to sound out the French on the idea of opening Southern ports exclusively to France for tariff-free commercial activity. This would, of course, necessitate the presence of a French fleet sufficient to shoot its way into Southern ports, thus forcing the blockade. In exchange for this aggressive action, the Confederacy would offer a "reimbursement" for their trouble. Benjamin suggested that the "reimbursement" might consist of a hundred thousand bales of cotton, which could be sold for over $12 million in French markets.

Apparently, the Confederate secretary of state wanted Slidell to approach this matter with his contacts in Paris because he failed to introduce the subject with Merciér. This is puzzling, considering the frustrating problems the Confederates had in sending and receiving messages. Benjamin could have asked Merciér to deliver the suggestion directly to his superiors in Paris in his diplomatic mail pouch. It is possible that Benjamin already knew Merciér would oppose any such action and wished to avoid any negative comments from Merciér that would undoubtedly accompany the proposal.[30]

Benjamin was well aware of Merciér's commitment to a "common market" concept between the North and South, should separation become permanent. For his own reasons, Benjamin did not approach the subject in his formal meeting with Merciér. Apparently in another encounter, either social or possibly another formal session, Merciér indirectly approached the subject by mentioning the need to give consideration to future borders between the Southern slave states and the North. Benjamin responded with a firm commitment to the existing state lines between the two sections, whereupon Merciér suggested, "Maybe you would succeed if you agreed to maintain commercial union throughout the former territory of the United States."[31] Benjamin patiently explained the long-standing differences between North and South over protective tariffs. Merciér continued to press his point by suggesting that if the North did reach the point of financial collapse, as Southerners expected, the reestablishment of commercial activity between the two sections would place the North in an economically dependent position to the South. Benjamin moved the conversation on to another subject, but the remarkable concept was not lost on the Confederate leadership.

It remained for R. M. T. Hunter, to whom Merciér confided this idea, to pursue the matter. The extraordinary implication of Merciér's "common market" plan is that the representative of the French empire was in the rebel capital of Richmond, in fact acknowledging the autonomous status of the Confederacy by suggesting a solution based on the political independence of the South, thus ending the war. Of course, diplomatic recognition would facilitate the process of negotiations.[32]

During his stay in Richmond, Merciér called on another old friend, Matthew Fontaine Maury. Of all his pre-war Washington acquaintances, he found Maury probably the most interesting, especially for his enthusiastic explanations of scientific ideas. Maury had suggested before the war that a hydrographical expedition, cosponsored by the French and Americans, be sent into the Antarctic. When Virginia seceded, the famous oceanographer and former head of the Naval Observatory in Washington rejected an offer from the Russians to sponsor his research abroad. Merciér made a similar offer to Maury during their meeting. He not only offered access to the French scientific community, but also told Maury he would be allowed to continue to work closely with his contacts in the Confederacy while pursuing his scientific endeavors in a peaceful France. Maury expressed his appreciation to Merciér and the emperor for the offer, but explained his commitment to Virginia and the Southern cause. He told his old friend he was deeply involved with his responsibilities as the director of the Confederate coastal defenses and reconfirmed for Merciér the single-mindedness of the Southern commitment to independence.[33]

Maury received Merciér graciously. After a brief renewal of their old acquaintance, Maury brought up the subject of the *Trent* affair. Even though the conversation was general, Maury pointed out the failure of the British to fully appreciate French support during the crisis. He told Merciér he expected a more conciliatory response, including a more sympathetic view toward the frustrating economic problems the American conflict was causing in France. Merciér warmed to the kind expression of support, which was completely consistent with his previously stated position. For the course of the conversation, Maury introduced an elaborate plan for a Franco-Confederate alliance, which he believed would have important commercial and economic rewards for the Second Empire. It was essentially the same proposal Benjamin had previously forwarded to Slidell, providing a large quantity of cotton in exchange for the presence of the French fleet off Southern ports. Maury enthusiastically pointed out the financial rewards and permanent commercial opportunities for the French inherent in the plan.[34]

Merciér diplomatically explained that the French were unable to take advantage of the Confederates' offer of free trade. The French merchant fleet was too small and had always relied on New England's merchant vessels to supplement its carrying capacity to and from Southern ports. Merciér, apparently, did not suggest the French navy might be inadequate for the task, particularly in light of the French commitment in Mexico. In his strongly worded argument against the Maury plan when reporting the conversation to Thouvenel, Merciér did mention the strong Union naval force existing off the Atlantic coast. Merciér continued by pointing out to Maury that France sought peace in America and that French interest could best be served by continuing active commerce with both the North and the South once peace was restored.[35]

After his meeting with Merciér, Maury provided Benjamin with a detailed report of the conversation. There is no direct evidence in Maury's papers to suggest he was requested by the secretary of state to propose the new cotton strategy to Merciér, nor does Benjamin make reference to any such request. It does appear remarkably consistent with the new Confederate strategy that a discussion of the *Trent* affair and the new cotton proposal would be unofficially broached by Maury, while Slidell was preparing to sound out officials in Paris along the same lines. Strangely enough, the subtle suggestion that the French were prepared to accept the Confederate government by engaging in conversations of international trade agreements and a free trade solution to create a separate nation seems to have been lost on the Confederate leadership.

When Merciér returned to Washington on April 24, he discovered the implications of his visit had produced an immediate response from his superiors in Paris.[36] Merciér called on both Lyons and Seward to communicate the results of his visit to Richmond. Lyons was relieved to hear that no exclusive arrangement was negotiated between the French and Confederate governments. On April 28, he informed Russell of his concern that Merciér might negotiate some commercial accommodation independently of Britain that would foreclose joint action and violate the Anglo-French agreement. Seward, on the other hand, after learning from Merciér of the strong Southern conviction to "take to the hills" in defense of their independence even if their cities were lost, explained the strong Southern sentiment as a desperate response to the increased military pressure from the Union.[37]

Merciér intended his report to Seward, Lyons, and Thouvenel to form the basis for further mediation and intervention moves. But Seward, again taking the initiative, published an account of Merciér's trip in the *New York Times* on May 6. In this account, Merciér was depicted as an agent of the U.S. government sent to Richmond to urge the Confederates to give up their efforts and return to the Union.[38] Seward hoped that this account would discourage any idea of intervention and cause the Confederates to question Merciér's motives. To a large extent, Seward was successful. After reading the *New York Times* article, Benjamin wrote to Slidell: "I am very much inclined to believe that he [Merciér] really came at Seward's request to feel the way and learn whether any possible terms would induce us to re-enter the Union."[39]

In any case, Merciér and Seward both got what they wanted from the Richmond trip. Merciér now knew the Southern determination to fight to the end, and Seward accomplished his goal of separating, at least temporarily, the two European powers to prevent any joint intervention. The jealousy and suspicions created in Great Britain over Merciér's visit to the Confederate capital were viewed by the Confederate envoys in Europe as an opportunity to introduce the idea of mediation and renew the recognition debate. Unfortunately for Merciér's credibility, Thouvenel first learned of his trip South from Lord John Russell on April 29. Thouvenel quickly recognized the potential danger to the British entente, to which he remained personally committed. Thouvenel was antagonized by Lyons's suggestion that the emperor had proposed the Merciér trip and that Thouvenel particularly wanted Russian Minister Stoeckl to accompany Merciér. Thouvenel immediately denied to the British through Flahault that either he or the emperor were involved in instructing Merciér to undertake the impromptu mission and dispatched a rather heated rebuke and a request for an explanation to Merciér.[40]

The Confederate agents were the most excited persons in Europe over the Merciér trip to Richmond. At first, Mason and Slidell believed Merciér was acting under secret orders from Napoleon and, of course, this delighted and encouraged them. Such a secret initiative was consistent with the earlier initiatives of Napoleon. When Thouvenel denied any official knowledge of Merciér's actions, Slidell reported to Mason that the foreign minister nevertheless appeared more friendly than usual.[41] After Slidell's interview, Mason suggested that Merciér was possibly acting as Seward's agent without Thouvenel's knowledge.[42] Slidell decided to pursue other sources of information within the official Paris community and received assurances from Flahault that "the Emperor and all the ministers are favorable to our cause, have been so for the last year, and are now quite as warmly so as they have ever been. M. Thouvenel is, of course, excepted, but then he has no hostility."[43] The two Confederate diplomats now returned to the conclusion that Napoleon was manipulating the situation and they should be content to wait for further developments.

The Confederate newspaper *Index*, under the direction of Henry Hotze, learned of Merciér's trip and published its account and opinion on May 1, 1862. Hotze claimed, "The visit of M. Merciér to Richmond is . . . extremely significant for the determination of the French government to put an end to the blockade."[44] Clearly, Hotze did not believe the report that Merciér went to Richmond in the interest of the Federal government. Consistent with his instructions from Benjamin to "plant" information in European journals favorable to the Confederate cause, he suggested that the rumor that Merciér represented the Federal government was a figment in the mind of the master propagandist, William Seward. The editorial in the *Index* was quickly followed by an article in the *Economist* agreeing with the Confederate commissioners that Merciér's actual purpose was to obtain relief for the suffering "commercial uneasiness in France."[45] The editors of the *Economist* did not believe France would use force to open Southern ports, but concluded that Napoleon could be expected to continue maneuvering to reopen trade with the South.[46]

Hotze and his staff not only published the *Index*, but were also in constant communication with influential British leaders sympathetic to the Southern cause. They entertained regularly and were frequently invited to various official and unofficial social functions. In the course of these social activities, Hotze and other Confederate propagandists dispensed money, favors, ideas, and influence to further the Confederate cause.[47]

Henry Hotze and the success of the *Index* represents one of the few successful diplomatic initiatives of the Confederacy. Hotze was remarkably sensitive to the feelings of the Europeans and, despite his youth, was accepted by the literary community. Hotze was born in Switzerland on September 2, 1833, and immigrated to Mobile, Alabama, in 1855 and became a naturalized U.S. citizen.[48] Hotze's strong racial views, as reflected in his writings, contributed to his acceptance in the social and intellectual circles of Mobile. He made powerful and influential friends, such as C. J. McRae, who later became the chief Confederate financial agent in Europe. He also worked as an associate editor for the Mobile *Register*, which was edited by the moderate Southerner John Forsyth. Because of his moderate views, Forsyth was selected by Jefferson Davis as one of the three Southern peace commissioners sent to Washington during the early days of the Confederacy.[49]

Hotze cultivated both conservative and radical Southern leaders. He was well acquainted with the fire-eating William L. Yancey and was respected by J. D. B. DeBow, editor of *DeBow's Review*. It was through the influence of such powerful friends that the young Swiss American was appointed secretary and chargé d'affaires of the American legation in Brussels. It is not coincidental that the American minister to Belgium was Gen. E. Y. Fair of Alabama. Unfortunately for the young diplomat, Congress refused to provide adequate funds in 1859 and he returned to Mobile in time to support Stephen A. Douglas for president in 1860.[50]

Hotze was appointed to the Mobile Board of Harbor in 1861 and was involved in Southern attempts to seize the Union transport vessel, the *Illinois*. As a result of his involvement in this aggressive Southern action, Hotze was noticed by L. P. Walker, the Confederate secretary of war. After Hotze served a brief stint in the newly formed Mobile Cadets, Walker selected him for a special mission to Europe in September of 1861. The mission was to determine why Confederate agents were so slow in obtaining munitions and other vital military supplies for which the Confederate government had advanced over $1 million. Hotze proceeded to Great Britain by way of an internal passage through Union territory into Canada and subsequently to London. Hotze selected this hazardous trip to evaluate public opinion in the Midwest toward Southern secession. The trip identified Hotze's special interest in public opinion and contributed substantially to his future interest in Confederate propaganda in Europe.[51]

After Hotze reached London, he conferred with his old friend William Yancey and determined that no unusual financial "shenanigans" had prevented the purchase and shipment of Confederate military supplies. The Confederate government naively expected traditional shipping and financial arrangements would not be disturbed by the outbreak of hostilities. While Hotze completed his assigned mission expeditiously, he was determined to request authority from the Confederate government to initiate a propaganda campaign in Great Britain. He returned home in the late fall of 1861 only to find his friend and mentor, Judah Benjamin, serving as secretary of war. It was probably Benjamin who recommended Hotze present his propaganda plan to Secretary of State Hunter. Hotze was appointed as a commercial agent on November 14, 1861. Hunter instructed Hotze in great detail to pursue influencing British public opinion through his own well-placed editorials while securing the cooperation of British newspaper and literary persons.[52]

Hotze was quick to sense a fundamental shift in the Confederate diplomatic strategy, even though his written instructions emphasized the continued reliance on cotton. It was probably Benjamin, in his discussions with Hotze, who first suggested that a shift in future Confederate policy would be necessary. It is, therefore, not surprising that Hotze was prepared on his return to England to work closely with Benjamin after his appointment as secretary of state. Hotze was remarkably successful with the Confederate propaganda campaign and founded the *Index* with little funding from the Confederate government. Most of the funding came from private sources in the Confederacy and Great Britain, as well as his personal resources. Hotze received only $750 as a contingency allowance and a $150 annual salary with which to conduct his propaganda campaign. Most of the financial assistance came from two wealthy friends, H. O. Drewer of Mobile and A. P. Wetter of Savannah.[53]

The young Confederate editor enjoyed powerful friends on both sides of the Atlantic and took full advantage of his association to conduct a remarkably successful propaganda campaign throughout the war. Unfortunately for Benjamin, Hotze's perceptive impressions of European attitudes were usually received belatedly. Hotze generally operated under the local supervision of James Mason and frequently did not benefit from timely or direct communications with the Confederate State Department. The absence of direct indications of a shift in Confederate policy required Hotze to often operate in an information vacuum. He obtained knowledge of Merciér's trip and Benjamin's new cotton strategy from Slidell around the first of May. The perceptive Hotze quickly seized the opportunity presented by the shift in Confederate policy and presented the new Confederate position in the *Index*.[54]

Benjamin's proposal to Slidell of cotton in exchange for the presence of a French fleet, which was confirmed in the Maury proposal to Merciér, signaled a change in the Confederate strategy. The new Confederate secretary of state was returning to his original suggestion in early 1861 that Confederate cotton in Europe could better finance and sustain the Confederacy than cotton on the plantations or in burning warehouses. The specific suggestions contained in the Benjamin and Maury proposal were unrealistic, but the seeds of a new cotton strategy were planted. When Slidell approached leading French officials with the idea, he found little interest.[55]

The conversations with financial leaders, however, took a slightly different turn and eventually led to a much-needed financial arrangement based on cotton bonds. The shift in Confederate diplomatic strategy, revealed to Merciér on his trip, was handicapped by the Confederacy's poor lines of communication. Slidell and Mason, operating on the scene in Europe, were pressing the blockade issue and the Lindsay initiative without any knowledge of the shift in cotton diplomacy. The information they received on the Merciér trip was obtained through unofficial sources and they did not receive Benjamin's dispatches until the middle of July. The effect of poor communications on the ultimate outcome of the blockade debate is uncertain, but the prolonged and insecure lines of communication hampered all Confederate diplomatic activity.

Chapter 8

Will the Emperor Help
Obtain Recognition?

In the spring of 1862, both Seward and Benjamin were induced to modify their diplomatic strategies to reflect the fortunes of war. Benjamin's effort to free the South from its economic dependence on Great Britain is revealed in the abandonment of the cotton embargo and in a new Southern strategy focusing on France. Seward's shifting strategy, emphasizing the differences between French and British interests, sought thereby to prevent joint intervention. Unlike Benjamin, Seward enjoyed the luxury of open and secure lines of communication with his representatives in Europe. Both secretaries of state benefited from a number of battlefield successes.[1]

The summer of 1862 allowed the Confederates an opportunity to briefly enjoy the support military victory provided for diplomatic initiatives. The welcome news of General Lee's success in May and June provided Hotze with real propaganda ammunition. Unfortunately for the Southern cause, victory in Virginia did not disguise the fundamental weakness of the Confederacy's diplomatic position. The absence of sufficient naval or economic power to compel intervention doomed the Confederate diplomatic offensive.

There was more than a hint of desperation, however, in Seward's behavior as he strove to convince the British that the North intended to press on with the struggle despite military failures in Virginia.

Seward's correspondence to Adams and Dayton reflects concern over the hardships caused Europeans by the absence of cotton. He continued to press for the withdrawal of belligerent status, which he believed would break the spirit of Southern resistance.[2]

The modestly financed but successful Confederate propaganda campaign in Great Britain and France produced a pro-Southern response from much of the public press in London and Paris.[3] Merciér's visit to Richmond stimulated editorial speculation in both capitals. A serious dialogue soon developed over the role the respective powers should play in the American conflict. The issue of intervention divided the French journals. The liberal press, led by the *Journal des Debats,* was against intervention. *The Constitutionnel,* which generally expressed the government's position, favored intervention and was controlled by Duke Fialin Persigny, the close friend of Slidell and advisor to Napoleon. The British papers were similarly divided; however, British press tended to more accurately reflect both the realities and public opinions on the issue.[4]

The environment in Europe seemed conducive to new Confederate initiatives despite the inability of the Confederate lobby to obtain Parliament's denunciation of the blockade. Thomas Dudley, U.S. consul in Liverpool, summed up the situation in May 1862 when he wrote Seward: "The people of this place, if not the entire Kingdom, seem to be becoming every day more and more enlisted [in the Confederate cause]."[5] From the legation in London, Henry Adams wrote his brother Charles in the Union army: "The feeling is universal here against us."[6] Even before the good news arrived from Virginia that McClellan was retreating from the gates of Richmond, Mason and Slidell decided to press the European powers for intervention or mediation.

The Union blockading squadrons forced the Southern representatives to act on their own initiatives. The absence of any reliable and timely information on military matters and other strategic materials forced the Southerners to act on hearsay information and stale news from the European papers. Judah Benjamin, undoubtedly the most qualified of the Confederate secretaries of state, frequently did not receive dispatches from his representatives in Europe until after delays of up to six months. Communications were particularly difficult during the critical period from late 1861 until mid-1863 and forced the tiny Confederate State Department staff to obtain overseas news from Northern newspapers, out-of-date European journals, and parliamentary publications.[7]

Benjamin spoke and read several foreign languages and was as aware of the historical precedents and national interests that influenced the Europeans as anyone in the Confederacy. Unfortunately for the Southern cause, he was severely handicapped by lack of fresh intelligence from Europe. In the absence of instructions from home, Mason and Slidell pressed on with their mission.[8] Not until the summer of 1863 was Benjamin successful in obtaining the services of a fleet of fast packet ships capable of running the blockade from Nassau and Bermuda, reopening fairly secure lines of communication with Europe.[9]

The Confederate State Department, unlike the War Department with thousands of employees, operated on a Spartan budget with a minimum number of employees. In addition to Benjamin, the department consisted of secretaries, clerks, and researchers and never numbered more than seven. Unfortunately for Benjamin, immediately after he took office, William M. Browne resigned as assistant secretary of state to become the aide-de-camp to Jefferson Davis. Browne's position was not filled and most of his duties fell upon Lucius Quinton Washington, the department's chief clerk. Benjamin and his chief clerk knew each other before the war, but working together in the State Department produced a warm and permanent friendship.[10] According to Washington's ledger book, the employees in the Richmond office and their monthly salaries on September 30, 1863, were as follows:

L. Q. Washington	Chief Clerk	$1,750.00
Wm. J. Bromwell	Disbursing Clerk	1,500.00
James B. Baker	Clerk	1,500.00
Geo. W. Paul	Messenger	750.00
Philip Green	Laborer	45.00

The salaries of agents and commissioners serving abroad were paid from the Treasury Department, while appropriations for special projects such as the propaganda campaigns of Edwin DeLeon and Henry Hotze, were paid from other sources within the government. Henry Hotze obtained funding from both private and personal sources, while DeLeon enjoyed substantial financial support from the government.[11]

The Confederate State Department was located in the handsome spacious pre-war U.S. Customs House in Richmond. The building was completed shortly before the war and was located on Main Street in the heart of the business district. When the Confederate provisional government moved to Richmond, it appropriated the building for use as the executive office building. Vaults on the first floor were used by Christopher Memminger and the Treasury Department. The elegant and spacious offices on the upper floor were reserved for Jefferson Davis. The State Department was located on the same floor as the president's office. As secretary of state and the president's closest friend in the Cabinet, Benjamin enjoyed an office adjacent to the Davis suite.[12]

One contemporary visitor to the Confederate State Department in 1864 recalled "entering the room and facing a black walnut table covered with a green cloth and filled with a multitude of State papers."[13] On the walls were hung a few maps and a tier of bookshelves. Benjamin's office resembled the State Department he operated and was without the typical trappings and furnishings of high-ranking officials. The books were largely concerned with international law and European history. Conspicuously absent were the classics Benjamin enjoyed and would again purchase after the war.[14]

Lindsay's parliamentary initiative was postponed without consultation with Benjamin. This decision strained the otherwise cordial relations between Mason and Slidell. The two men decided to continue working closely together but to pursue recognition independently in London and Paris. Slidell was optimistic that he could succeed in persuading Napoleon to act independently and recognize the Confederacy. He also believed that despite the cooperation Mason was receiving from a strong and influential group of Southern sympathizers in England, they would remain timid, allowing Palmerston and Russell to avoid the gamble of recognition. Slidell wrote Benjamin, "I think that it is now more evident than ever that England will do nothing that may offend the Lincoln government and I shall await as patiently as I can the course of events."[15]

When news arrived of Confederate victories, Mason was convinced that Spence had counseled correctly. Hotze moved to capitalize on the news and, after consultation with Spence, wrote: "Surely a people who numbered eight millions, inhabited a large and distinct country, and who have proven their determination and ability to maintain their independence, constituted a nation."[16] The implication, of course, was that a nation in possession of these characteristics had a right to recognition from other nations. The *Morning Star* confirmed "the men of the South have undoubtedly gained a considerable advantage over the men of the North."[17] Despite this good press, Spence still counseled delay of Lindsay's often-postponed motion. He wrote Mason on July 11 that public opinion was "ripening fast," but the atmosphere in the House of Commons was not quite right yet. Nevertheless, if McClellan was about to surrender his army to Lee, as was rumored in London, Mason could make a formal demand for recognition and expect success following the subsequent debate in Parliament.[18]

Adams and the Union sympathizers among the British did not intend to allow Mason and the Confederate lobby to go unopposed. As if to ensure Adams would appreciate the seriousness of the situation, a report was brought to his attention on July 17 by Consul Morse that the Austrians were proposing an Anglo-Austrian scheme to summon an international conference to settle the American question.[19] Morse suggested that Adams immediately explain to the Austrian ambassador that the benefit of a separated United States would accrue to the British—not the Austrians—and to Palmerston in particular. Adams reported the entire conversation to Seward and suggested that the war aims of the United States be restated and clarified. Slidell believed the failure of mediation, if in fact it was proposed, should be laid at the feet of the Confederates. It was the South, not the North, that had started the war and refused to come back into the Union.

A litany of problems, such as boundaries, slavery, trade, open cities, and the nature of a cease fire, existed within any mediation proposal. The international community was obviously aware of these problems, and Adams feared the British would reestablish a presence in the Western Hemisphere.[20] Hoping to slow down the Confederate movement, Adams had directed one of his staff to write Thomas Dudley in Liverpool requesting a thorough inquiry into Lindsay's possible association with blockade-running. Benjamin Moran wrote Dudley that just one case could discredit the Southern sympathizer and his following; but, alas, Dudley was unable to come up with any evidence of illegal activity.[21]

On the day of the mediation debate in Parliament, rumors appeared in London newspapers that McClellan had surrendered. As a result, Adams had to devote the afternoon of July 18 to reassuring worried and nervous Union sympathizers in the Commons. To discredit the inaccurate rumors about McClellan, Adams distributed copies of the July 5 edition of the *New York Tribune*. Mason, however, hoped to make use of the rumors in the House of Commons debate, regardless of their authenticity.

Adams asked Benjamin Moran to attend the session of Parliament and observe the proceedings. Moran provided a colorful account of the event, reporting that the galleries were packed and the Confederates conspicuously present. According to Moran, "Mason was overdressed and one of his companions underdressed, having forgotten to button his trousers."[22] The seriousness of the debate, however, was no laughing matter. Lindsay led the debate and presented his motion. He was supported by William Gregory and James Whiteside, both of whom were eloquent and forceful in speaking for the motion. Von Tempest, according to Moran, appeared the worse for drink and stumbled through his pro-Southern litany. The only new argument presented came from Gregory when he suggested that mediation would allow Northerners to speak out in opposition to the war. Undoubtedly, Gregory was again coached by Hotze. This new wrinkle came directly from Benjamin, who had at last made a contribution to the debate.[23]

Mason probably did not understand the partisan dilemma confronting British politicians, but he did sense an opportunity through the issues articulated by Derby to secure a Conservative report. It is unlikely that any diplomat could have positioned the players well enough to carry the debate, but the master of the game with sufficient perceptive skills to succeed was Judah Benjamin. Unfortunately for the Union diplomatic effort, Benjamin knew little of the debate and the blockade squadron prevented any serious participation on his part.

Slidell was unaware that Thouvenel had continued to pressure Merciér to offer mediation to Seward at the earliest opportunity. Merciér did in fact approach Seward on July 1 but reported that the secretary of state was adamant in his rejection of the proposal. While assuring Merciér of his hope for continued good relations, Seward warned him not to "compromise his attitude which is of such grave importance to you."[24] Even though Slidell was not aware of Seward's official response, he certainly was aware of the persistent attempts by the emperor to intervene in the American war.[25]

On July 15, after further consultations with Persigny, the Confederate commissioner departed for the interview with Napoleon in Vichy. Slidell arrived on July 16. When the interview began, Slidell was astonished by the bold and frank opening remarks of the emperor, which were generally sympathetic to the Southern cause. The emperor praised the courage and determination of both the civilian population and the armies in the field. He demonstrated a remarkable knowledge of the strategy and campaigns when alluding to Lee's victory over McClellan on the peninsula. The emperor continued to set the candid tone of the interview by pointing out that France had always hoped a united America would provide a counterpoise to England; nevertheless, he believed that under the circumstances, French sympathies should continue with the South. In his opinion, Southern victory was inevitable. Unfortunately, said the emperor, there was no safe way to properly express French sympathies for the Southern cause. Although he wished to intervene, he could not do so without the cooperation of England. As Slidell knew, England had rejected numerous French requests to cooperate on the American question. France would "not draw England's chestnuts out of the fire." Napoleon repeated, at this point, his resentment toward England as a result of their coolness after the *Trent* affair. Slidell, of course, hoped to take advantage of the emperor's sentiments and obtain independent action from the French.[26]

Delighted with the emperor's observations, Slidell respectfully requested to continue the interview in English. Although Slidell's French was excellent, he flattered the emperor by acknowledging Napoleon's mastery of the English language. In support of the emperor's statement that Southern independence was a foregone conclusion, Slidell pointed out that the Confederacy had about 350,000 men under arms, with additional men available if needed to combat the Union army. The desperate need was not for troops but for arms, clothing, and the necessities of war. Southern men were better fighters, explained Slidell, because they were native to the South and were fighting in defense of their homes, while most of the Northern troops were foreigners, mercenaries, and soldiers of fortune.[27]

Slidell asserted that European acceptance of the paper blockade was a violation of neutrality. The French tradition supporting neutral rights, as articulated as recently as January 1862 in the aftermath of the *Trent* affair, was being renounced and France was failing to uphold international law. Probably to Slidell's surprise, the emperor replied, "I have committed a deep error, which I now deeply regret. France should never have respected the blockade; the European powers should have recognized you last summer when your ports were in your possession and when you were menacing Washington."[28] Slidell hastened to point out that much of the Southern coast was not yet blockaded and the option for France to declare the blockade illegal still existed. These unblockaded points could be used to reestablish open lines of communication and trade by using the French navy to convoy neutral merchant ships. "After all," Slidell said, "the North would probably back down as it did in the *Trent* affair." Again, the emperor agreed with Slidell; but regrettably, he said he needed to maintain for "many reasons why I desire to be on the best terms with her [England]. I am, consequently, obliged to look forward to the possible contingency of not always having the same friendly relations as now exist."[29] Slidell accepted this as a reference to the Anglo-French disagreement over the Mexican expedition. Seizing the opportunity,

Slidell decided to pursue, on his own initiative, a Southern alliance with France against the Juarez government in Mexico.[30]

Slidell told the emperor, "I do not hesitate to say that it [the military expedition to Mexico] will be regarded with no unfriendly eye by the Confederate States; they can have no other interest or desire than to see a respectable, responsible, and stable government established in that country."[31] Slidell then mentioned Seward's proposed Corwin Treaty that would place $11 million in the hands of Juarez to fight the French, implying that U.S. aid would be used to fight Napoleon's armies. Napoleon, obviously angered, suggested that the American Senate would not ratify the treaty. Slidell disagreed and pointed out that Consul-General Robert W. Shufeldt had left his position in Cuba and was in Mexico prepared to give Juarez $2 million as the first installment on a new loan. Slidell pressed his point home by suggesting that a number of Orleanists were serving in the U.S. army.[32]

After repeating he had no official instructions from his government, Slidell suggested an alliance between the South and France "against the common enemy." He told the emperor that "the Lincoln government is the ally and protector of your enemy, Juarez. We can have no objection to make common cause with you against the common enemy." Slidell expected that an alliance with France against Juarez would create a corresponding alliance against the Union navy.[33]

Slidell then redirected the interview toward Benjamin's cotton offer. He first asked the ruler if he had heard recently from Persigny. The emperor said he had not. Slidell proceeded to describe the offer of cotton in return for war supplies from France. Napoleon was interested and asked Slidell, "How are you to get the cotton?" Slidell replied, "Of course, that depends on your Majesty."[34] The Southern agent then proceeded to flatter the emperor by explaining that the French navy, which would hopefully soon be off the coast of the United States, was powerful enough to hold New York and Boston at its mercy. Slidell further emphasized that the cotton proposal was limited to France and, as yet, no offer was being made to England. In other words, the preferred status of France depended on the willingness of the emperor to use his fleet.[35]

The emperor continued with a rather lengthy discussion of recognition and mediation. After responding carefully to the emperor's questions, Slidell decided to take the initiative and terminate the interview. Slidell told the emperor, "I have prepared a formal demand for recognition in which they [all the previously stated arguments] are embodied, and I intend to present them to Mr. Thouvenel."[36]

Slidell then asked the emperor if he had any objection to this course of action. To Slidell's delight, the emperor said he did not and hoped that in the future Slidell would have less difficulty in obtaining an audience with him.

The interview lasted about an hour and is remarkable for several reasons. It provided Slidell with what appeared to be a clear statement of Napoleon's sympathy for the South and confirmed that a willingness to intervene still existed. Taking it upon himself to offer a military alliance against Juarez without defining precisely what the Confederacy expected in exchange, Slidell had probably realized the illegal blockade debate was a dead issue. Nonetheless, he dutifully presented the anti-blockade argument using the information Benjamin had furnished in his instructions of April 8 and April 11, 1862. The information contained in these instructions arrived belatedly, and Slidell decided to build on the cotton initiatives outlined by Benjamin in his March 18 dispatch. Slidell came away from the meeting with Napoleon convinced that the emperor might soon attempt intervention independently of England. Napoleon clearly left the impression with Slidell that he desired to intervene on behalf of the South.[37]

After the interview, Slidell quickly wrote Mason a sketch of the conversation but omitted any detail of either the cotton proposition or the Mexican proposal. Slidell later explained that he feared the sensitive proposals he made to the emperor would fall into the hands of Federal agents operating throughout Europe, who were constantly watching every Confederate operative. Slidell's extraordinary proposals remained secret for the time being. The implications, should the French accept either or both of the proposals, certainly would have altered the course of the war. The French providing the Confederacy with much-needed naval support was an exciting prospect for Slidell's cause; but, as important for its international implications was the Franco-Southern alliance against Juarez.[38]

The Lincoln administration had expressed opposition to French actions in Mexico, but to openly aid and support the enemies of Napoleon was another matter. Slidell hoped that by tying the Union to Juarez he could not only obtain the support of the French, but also secure commitments from other European nations sympathetic to France. There is little evidence to suggest that the Confederate government would have sustained Slidell if the French had accepted his proposal; but Slidell, always the realist, seized the opportunity because other diplomatic initiatives had proved inadequate to provoke intervention.[39]

Slidell was now ready to present Thouvenel with his recognition demand and wrote Mason that he would present his demands on Monday or Tuesday. Mason replied that he would be prepared to present his note to Russell after the Lindsay debates. In the middle of July, Slidell and Mason were excited about the prospects for either a joint Anglo-French action or, if the British continued to delay, an independent action by Napoleon. The expectation that Napoleon would ignore the international realities and intervene without the cooperation of England was remarkably naive, especially in light of Napoleon's repeated statements that he could only act in cooperation with Britain. The Confederates actually had little to offer Napoleon that would assist him militarily in Mexico. They could only tender cotton and preferred trade status in return for a naval assault on the Federal blockade. Slidell desperately hoped that his recognition demands would meet with some degree of acceptance.

The anxious Slidell requested an interview with Thouvenel on July 20, 1862, the same day the French foreign minister returned to Paris. It was granted for Wednesday, July 23, at 7:00 P.M., at which time Thouvenel heard Slidell's account of the interview in Vichy. When Slidell first approached the subject of his meeting, Thouvenel discouraged what he called a premature recognition request and suggested that Slidell wait until the military situation could more clearly define the issues. To Thouvenel's surprise, Slidell explained that the emperor had heard all of the arguments favoring intervention and endorsed the request for recognition. A shocked Thouvenel retreated from his first position. He even expressed a feeling that no one in France believed in the possibility of reunion and thought that sooner or later recognition would come. As the interview came to a close, Slidell asked Thouvenel if the French dispatch case going to French consuls in Southern ports might carry some official dispatches and communications to the Confederate government. Thouvenel explained that even French citizens were denied that privilege but that as soon as the expected recognition occurred, the issue might again be discussed.[40]

Slidell's request again illustrates the desperate need for secure communications between Richmond and its European representatives. The fact that Slidell, a representative of a nation seeking full diplomatic recognition, would need to have his nation's diplomatic communications protected by another power undermined his arguments for Southern sovereignty. Thouvenel's reply, however, implied that a favorable response to Slidell's recognition demand would be forthcoming. Meanwhile, Thouvenel said, he would forward a copy of

Slidell's request to the emperor and provide a reply sometime after his return from a trip to Germany. He also asked for the specifics of the cotton proposal and asked if a similar offer had been made to the British. Slidell stated that even Mason did not have knowledge of the specifics of the proposal and that he was sure the foreign minister could appreciate the need to exercise discretion with the information. Slidell left his meeting with Thouvenel excited and optimistic. Two days later, he wrote Benjamin, "I am more hopeful than I have been at any moment since my arrival in Europe."[41]

Thouvenel, however, remained sympathetic to the Union cause, even though he believed that the South would ultimately achieve its independence. He was further committed to localizing international issues to avoid French involvement in areas beyond their control. The American Civil War provides a clear example of the Thouvenel concept of diplomacy, although the experienced foreign minister sometimes found himself opposed by the emperor. In Imperial France, this could be dangerous. Nevertheless, Thouvenel carefully balanced his perception of French interest with the need to placate an impulsive and ambitious emperor. Having recently returned from London, where he had observed with interest the public debate on the American question, the French foreign minister was keenly aware that any French overture to the British on the matter would be rejected. He agreed with Merciér that recognition of the South would likely produce war with the North and urged the emperor to postpone any action until his return to Paris. Thouvenel provided this information to the French ambassador in London, Count Auguste Charles Joseph Flahault, in a letter dated July 26. He closed his letter by declaring, "I shall perhaps need your help in order to guard us from an adventure any more serious than the Mexican one."[42]

It was not until August 19 that Slidell learned from Thouvenel that the foreign minister "did not want to send an unmeaning reply to his demand for recognition; that at present he could make no other, that unless Slidell insisted, he intended to remain silent."[43] Slidell was again dejected and frustrated and went straight away to consult with Persigny. The two men decided to await more battle reports and the emperor's return before pursuing their demands. There is no evidence that Persigny or Slidell had any indication at this time of Thouvenel's impending difficulties within the Imperial court.[44] Slidell wrote on August 24 to Benjamin, "you will find by my official correspondence that we are still hard and fast aground here. Nothing will float us off but a strong and continued current of important successes in the field."[45] Both Slidell and Mason were in a state of utter despair and frustration over their inability to make any progress.[46] They, particularly Slidell, continued nonetheless to receive unofficial encouragement from Southern sympathizers. Little did the two Confederate agents know that a very serious debate over the American question was brewing in the British Cabinet, while in France, Thouvenel's days at the Foreign Ministry were numbered.

Chapter 9

The Lost Diplomatic
Opportunity of 1862

During the months of September and October
1862, the British came close to voluntary involvement in the American Civil War. Confederate diplomacy, however, played no part in the
events unfolding in Britain. The debate over the blockade left the
Confederates completely unaware that Russell and Palmerston supported the blockade because of a commitment to past precedent.
Future diplomatic crises might again require the British lion to roar
from a powerful blockade fleet.

James Mason was completely in the dark as Russell and Palmerston
made secret moves to organize a British-led proposal by the European powers for mediation to separate the Southern states from the
Union. Ironically, Napoleon, who had been seeking the cooperation
of the British, failed to exploit the best opportunity he would have to
secure British intervention.[1]

Charles Francis Adams, the U.S. representative in England, sensed,
after Russell and Palmerston deflected the initiatives of the Southern
lobby in July, that the battle was not over. He was not aware, however, of Russell's complete shift from a policy of noninvolvement into
an enthusiastic proponent of intervention. Russell's conversion probably occurred gradually during August and was complete with the
news of the Confederate victory at second Bull Run.[2]

The series of humiliating defeats for the Union army that took place during the summer of 1862 was skillfully used by Hotze to encourage the widely held conviction in England that the Confederacy could not be conquered. News arrived of a Southern victory at Murfreesboro, Tennessee,[3] and of McClellan's demotion after the failed peninsula campaign and his subsequent reappointment as commanding general in the East after the failures of his successors. Not only did Europeans perceive that the Federal military effort was in disarray, but they also read in their newspapers of a North deeply divided over the issue of emancipation. Lincoln's political popularity slumped, and the Peace Party expected substantial gains in the off-year congressional elections of 1862. Arbitrary arrests and suspension of civil rights by the Lincoln administration provoked dissent throughout the North. Both the Union and Confederate diplomats in Europe sensed that a diplomatic breakthrough leading to recognition might tip the balance in the fall Congressional and state elections in favor of the Northern Peace Party, thus securing the division of the United States.[4]

It was in this atmosphere that Russell wrote Palmerston on September 14, 1862. He recommended mediation "with a view to the recognition of the independence of the Confederates. In case of failure, we ought ourselves to recognize the Southern States as an independent State."[5] Russell thought that a Cabinet decision would be required, and he therefore suggested a meeting be arranged for October 23 or October 30.

Russell was greatly surprised when the French failed enthusiastically to embrace his informal overtures in favor of joint mediation in the American conflict. After all, had not the French been recommending just such an Anglo-French alliance to force mediation? On September 16, Russell instructed the British representative in Paris, Lord Cowley, to approach Thouvenel privately on the idea of "an armistice without mediation." Cowley was further instructed to make certain the French would not be threatened by suggesting that there was "safety in numbers."[6]

Other European powers would be invited to join the coalition, including Russia. The latter proposal for multilateral involvement was put forward by Palmerston, who said, "A refusal would be followed by the recognition of the Southern States, the certainty of such recognition by all Europe must carry weight with it."[7] To the surprise of the British, once more, Thouvenel suggested delaying mediation until after a Northern collapse, thus avoiding international war. Thouvenel suggested that the forthcoming election would provide an indication of American public opinion on the war.[8]

Thouvenel's reluctance to embrace the British proposal may have stemmed from the offer to include Russia as a concession to the North. In late July, the French were in fact resoundingly and unceremoniously rejected when they presented a similar proposal to the Russians. Undoubtedly, Russell was completely aware of the Russian position and chose to ignore their previous commitments, believing that a multilateral proposal would bring the Russians along. It is more likely that Thouvenel, who was increasingly at odds with the emperor on the American question, as well as on policies toward Italy and Austria, chose to doggedly pursue his perception of French interest. Thouvenel was convinced that the emperor had overextended French resources in Mexico and was deeply concerned with the emperor's commitment to Italy. He believed that the separation of the United States was inevitable and admitted to Dayton on September 12 that "the undertaking of conquering the South is almost superhuman."[9]

The timing of the British initiative was not auspicious for Southern interests. Napoleon was absent from Paris, Russell was absent from London, and Thouvenel was well aware that he was facing a confrontation with the emperor. Although the atmosphere in the United States, both militarily and politically, suggested an opportune time for the British to consider intervention, conditions in Europe ultimately prevented any joint action.[10]

Mason and the Confederate lobby in London, had they been aware of the policy shifts in the Cabinet in early September, might have influenced the outcome. The Confederacy might have put forward a clear policy statement, should intervention occur, explaining their position on future national boundaries, trade policy, slavery and emancipation, and other practical issues to be negotiated. The British, however, sought peace in the United States to protect their interest in Canada and provide a stable environment that would not drag them into a war should Europe explode; thus, they prevented their need to defend their interest in North America.

Mason and his colleagues contributed little substance to the debate, either because they were unaware of the situation in the British Cabinet or did not understand how to support their advocates. Mason did not understand the British motivation, nor did he realize that Russell and Palmerston were concerned not with a cotton shortage, but with the need to protect against a two-front war. If they were required to fight to protect their interest in North America and a war broke out in Europe, the British navy and small army would be less effective. The ability of the British to influence political and diplomatic decisions on the Continent would be reduced by any involvement in North America, even if hostilities did not actually begin in Europe. The Confederates in Europe failed to recognize and seize the opportunity presented for their cause in September and October 1862. The Confederate agents, after engaging in a year of frustrating debate, missed their best opportunity to influence the course of diplomacy.

On September 10, 1862, James Mason wrote Slidell of the defeat of John Pope's army at the Battle of Bull Run. Slidell had also recently received some good news and wrote Mason on September 12 that several British correspondents and friends informed him that the British Cabinet was going to take up the question of recognition in the early part of October. Slidell informed Mason of his intention to push for an answer to his earlier note to Thouvenel demanding recognition as soon as the emperor returned to Paris. Slidell believed that Napoleon, encouraged by the military successes of the Confederacy, would now approach the British Cabinet with an official proposal for joint intervention.[11]

After consulting with Persigny, Slidell decided to write a memorandum for him to deliver to the emperor immediately. Because the emperor was not planning to return to Paris until the first week in October, Slidell urged Napoleon in the memorandum to put his proposal before the British Cabinet right away to prevent Russell from claiming that the French government did not support intervention. Even if the Confederate army succeeded in capturing Washington, he asserted, the war would end only if the Peace Party received sufficient backing to win the election and end the struggle. Joint recognition by the European powers of the Confederacy's legitimacy would secure victory for the Peace Party. The bloodletting would not cease until the war party of Lincoln and Seward suffered an election defeat. Slidell, unlike his colleague in London, was moving to affect the outcome of the issue.[12]

Slidell was further encouraged on September 29 when the Earl of Shaftesbury, Palmerston's son-in-law, passed through Paris and called on the Southern representative. He told Slidell that the government was seriously considering intervention and that it might make a move shortly.[13] After returning home, Shaftesbury investigated further and reported to Slidell that "there is every reason to believe that the event you so strongly desire and of which we talked when I had the pleasure of seeing you in Paris is very close at hand."[14] Slidell was so excited over Shaftesbury's letter that he hurried to see Thouvenel at the foreign office. He was surprised to find the foreign minister closeted with Dayton. Later in the day, Slidell received from a "confidential friend" in the foreign office a message from Thouvenel assuring him that the South might expect recognition soon. The communication also suggested that correspondence was underway between the British and French foreign offices on the matter of Southern recognition.[15]

Just at this juncture, however, Slidell was confronted by two discouraging events. First, news reached him that Thouvenel was about to leave the Cabinet because of a disagreement with the emperor over the Italian crisis. From a long-term Southern perspective, Thouvenel's departure could not be seen as bad because he was committed to nonintervention. Thouvenel's resignation, however, would delay progress in the negotiations underway with the British. His successor would need to be thoroughly briefed and, while possibly viewing the prospect of intervention more favorably in the long run, might require more time to prepare.[16]

The second piece of news was as disappointing for Slidell as the first. Lord Cowley now denied that there had been any correspondence between Great Britain and France concerning a joint action in the Civil War. Thouvenel, when he heard the news, hastened to assure Slidell that Cowley's denial was only a poor joke and that there had been serious conversations.[17] Cowley's denial was consistent with both British and French diplomatic policy to deny any unofficial communications and acknowledge only formal proposals and communications. Slidell hardly knew what to believe or how to proceed at this point.[18]

At the earliest opportunity, Slidell called on Thouvenel's successor, Edouard Drouyn de Lhuys. On October 26, the new foreign minister admitted that he had not been fully apprised of the American question and requested a thorough briefing from Slidell. The Southerner reviewed his diplomatic activities since meeting the emperor at Vichy. Undoubtedly, Slidell reflected the Confederate view of the British denial of the French mediation proposal. Drouyn de Lhuys agreed that the denial misrepresented the facts but said he was not yet prepared to discuss the Cowley-Thouvenel conversations. Slidell suggested that the evasions of the British indicated that Great Britain had no intention of joining the French in undertaking any action in the American war. He pressed Drouyn de Lhuys to take action independently of Britain. The minister, like his predecessor Thouvenel, said such a course was out of the question.[19] Slidell's suggestion probably reflects his frustration with what he perceived as an unreasonable delay by insincere, cynical Europeans. Despite his understandable impatience, Slidell made a tactical mistake in suggesting that the British were not prepared to join the French.[20]

Drouyn de Lhuys needed encouragement to continue a dialogue with the British consistent with the emperor's wishes. Slidell might have offered, using his unofficial connections, to continue indirect communications to the British Cabinet, bypassing Cowley. It was vital to the Southern diplomatic effort that negotiations continue and that the British Cabinet join the French initiative, avoiding the responsibility of joint mediation. Although other factors influenced the French decision not to intervene, Slidell's insensitivity to the diplomatic traditions of Europeans contributed to that conclusion. He could not understand the difference between official and unofficial dialogue; but, to his credit, Slidell was active and involved in the diplomatic effort to obtain recognition.

In the meantime, Russell prepared another memorandum for Cowley to use in his private, unofficial conversations with the French. On September 22, Russell forwarded to Palmerston a copy of this memorandum along with Cowley's dispatch reflecting the results of his initial interview with Thouvenel. He included an outline of his plan to obtain the approval of France, Russia, Austria, and Prussia. Since Palmerston had proposed such a strategy to Russell earlier, it is not surprising that he replied, "Your plan of proceedings about the mediation between the Federals and Confederates seems to be excellent. Of course the offer would be made to both the contending parties at the same time."[21] Palmerston also brought up the possibility that if Russia were included in the first mediation proposal, it might present problems in the negotiations. The Russians, more supportive of the North, might more readily accept positions favorable to the North, but, at the same time, they might make the North more willing to accept a mediation settlement. The prime minister further confirmed Russell's position that "events may take place which make it desirable that the offer should be made before the middle of October,"[22] in order to arrive in Washington before the fall elections in the North.

It appears at this stage of the negotiations that the only members of the British government involved in the mediation negotiations were Russell, Palmerston, Cowley, and possibly Gladstone. Nevertheless, Seward and Adams sensed something was afoot. Seward wrote Adams on August 16 to break off relations in Europe if Britain recognized the South.[23] Despite the strenuous denials by Cowley that negotiations were proceeding, both Slidell and Mason learned through their contacts of Russell's shift in strategy. Mason knew from confidential sources that the British Cabinet would pursue intervention in some form, but failed to acquire detailed information that would assist in formulating a Confederate strategy to influence the outcome. Slidell, on the other hand, did take action and sought an interview with Napoleon. Mason remained remarkably inactive and insensitive.[24]

On September 24, Lord Russell planned to inform the other members of the Cabinet of the new mediation initiatives. Palmerston wrote Gladstone that he and Russell had decided an offer of mediation should be made by Great Britain, France, and Russia, and that the time was fast approaching when a mediation proposal might meet with some success.[25] On September 26, Russell wrote Gladstone and other members of the Cabinet fully outlining his proposed plan and suggesting October 16 for a Cabinet meeting to decide the issue. Both Palmerston and Russell correctly assumed that Gladstone favored intervention and would support their strategy in the Cabinet. In his reply to Russell, Gladstone mentioned his concern that Southern military victories might so encourage the South that they would be reluctant to settle on satisfactory terms.[26]

Granville was the first member of the Cabinet to object to Russell's plan. He wrote Palmerston that if the war continued for any length of time after British recognition, it would be impossible to avoid entanglement.[27] Palmerston, after receiving Granville's September 27 letter, apparently adopted a more cautious position. Palmerston's cautious approach was confirmed when news arrived of Lee's strategic defeat at Antietam.

Gladstone, apparently losing touch with the Cabinet in the last week of September and the first week of October, delivered a speech on October 7 in Newcastle. The speech was not entirely devoted to the Civil War, but at least one-third addressed the American conflict. In his speech, Gladstone said, "Jefferson Davis and other leaders of the South have made an army; they are making, it appears, a navy; and they have made what is more than either—they have made a nation."[28] Gladstone's comments, seemingly reflecting the position of the Cabinet, heightened Southern expectations for a forthcoming mediation proposal, but other members of the Cabinet quickly disavowed any official responsibility for Gladstone's remarks.[29]

On October 13, six days after Gladstone's speech, Russell felt compelled to circulate a "memorandum on America." Russell's memorandum asserted that the South had conclusively shown its power to maintain a successful defense. Seward's claim that a strong pro-Northern element in the South would soon revolt had proved incorrect and, perhaps more importantly, denounced the Emancipation Proclamation as no humanitarian or idealistic measure. Russell returned to his old premise that the Emancipation Proclamation would incite a servile war and was a "most terrible plan." For all these reasons, Russell urged the great powers to consider seriously a proposal for "the suspension of arms."[30] Despite what appeared to be an unauthorized statement by Gladstone, Russell was supporting the basic position stated in the Newcastle speech. Moreover, Russell seemed to be removing slavery as an obstacle to mediation or recognition.

The minister of war, Cornwall Lewis, vigorously opposed any intervention in the American War in a speech at Hereford on October 14. Declaring that the Cabinet had not reached a decision on the matter, Lewis maintained that a policy of noninvolvement was the best one for British interests. Lewis's speech motivated Palmerston to consult the opposition. Through Lord Clarendon, he contacted Lord Derby, who replied on October 16 that he opposed intervention. Lewis was Clarendon's brother-in-law, and throughout the Cabinet crisis Lewis remained in constant communication with the Conservatives. Lewis, as much as any member of the Cabinet, led the opposition to Russell's proposals and penned a response to Russell's October 13 memorandum in which he claimed the partisans in the United States could not be expected to react passively to any mediation proposal. The result, he claimed, would be to embroil the British in the conflict.[31]

A series of position papers and letters circulated within the British Cabinet, with Russell and Gladstone proposing mediation or the good offices of the European powers. Lewis, Argyll, and Granville, on the other hand, stubbornly defended the existing policy of neutrality. On October 28, Sir George Gray, the home secretary, wrote Russell of his opposition to mediation. It now appeared that any debate would at best result in a stalemate in the Cabinet. Hence, Palmerston decided to let the matter rest at least until the spring of 1863.[32]

About this time, Napoleon decided to request an armistice. The emperor placed a great deal of confidence in Merciér. For advice on the American question, he relied more on the minister than on Thouvenel or his successor, Drouyn de Lhuys. On October 31, Napoleon officially proposed to Russell, through Cowley, that a joint offer of an armistice be presented to the belligerents in the United States. Napoleon made the proposal despite his knowledge that Russia would refuse to participate. On November 2, Palmerston wrote Russell that the French proposal should be discussed in the Cabinet on November 11. He personally did not believe the Federals would consent "to an armistice to be accompanied by a cessation of the blockades which would give the Confederates means of getting all the supplies they may want."[33] He counseled that any attempt at mediation should be delayed until after the elections in the United States. By this time, Russell, too, was beginning to back away from his earlier position. On November 3, he wrote Palmerston enumerating several conditions to the French proposal. On November 7, Lewis came out with a strong statement against Napoleon's offer. It was in this atmosphere that the debate took place in the Cabinet on November 11.[34]

In the meantime, the Confederates were under the impression that mediation would shortly be offered. Mason wrote Benjamin on November 7 that the cotton famine was succeeding and was "looming up in fearful propositions."[35] He continued to express high hopes when he wrote Slidell the next day that "it is hardly probable that she [Great Britain] will refuse her concurrence" in Napoleon's offer of joint intervention.[36] Both Mason and Slidell remained optimistic as the Cabinet debate on the French proposal began November 11.

The Russians sent word that they would not join in a mediation proposal but would not oppose it. Russell argued in favor of accepting the French proposition to prevent France from joining Russia and isolating Great Britain. Lewis countered that any armistice would be an unneutral act favoring the South. Therefore, it would be unacceptable to the North and could only provoke added conflict. The Cabinet decided to reject the French proposal. Russell informed Cowley on November 13 of the Cabinet's decision and provided two reasons for the British action: First, Russia refused to join, and, secondly, the North's rejection of the proposed armistice appeared certain.[37]

In a cynical attempt to find a scapegoat for the economic troubles within France, Napoleon blamed the Civil War and the cotton famine for recession and unemployment. Encouraged by Slidell, he published his November 10 proposal in the Paris newspapers. On November 13, he published the full text of the notes received from the various countries responding to his offer.[38] For the Confederate agents in Europe, the British Cabinet's decision negated a year's work in pursuit of Confederate objectives. Initially, Slidell maintained some hope that all was not lost and wrote Mason on November 14: "I think that Russia will act with France, perhaps with some reservations."[39] He then wrote Mason on November 16, stating that, even if Britain remained passive, he believed France would act alone.[40] In London, too, the Confederate lobby was not prepared to admit defeat. They decided to take the position that the emperor had been "sold out" because Russell, after encouraging Napoleon's proposal, calculatingly rejected and embarrassed the emperor.

The new Confederate diplomatic strategy encouraged the French to act alone out of wounded pride and to propose mediation without the cooperation of the other European powers. Lindsay supported this strategy in a letter to Mason on November 20, in which he called Russell's communication rejecting the French offer a "most cowardly one."[41]

Slidell wrote Benjamin a few days later, saying, "I shall be surprised if he [Napoleon] does not soon prove that her [Great Britain] cooperation may be dispensed with. If, on the contrary, he did not expect the acceptance of his proposition, judging from his character and antecedents, he will not be disposed to leave his work unfinished and will act alone." Even John Bigelow, the U.S. consul general in Paris, shared the belief that Napoleon would act alone. He wrote Seward on November 21, 1862, that the emperor "will compel us to make peace or fight him."[42]

The campaign for European intervention, which began in the aftermath of the *Trent* affair in early 1862 and proceeded through the debates of the summer, ultimately failed in November to produce any meaningful change toward the war. The campaign did succeed in winning Russell to the mediation side of the issue, but correspondingly produced a determined Cornwall Lewis in opposition to Russell. The Confederate defeat at Antietam was not the determining reason, although it was a contributing factor to the British policy of continued neutrality and inaction. The disruptions in Europe and the perception that Great Britain possessed limited power to effect changes sufficiently beneficial to British interests were the overwhelming reasons for nonintervention. Lewis acknowledged the Confederacy's ability to defend itself and generally accepted Gladstone's opinion that the South was creating a nation. He was not prepared to support military or naval action to shorten the war. If the South was successful, Lewis believed British interest would be served. If and when the Americans took the initiative and requested some form of mediation, Great Britain would cooperate. In the meantime, he convinced Palmerston that the prudent stance, contrary to Russell's position, was to remain neutral.[43]

The thorny issue of slavery and the subsequent Emancipation Proclamation, like Antietam, were contributing factors, but by no means did they determine the result.[44] Russell interpreted Lincoln's decision as a desperate maneuver to provoke slave revolts, forcing Southern manpower away from the front to maintain domestic order. Russell's position, stated early in July, provided Mason and the Southern lobby with an opportunity to propose a plan that would improve the chances of mediation by demonstrating a more aggressive plan for emancipation while preventing a slave revolt. A proposal of gradual emancipation with compensation would have shown a Southern commitment to action. The Union could only issue proclamations without control of the slaves or the governing apparatus to force emancipation. As a practical matter, it is doubtful that the Confederate Congress would have passed such a proposal, but at least Mason and Slidell could have proposed a plan. Both Mason and Slidell were committed to slavery and it is doubtful that either man, at least at this stage, would have been a party to any proposal to eliminate the South's "peculiar institution."[45]

Napoleon, possibly because of Thouvenel's action or planned inaction, missed his best opportunity to obtain British cooperation. Because of the Mexican adventure in 1862, France was in a position to benefit greatly from Southern recognition. The presence of a more sympathetic and aggressive French foreign minister who saw French interest more as did the emperor might have enabled Southern sympathizers to overcome British resistance to the mediation proposals.

The Europeans possessed the naval power to engage the Union blockading force and the industrial power to allow the Confederates to rapidly construct a naval fighting force to harass the Union fleet. The two armies engaged in the American Civil War were approximately the same size and equally well led.[46] European intervention would have assisted in the supply and maintenance of the Confederate army, certainly prolonging the war if not changing the outcome. Recognition of the Confederacy by a major European power during the fall of 1862 might have changed the outcome of the American elections and weakened the will of the North to pursue the war. The failure of the Confederate diplomatic initiatives in 1862 substantially affected the war in America.

Chapter 10

The Diplomacy of Finance and the Erlanger Loan

The Confederate commissioners in Europe increased their involvement in Confederate finances while vainly awaiting unilateral French intervention in the American conflict. They hoped for success based on the coercive economic powers of King Cotton. Back on January 17, 1862, Benjamin had written E. J. Forstall in New Orleans, a representative of a foreign banking house, supporting a loan with cotton as collateral. The Confederacy would pay interest, commission, and warehousing fees and "the cotton would remain on this side until the blockade is raised."[1] Unfortunately for Benjamin's proposal, New Orleans fell to the Union before arrangements could be completed.

The idea of trading cotton for recognition was afterward discussed with Merciér during his spring visit to Richmond, and Slidell broached the subject in Paris. The economic benefits to European speculators were obvious with cotton at fifty cents a pound in London. The political advantages of obtaining cotton to relieve the hardships within the textile-producing communities of Europe would not be lost by Europe's leaders, but they were not directly responsible to a voting electorate.

The Confederacy sent a host of purchasing agents under the direction of the Navy Department, the Treasury Department, and the War

Department to Europe to spend rather than to raise money. By the summer of 1862, the Confederacy was completely without hard currency. The need to improve credit to continue the acquisition of much-needed supplies was obvious to the Richmond government. After much debate and confusion, Secretary of Treasury Christopher Memminger decided to leave the responsibility of securing foreign credit with cotton as collateral to the secretary of state. Benjamin then centralized Confederate financial operations in Europe by requiring all purchasing agents to cooperate with James Mason in London.[2]

In the summer of 1862, Secretary of the Navy Stephen R. Mallory sent George N. Sanders to Great Britain to contract the construction of ships for the Confederacy. Sanders arrived in Great Britain about July 15 with a contract to build several fast postal ships. Authorized by the Navy Department to use cotton bonds instead of money, Sanders went to William Lindsay to seek advice on how best to utilize the bonds to raise needed funds. Lindsay said he was not authorized to discuss the matter with Sanders but would contact James Mason.[3]

Quite excited with the idea in principle, Lindsay told Mason a designated price should be included for the benefit of the bondholders instead of a market price at a Southern port. Lindsay believed the increased speculative value of a designated price would create a broader interest in the bonds. He proposed to Mason that a price of eight cents would enable a purchaser of the bonds to earn four times their investment. Mason, however, was reluctant to accept the responsibility of designating a specific price for the bonds and dispatched Sanders back to Richmond to discuss the idea.[4]

Like Lindsay, Mason was excited with the prospect of the cotton speculation bond as a means to raise money. Comdr. George Sinclair had also presented a similar bond proposal by this time to Mason, and the Confederate commissioner decided to write a dispatch to accompany Sanders on his return to Richmond. He wrote Benjamin: "I venture to suggest, therefore, that money may be commanded here by the use of obligations for delivery of cotton by the government on terms such as proposed by Lindsay."[5]

Sinclair, like Sanders, arrived in London with the authority to construct a ship. Unlike Sanders, Sinclair would take command of the new ship and was instructed to seek out James Bulloch for assistance in financing construction by converting Confederate bonds into money. Bulloch merely sent Sinclair to Mason, who sent the naval officer to Lindsay with instructions to issue £60,000 in cotton bonds at a fixed price. Mason assumed the authority and endorsed the bonds. The Sinclair Bonds, therefore, became the first cotton bonds used by the Confederacy. Sinclair enjoyed the confidence and support of both Mason and Lindsay. Sanders, on the other hand, was suspected by both men of pursuing a personal profit-making agenda.[6]

By October 22, Sanders had returned to Richmond and delivered Mason's dispatch to Benjamin. The secretary of state immediately called on Memminger, and the two men decided to adopt Lindsay's idea of a fixed price and a designated Southern port where the cotton could be warehoused to await shipment. In addition, they decided that an agent was needed to coordinate the cotton bonds in Europe. James Spence was selected because he was "the most energetic and resourceful friend the Confederacy had in England."[7]

Spence was an extraordinarily well qualified man for the job. He was a merchant, shipper, banker, and stockbroker and could provide sound advice for the financially inexperienced Confederate commissioners in Europe. Spence was quick to seize the opportunity and formally applied for the job as financial agent for the Confederacy. Mason, in recommending that Spence be confirmed for the position, pointed out that he had written extensively and spoken in the House of Commons on behalf of the Confederacy.[8] Benjamin was well aware of Spence's connections and had heard from Hotze that Spence had disposed of ordinary bonds sent from time to time from the Confederacy. Therefore, Benjamin notified Mason on October 28, 1862, of Spence's appointment as "financial agent" for Europe.[9]

By December 1862, a dispute arose within the Confederate Cabinet following the failure of the abortive British and French intervention movements. The problem resulted from the appointment of Spence to handle all finances abroad. Benjamin expected Spence to be reporting to the State Department through Mason, but Memminger wanted him responsible to the Treasury Department. Meanwhile, Mallory sent Captain Murray to Europe with blanket authority for himself and all other naval agents to use "the sky as the limit" in using bonds to obtain ships and money.[10] It appeared that Spence would be involved with various agents.

Finally, the tenacious Benjamin obtained a commitment from Davis and Memminger that all agents would work through Mason in Great Britain. Furthermore, Mason would coordinate the liquidation of the bonds with Spence as the financial agent. Mason would also act as a liaison between Spence and Fraser's firm in Liverpool, Trenholm and Company. Mason had previously written to Benjamin on December 10 that the multitude of agents and contractors operating independently in Europe was causing wasteful confusion. "All money should be dispersed through that agency [Spence] subject to his [Mason's] own general supervision," he wrote.[11] Before receiving Mason's recommendation, Benjamin wrote his envoy in Great Britain on January 15, 1863, stating that before any bonds were liquidated, Spence should be consulted and all agents, including those of the War Department who had subsequently been given authority to issue cotton certificates, should consult with him "before any step was taken."[12]

Eventually, C. J. McRae from Alabama was given the responsibility for all foreign credit and disbursements in Europe, reporting to Mason and Slidell. Even before McRae's appointment, however, Spence's authority was gradually constricted until finally he was unceremoniously advised that his services as financial agent were no longer needed.[13]

As long as they were authorized to do so, both Spence and Lindsay served very effectively as Confederate financial agents. Lindsay was particularly valuable because of his wealthy friends. In fact, he placed the entire Sinclair Bond issue secretly using only three investors. Clearly, in 1862 the cotton speculation bonds appealed to British investors.[14]

In early September 1862, Caleb Huse, frustrated with the confused financial situation in Great Britain, wrote Slidell requesting money to pay for ships and munitions he had purchased.[15] Slidell, apparently unaware of the Sinclair cotton bonds or the details of the Sanders mission, wrote Mason on September 26. He stated that if cotton could be used for obtaining recognition, he saw no reason why a portion of the 100,000 bales recently offered Napoleon could not be used to purchase the "necessary munitions."[16] Mason promptly responded with a letter explaining in detail the Sinclair arrangement and the proposal being carried by Sanders to Richmond.

Realizing both the political and economic benefits that a large bond issue supported by cotton would secure for the Confederacy, Slidell was already engaged in conversations with officials of the prestigious Erlanger and Company hoping to obtain favorable financing. Now encouraged by the news from London, and ably assisted by Caleb Huse, Slidell drafted a contract to present to his friend Baron Emile Erlanger. The preliminary contract was forwarded to Mason for his review and signature as chief financial agent for the Confederacy in Europe.[17]

Huse pointed out to Slidell that the terms of the £5 million bond issue were too harsh to be accepted by the Richmond government. Erlanger's profits would be huge if the loan was successful because of the 30 percent discount the banking house would receive. The investor would receive 8 percent until the bonds were redeemed. In addi-

Louis Napoleon III, emperor of France during the American Civil War.
Courtesy of The Abraham Lincoln Museum, Harrogate, Tennessee.

tion, Erlanger and Company would receive a 5 percent commission
for disposing the issue and 1 percent commission for handling the
sinking funds and interest payments. Bond redemptions would begin
on July 1, 1863, requiring the Confederate government to produce
one-fortieth of the original face amount. As a result of these expensive terms, the Confederacy would receive only about £3.3 million
out of the £5 million issued. Despite Huse's concern that the loan
would be jeopardized in Richmond as a result of the conditions Slidell
had negotiated with Erlanger, Huse and Slidell remained committed
as much for political and personal reasons as for economic ones.[18]

Baron Emile Erlanger, a German, made his home in Paris and
operated his large banking house with the cooperation and full knowledge of the French government. Erlanger and Company maintained
branch banks in practically every major city in Western Europe, including London. Slidell believed that Confederate interest would
benefit substantially from the financial commitment and prestige of
an association with "one of the most extensive and responsible houses
in Europe."[19]

When Mason received the proposed contract from Slidell and

Huse, he was reluctant to sign and recommend it to the Confederate government because Lindsay had recently offered a substantially less expensive proposition. Moreover, the proposed Erlanger loan was signed by Caleb Huse, who remained, as far as Mason was concerned, under a cloud of suspicion as a result of allegations by one W. G. Crenshaw. Mason reported that Huse "had contracted for 50,000 muskets at $4.00 above the current price, leaving $200,000 commission for whom? And that he really seems to be throwing obstacles in the way of Mr. C., who is endeavoring to procure commission stores in England."[20] The potential for corruption was clearly present, but often hidden costs such as bribes and kickbacks were included in the so-called "commissions."

Mason declined to sign the Erlanger agreement. At Slidell's insistence, Mason forwarded it to Benjamin with an explanation that he had no personal knowledge of Erlanger and Company and that his signature would commit him to the Erlanger proposal. He included in his dispatch the outline of Lindsay's proposal and stated, "It certainly seems to me that the London plan offers the best scheme of finance."[21] Mason did not reveal, however, that no substantial British banking house had indicated a willingness to underwrite a loan along the lines suggested. Lindsay thus far had only been successful in placing relatively small and short-term loans.

The two proposals from Mason and Slidell reached Benjamin on December 31, 1862. In the meantime, Erlanger and Company sent three representatives led by Jules Beer across the Atlantic Ocean to lobby and negotiate the contract.[22] After receiving notice of Mason's refusal to recommend the Erlanger proposal, Slidell wrote Benjamin on November 11 that "Messrs. Erlanger & Company have sent three special agents, who are now on their way to Richmond, in relation to their proposal for a loan. This fact proves, at least, that they are very much in earnest about the matter."[23] The Erlanger agents did not arrive before Mason's dispatch outlining the two loan proposals, to which the Confederate government's initial reaction was very cool. Although the government was committed to cotton bonds or a redeemable certificate, there were strong objections to the low price of cotton set by both Lindsay and Erlanger.

Despite their reservations, Benjamin was able to write Slidell on January 15, 1863, that "notwithstanding our desire to ratify the outline of the contract drawn up in Paris, it is impossible to obtain the sanction of Congress."[24] The secretary of state pointed out that after consultations with Erlanger's agents, it seemed plain that the contract was really a loan and not a cotton purchase. The Erlanger proposal containing the traditional characteristics of a loan could demand payment completely in cotton at the low fixed price, despite the Confederate's expectation that after the war cotton production would be drastically reduced for a period of reorganization and resettlement and prices would rise substantially above present levels. The financial merits of the Erlanger proposal fell far short of a reasonable business proposal.[25]

Benjamin's response to the details of the Erlanger proposition reflected the fundamental fallacies in both Confederate diplomatic policy and financial strategies. The Confederacy needed King Cotton to solve its problems more than did the Europeans. Not only was the Confederate leadership overly optimistic in its appraisal of the power of cotton, but failed completely to use the commodity to establish a financial basis for the procurement of war supplies in Europe.

Ultimately, the Confederate government was impressed with Slidell's argument that the political advantages far outweighed the monetary cost of the Erlanger proposal, and the Confederates decided to allow Erlanger to sell only £3 million instead of the negotiated and authorized £4 million of bonds. Rather than the original £5 million proposed, Erlanger was to receive 23 percent instead of the original 30 percent discount on the bonds. The interest rate to bearers of the bonds was reduced to 7 percent from the originally proposed 8 percent. Despite the reluctant acceptance of the Erlanger loan, the Confederate commitment was immediate and complete once the decision was made. During the winter of 1863, the secretary of Treasury informed Benjamin that he was actively at work purchasing cotton for European shipment in order to be prepared to satisfy the sinking fund commitments. The Erlanger loan, after conversion at the prevailing rate into Confederate dollars from either pounds or francs, equaled approximately $14,550,000 at the exchange rate.[26]

Benjamin wrote Mason that it was Slidell's expectation of receiving political favors in Paris that swayed the Confederate government to accept Erlanger's proposition.[27] Ironically, shortly after the Confederates accepted a watered-down version of Erlanger's proposal, Baron Emile Erlanger began to distance himself from the transactions. Erlanger held large amounts of the notes for his personal account. The highly speculative and questionable legal standing of the notes could have adversely affected his future business dealings.[28] Moreover, it began to appear doubtful whether a loan of the size required by the Confederates would be fully subscribed in Europe. As events proved, the winter and spring of 1863 provided the last favorable opportunity to obtain this kind of financial support for the embattled Confederacy.

Slidell's enthusiasm for the loan was supported by his expectation that the image of the Confederacy would be elevated because of its association with such a prestigious firm as Erlanger and Company. Undoubtedly, his daughter Mathilde's marriage to the Baron contributed to the friendship with Erlanger. Although Erlanger expected to profit handsomely from the transaction, he was already successful and did not need to complete the transaction to sustain his fortune. The desire to assist his father-in-law in obtaining financing for his beloved Confederacy was probably a contributing factor to Erlanger's original offer to float the bonds.[29]

On February 7, 1863, rumors that the Erlanger loan had been accomplished reached Europe.[30] The details of the loan and the money from the sale of the bonds were, of course, not yet available. Throughout the protracted negotiations, the problems for Mason, Slidell, and the Confederate purchasing agents magnified. On January 28, Mason wrote Slidell that Confederate agents could not wait any longer for funding. On January 12, Mason had expressed an urgent need for £500,000 or the Confederate government's credibility would be significantly eroded. To Slidell's suggestion that Spence, as the Confederate financial agent, place a short term loan until the Erlanger proceeds were available, Mason retorted that, under the circumstances, it would not be wise to confuse the markets by issuing a new security before the Erlanger offering.[31] In February, Mason was finally forced to allow Huse to issue cotton scrip amounting to nearly £2 million to settle supply debts. On February 5, Mason wrote Benjamin that Huse had contracted to deliver 2.3 million pounds of cotton for new purchases and 5 million pounds as payment for supplies already purchased and shipped.[32]

On March 15, Erlanger wrote Slidell from London that he had arranged on a recent trip to Liverpool for Fraser and Company to represent the loan there, and J. H. Schroeder and Company would bring out the loan in London. He expressed concern that the official Confederate government document of authority, known as the "act of ratification" had not arrived. Erlanger was confident that an advance could be arranged as soon as the solicitor "received the ratification order." The official copy finally reached Great Britain on March 18. On March 19, the bonds were put on the market in London, Liverpool, Paris, Frankfurt, and Amsterdam. During the first three days, $16 million worth of bonds were sold.[33] The immediate success of the loan allowed Erlanger to write Slidell on March 18 that "the

Baroness Mathilde Slidell de Erlanger, daughter of John Slidell and
wife of Baron Emile de Erlanger. Courtesy of the Chattanooga
Regional History Museum.

Confederate government will have gained a moral battle with less
bloodshed and perhaps as great an advantage as any of the gallant
triumphs!"[34] Slidell wrote Benjamin that "you will before this dispatch can reach you have seen by the newspapers the brilliant success
of Erlanger & Company's loan. It is a financial recognition of our
independence, emanating from a class proverbially cautious and little
given to be influenced by sentiment or sympathy."[35] Slidell's comment reflects the traditional Southern negativity toward bankers and
money managers. The failure to appreciate the financial environment
in which they were operating, combined with a general disdain for
financiers, prevented the Confederate diplomats from implementing
a sound overall financial strategy that certainly would have contributed to the war effort.

The Erlanger loan apparently caught the U.S. diplomats in Europe by surprise. John Bigelow, the U.S. consul general in Paris, responded quickly, planting stories in the French press about Jefferson

Davis's involvement in the 1840 Mississippi bond repudiation incident. The rumors of the Confederate president's involvement in financial shenanigans spread to Great Britain and threatened to undermine the credibility of the Erlanger bonds. Edouard DeLeon challenged the reports in the European press and conducted a relatively successful campaign in both France and Great Britain to dispel the threat to Davis's reputation.

DeLeon originally from South Carolina, was a close friend of Jefferson Davis. He was well acquainted with the president from their days together in the Pierce administration. DeLeon served in the pre–Civil War diplomatic corps as consul general to Egypt and maintained an active correspondence with Davis while they served President Pierce. When the Civil War broke out in 1861, DeLeon turned in his resignation and left Egypt, going to France where he quickly recognized the need for an organized propaganda effort on behalf of the Confederate cause. He decided to return to Richmond and seek financial support, as well as an appointment from his old friend, Jefferson Davis.[36]

The South Carolina diplomat arrived in Richmond, unaware of the activities of Henry Hotze in London, and presented his proposal. The Confederate State Department was under the direction of R. M. T. Hunter at the time, while Davis was concerned with the recent loss of Forts Donelson and Henry. Therefore, DeLeon's proposal had to wait for the appointment of the energetic Judah Benjamin as secretary of state. Benjamin was not fully aware of the effectiveness of Hotze and the *Index* in London. Although not enthusiastic about DeLeon's appointment, he decided to accept the president's recommendation that DeLeon be appointed to the post of propaganda chief in Europe.[37]

Benjamin had only recently informed Slidell that he had been appointed as propaganda chief in Europe in addition to his other duties. Unfortunately, within a matter of days, DeLeon arrived with a letter from the Confederate secretary of state naming himself to the position. While both Benjamin and Slidell appreciated the need for a separate person to engage in such press debates as the extremely competent John Bigelow could initiate, the arrangements and circumstances of DeLeon's appointment were poorly handled.[38]

The new European propaganda chief was well financed with funds from the Confederate Secret Service account, managed at the sole discretion of the president. Hotze was offended. He was struggling to support the *Index* with contributions from British sympathizers and his personal funds while DeLeon continued to meddle in his affairs. Slidell was irritated, not only because his authority had been overruled, but because DeLeon arrived in Paris and presented the dispatches from Benjamin with the seals broken. DeLeon's propaganda efforts, no matter how well conceived or well financed, were destined to be ineffective. He had made three powerful enemies within the Confederate diplomatic corps and did little to redeem himself in the eyes of Slidell, Hotze, or Benjamin.[39]

DeLeon did enjoy some success, however, during the campaign to restore the credibility of President Davis in the eyes of the European financial community. He prepared and published a pamphlet entitled "A Familiar Epistle from an Old Acquaintance," in which he defended the president and demonstrated that Davis was not directly involved with the repudiation of the Mississippi bonds of 1840. Over 10,000 copies of the pamphlet were distributed in Great Britain alone. Unfortunately for DeLeon's relationship with Hotze, he pointed out in correspondence to Benjamin that he decided not to use the *Index* as a platform to reply to the Union accusations because the Confederate newspaper's circulation was too small. In fact, DeLeon repeatedly criticized the *Index* and recommended it be discontinued because of its limited circulation. It is possible that DeLeon's propaganda efforts on behalf of his old friend Davis did contribute to the favorable reception of the Erlanger loan, but his work was generally relegated to the periphery of the propaganda campaign.[40]

The early success of the Confederate loan in Europe was nevertheless encouraging to the people of the South. Conditions were serious at home, inflation was out of control and shortages abounded. Flour, when available, was $30 per barrel. Butter cost $3 per pound, eggs were $2 a dozen, a turkey was $15, and bacon and beef were unattainable.[41] The hope in Richmond was that the proceeds from the Erlanger loan would sustain the war and stop the ever-downward spiraling of the currency. The early jubilation, however, quickly faded.

In April, the bonds had fallen to a discount of 86 percent, 4 percent below par. The fear that investor confidence was eroding due to an increased Federal propaganda effort contributed to a decision by Mason to enter the market and buy the bonds to sustain prices. Erlanger, encouraging Mason to "bull the market" claimed to be following Slidell's advice. It is likely, however, that Erlanger, already breaking away from his commitment, was anxious to dump his private Confederate bond holdings. By encouraging the inexperienced Confederates to go against the advice of Spence and other long-suffering friends, the baron fulfilled Slidell's earlier appraisal of the cynical bankers. It is difficult to understand how a firm "making a market" in a security would not provide, indirectly through their facilities, favorable terms to liquidate a security of doubtful value. The prestigious Erlanger firm acted unprofessionally because it quietly unloaded its large holdings on the unsuspecting Confederate agents when the market began to collapse.[42]

On April 7, Mason and Erlanger entered into an agreement that allowed Erlanger and Company to buy "up to £1,000,000, or any smaller sum that might be deemed necessary to restore the value of the bonds." The resourceful Erlanger, in this agreement, was allowed to resell the bonds from the Confederate account at par or better and retain the profits. The Confederates stood to suffer the loss in a collapsing market, but should events produce a recovery, their potential for profit was limited to par.[43] Between April 9 and April 24, the Erlangers bought £1,388,500 worth of bonds.[44]

The bonds continued to be quoted at a reasonable discount because of the Confederate inside support. But, as the news of military disasters during the summer of 1863 at Vicksburg and Gettysburg reached Europe, there was little hope to sustain Confederate creditworthiness. Beginning in late May of 1863, the bonds had a shadowy and speculative character in European financial markets. New money could not be raised, and frequently the bonds were only valuable to pay contractors for supplies. The suppliers were unable to obtain payment by any other means and usually overcharged the Confederates in order to sell the cotton certificates at substantial discounts without suffering a loss. The bonds, like all Confederate financial arrangements, ended in disaster.[45]

If the Confederate government had proclaimed cotton as King and allowed him to reign in exile, the course of the war would have been affected. Had cotton been placed in European warehouses and the huge crops of 1861 and 1862 exported promptly rather than embargoed, Confederate agents could have used their greatest asset to purchase munitions and supplies from anxious vendors. Access to cotton as a cash equivalent would not have protected the Confederacy from a clumsy and ill-conceived purchasing system. Despite the need of vendors and suppliers to overcharge to compensate for the risk factor, bargains might have been available if cotton had been on hand instead of only partially available. A stable currency based on a managed cotton supply would, undoubtedly, have improved the chances of Confederate recognition.

Chapter 11

The Burden of Multiparty Diplomacy: The Roebuck Initiative

The failure of the Confederate commissioners and their friends in London to obtain European intervention through Napoleon's proposal of joint mediation in the fall of 1862 was naively viewed by the Confederates as a temporary detour along the road toward recognition. On December 11, 1862, Mason wrote Slidell that "gigantic strides" in the cotton famine, coupled with "events which are maturing, must lead to some change in the attitude of England."[1] Mason believed that Parliament would force the government by February to relieve the suffering caused by the shortage of cotton. The Confederate agents, not nearly as discouraged by the failure of their November initiatives as they should have been, decided to pursue their objective vigorously as soon as the military news improved.[2]

Throughout the fall, the Confederate government was unaware of the rapid flow of diplomatic events in Europe. The inability of the Confederates to communicate readily through the blockade delayed instructions that would have benefited the diplomatic process. Mason's correspondence detailing Russell's rude and inconsiderate attitudes toward him, sent to Benjamin on April 8, 1862, was not received in Richmond until early October. Benjamin's instructions to Mason of October 31 regarding the blockade and complaining about Russell's

"inexcusable behavior" toward Confederate representatives were irrelevant to the debate in progress during the fall of 1862.[3]

Despite the fact that Benjamin was not aware of recent events,
Mason decided to act on the secretary of state's instructions. On
January 3, 1863, he sent Russell a letter conveying the resentment
felt within the Confederate government toward the British rebuffs.
In concluding his October 31 dispatch, Mason stated, "The President has further under consideration the propriety of sending out of
the country all British Consuls and consular agents, and I will give
you early advice of his conclusion on this point."[4] The contents of
Benjamin's dispatch are significant, not only because it contains the
most articulate, legalistic indictment of the blockade under the Declaration of Paris, but also because Benjamin expresses the general
dissatisfaction within the Confederacy toward British policy. It is clear
that both Benjamin and Davis were prepared to force a "diplomatic
break" if recognition or some form of intervention did not occur in
the near future. Such a position appeared to the British as the height
of arrogance, since no official diplomatic relationship existed to break.[5]

While Mason awaited Russell's response to his January 3 letter,
news arrived of President Davis's December 6, 1862, address to Congress. The Confederate president openly chastised the two powerful
European nations for their complacency in the blockade, accusing
Britain and France of securing Confederate compliance to the Declaration of Paris and then refusing to take appropriate action when the
covenant was violated. The two European governments had acquiesced in the "outrages of neutral rights committed by the United
States with aggressive and unceasing arrogance during the whole period of the war."[6] Davis accused the U.S. Navy of being incapable of
blockading the ports of any single state, much less the Confederate
coastline from Virginia to Key West.[7] Davis's speech, when viewed
along with Benjamin's angry directions to Mason, reflects the increasing frustration caused by the failure of European governments
to recognize the legitimacy of the Southern cause.

The inability of the Confederates to communicate in a timely manner between Richmond and Europe probably prevented a diplomatic
break at this early point. Had Davis and Benjamin been aware of the
complete failure of the Confederate lobby to achieve a breakthrough
in October and November, Mason might well have been ordered to
depart from England immediately. Both Mason and Slidell, however,
remained optimistic that intervention could be achieved within the
next few months.[8]

Slidell was encouraged by the influence exerted by Dudley Mann in Brussels. When Yancey and Rost were recalled at the end of 1861, Mann was ordered to go to Brussels to pursue Confederate interests at the court of King Leopold. On January 5, 1863, Mann presented formal demands for recognition to the Belgium foreign minister, M. Rogier. King Leopold, the uncle and close advisor of Queen Victoria, responded by urging Napoleon to intervene to protect the cotton operatives in both countries. The environment in Belgium was generally friendly toward the Southern cause, despite the efforts of the American minister, Henry Sanford. Sanford was not as effective on his home turf in Belgium as he was roaming other European capitals organizing and financing the clandestine operations of the U.S. government.[9] Mann, on the other hand, concentrated his efforts during the fall of 1862 and winter of 1863 on the royal court in Brussels and was able to maintain cordial and sympathetic relations. Leopold influenced and advised Queen Victoria and Napoleon III on foreign-policy matters. The Belgium monarch's advice was appreciated, but the modest economic and military power of his small nation tended to moderate his influence. Nevertheless, Mann's diplomatic initiatives in Belgium must be considered successful even though Belgian foreign policy did not affect the ultimate decision of the European powers to remain neutral.[10]

Apparently, Napoleon was influenced by Leopold's communications. On January 9, urged on by Slidell, the emperor instructed Drouyn de Lhuys to write a letter instructing Merciér in Washington to take up the question of mediation with Secretary of State Seward.[11] In instructing Merciér, de Lhuys told him to pick his time carefully and suggested that the two warring American sides elect commissioners to conduct negotiations. The problem in the past, at least as Drouyn de Lhuys understood it, was the advantage gained by the Confederacy during any armistice. The solution to this dilemma would be the appointment of commissioners to negotiate while hostilities continued.[12]

On January 12, Napoleon followed up his diplomatic initiative in a speech before the chambers in which he denounced the bloody American war as the cause of the hardships in "one of the most fruitful of our industries." He continued by pointing out that his mediation attempt of November 10 had been rejected by the "maritime powers," who apparently did not view the economic crisis in France with the same degree of concern.[13] The text of Napoleon's speech, when it appeared in London, provoked negative editorial comment and suggested Napoleon was not prepared to accept the responsibility for the economic hardships caused by his government's economic policies. The *Index* responded to these criticisms by fully supporting the emperor's demand for intervention and identifying Napoleon's humanitarian objectives, both within France as well as the war-torn United States.[14]

The emperor made no specific reference in his speech to his mediation proposal sent to Merciér on January 9; but on January 29, the *Constitutionnel* suggested the offer might be made in the future. A concerned Slidell hurried to visit with Count Persigny to confirm that the offer had already been forwarded to Washington. In fact, the offer had not only been sent, but soon newspapers throughout Europe would carry the news that Napoleon was again involved in a plot to involve the European powers in the American conflict.[15] The *Index* of January 29 printed the full text of Napoleon's mediation offer. Dayton, acting on instructions from Seward, first confirmed the proposal and then flatly rejected it. The offensive and abrasive tone of the U.S. rejection offended Drouyn de Lhuys and encouraged Slidell.[16]

The French Foreign Minister, who had leaked the news to the press and then allowed Slidell to confirm the emperor's mediation offer, did not disclose the entire grandiose Napoleonic scheme to resolve the American problem. The emperor expected to establish a confederation of American states consisting of four roughly equal parts: the North, South, West, and French Mexico. Napoleon, like many leaders of his day, was committed to the concept of a balance of power. His proposed four-nation realignment was designed to curb imperialistic tendencies in both the Northern and the Southern states, and would allow for the expansion of French-controlled Mexico into Texas, Louisiana, and Central America.[17] Unfortunately for Napoleon's scheme, his foreign minister lacked commitment and was very careful that the details of Napoleon's plan not be exposed. Seward's firm rejection of any form of intervention and Napoleon's commitment to act only with the cooperation of Great Britain doomed the American confederation plan. This left Napoleon with only one unsatisfactory option, to act alone by recognizing and allying France with the Confederacy as Slidell and other Confederate agents had long urged.[18]

Slidell failed to appreciate the potential support for the Confederacy within the group of Frenchmen anxious to secure the success of Napoleon's Mexican strategy. While this group was not particularly sympathetic to the Confederacy, their interest in the success of the Mexican venture made them possible allies. Although Slidell, much like Seward, probably feared the success and reestablishment of a strong European power in North America, he was not reluctant to offer cooperation with the French forces in Mexico in exchange for assistance from the French fleet against the Northern blockade.[19] Although his previous offer was unauthorized by the Richmond government, Slidell clearly was prepared to run the risk of a strong French presence in Mexico in order to secure active support for the Confederacy. It is difficult to understand why he did not try to enlist the support of those close to the emperor who were committed to the Mexican strategy, unless he feared the French success in Mexico more than the failure of the Confederacy. Of course, at this point, he did not yet fear Confederate failure.

While Slidell was finding the diplomatic atmosphere in France sympathetic to the Confederate cause, Mason received no encouragement at all from the British government. Despite the news in early January 1863 of the resounding Confederate victory by Gen. Robert E. Lee at Fredericksburg, Mason was counseled by his British friends in Parliament to delay his push for recognition. Mason's optimism, demonstrated in his December and early January correspondence to Slidell and Benjamin, changed to feelings of discouragement and despair by early February.[20] Russell replied to Mason's blockade note on February 10, sidestepping the blockade, while assuring Mason that no offense was intended by his failure to respond to the Southerner's earlier notes of January 3 and January 7.[21] It was clear to Mason that Russell had given up his ideas of mediation. Indeed, the British foreign minister wrote Lyons that "until both parties are heartily tired and sick of the business, I see no use in talking of good offices."[22] Lord Derby, speaking for the opposition in a speech to the House of Lords on February 5, supported Russell's position of non-intervention and argued that recognition represented a breech of neutrality, bound needlessly to provoke the United States.[23]

Despite the encouraging news from France, the favorable reception of the Erlanger loan, and excellent military reports from home, Mason accepted the advice of the Confederate lobby against pursuing a parliamentary motion for the time being. Gregory, a longtime supporter of the Confederate cause in Parliament, advised Mason that "the House of Commons is opposed to taking any steps at present."[24]

The world was not willing to stand still while awaiting the outcome of the American Civil War. Events in Europe forced the resignation of Thouvenel and many of his colleagues at the French foreign ministry in the fall of 1862, handicapping Napoleon's intervention proposals. February 1863 brought the Polish uprising against Russia, requiring the attention of European diplomats.

Napoleon's strong stance in support of the Poles exacerbated the already strained relationship with Austria and raised suspicions of Napoleon's motives both in Russia and in Prussia. Requiring the goodwill of the British more than ever, Napoleon made clear to the Confederates throughout late February and March, through both official and unofficial sources, that he could only act on the American question jointly with Great Britain.[25]

Despite the changing political scene in Europe, Slidell continued to encourage independent French action. As the Polish problem diminished in April and May, the good news of Hooker's defeat at Chancellorsville arrived in Paris, further encouraging Slidell. Rumors abounded that Lee was preparing to invade the North again, and Mason sent word that the Confederate lobby was interested in a new recognition initiative.[26]

The revival of Mason's spirits prompted him to suggest a meeting with John Roebuck and William Lindsay at Shepperton Manor, Lindsay's estate just outside London, to devise a strategy for another drive toward intervention. By this time, Lindsay had succeeded William Gregory as the unofficial leader of the Confederate lobby in London. Gregory, although committed to the Confederate cause, found it necessary to focus most of his attention on European developments.[27]

Lindsay was a remarkable man. Unlike many Europeans who supported the Confederacy, Lindsay's sympathies came from the heart and were not always based on financial self-interest. He believed that the Southern states were committed, as he was, to free trade. Even though his huge shipping interest would directly benefit from an independent South, his sympathies had already cost him dearly in his business dealings with the North. His contemporaries in Parliament and the British press frequently accused him of "pecuniary or selfish motives."[28] Lindsay was not born into the British aristocracy or the landed gentry, but had conquered poverty by a combination of hard work, good fortune, and innate intelligence. He managed to purchase for himself a position of prestige and power and was willing to risk it all for the Confederacy.

During the strategy meeting at Shepperton Manor, both Lindsay and Roebuck warned Mason to proceed cautiously. The two Englishmen were convinced that the support of the opposition Conservative Party was vital to the success of any recognition campaign. Roebuck was sufficiently convinced, after conversations with Disraeli, that modest support would be forthcoming if he moved in Parliament for Confederate recognition. The three men decided to encourage, and

even bribe, certain popular leaders to stage large gatherings throughout the economically troubled areas around Manchester. They hoped
that these demonstrations would garner support for Roebuck's motion. Henry Hotze was directed to conduct a propaganda campaign
consisting of posters and placards showing the Union Jack and the
Confederate battle flag crisscrossed together. The "Shepperton strategy" also called for Hotze to pursue editorials in Tory publications.
As it turned out, Hotze was remarkably successful in publishing regular
editorials in the *Morning Herald* and the *Standard* supporting
Roebuck's proposed motion.[29]

Eduord DeLeon, having already antagonized Slidell and Mason
with his arrogant attitude, again counseled Mason and Roebuck to
move slowly until Tory support was certain.[30] In fact, DeLeon worked
against Roebuck by suggesting to his British friends that they "mus-
sel [*sic*] Roebuck whose honest bark on this occasion may only serve
to warn the burglar."[31] DeLeon was, obviously, not fully committed
to the Roebuck-Lindsay initiative. He managed to convince Mason
that one of two things should occur before Roebuck's motion had a
chance of success in the Commons. Only a French invitation to join
them in intervention, or an overwhelming military victory by the
Confederacy, could rescue Roebuck's motion.[32]

It was with these ideas in mind that Roebuck determined to go to
Paris to pursue a French-led initiative. While Roebuck's trip was under consideration, rumors began to circulate in London that Napoleon was no longer interested in recognizing the Confederacy. Roebuck was anxious to dispel such rumors. If any suspicion existed that
French support would not be forthcoming, Roebuck's motion was
doomed to embarrassing failure. Although known to be an outsider
and independent thinker, Roebuck was a man of some means and
influence. He had little trouble obtaining an interview with the emperor. In order to give his mission as much credibility as possible, he
persuaded Lindsay to accompany him to Paris. Lindsay agreed with
some reservations, for his previous experience with the emperor had
led him to suspect Napoleon's motives in granting the interview.[33]

Slidell, in an attempt to create a favorable atmosphere for the up-
coming Roebuck visit, asked for an earlier meeting with the emperor.
In his letter to the emperor, Slidell again made reference to the diver-
gent interests of Great Britain and France and pointed out that two
strong American republics would help France challenge British mer-
cantile and maritime power. The quickest way to end the American
war, Slidell declared, was for France, joined by other continental powers, if not by Great Britain, to recognize the Confederacy.[34] Clearly,

Slidell did not hold much hope for the success of Roebuck's motion in the Commons. The most perceptive of the Southern diplomats believed, correctly, that Great Britain would remain neutral until the Confederacy secured victory. He further believed that the rumor and suggestions that Napoleon was no longer prepared to support recognition was a plot by the Palmerston government to undermine the legitimate attempt of Roebuck to pass a recognition motion.[35]

Slidell met the emperor on June 18 and quickly discovered that a sympathetic Napoleon had no intention of antagonizing the North without the protection of the British navy. Slidell mentioned the Roebuck motion, adding his belief that the rumors that Napoleon was no longer for intervention were a Palmerston plot. He then asked the emperor to confirm that his position had not changed. Napoleon responded that he continued to support mediation and recognition and Slidell was authorized to report the French position directly to Roebuck.[36]

The Southerner then requested an interview for Roebuck and Lindsay. The emperor replied that he would "be pleased to converse with them on the subject of Mr. Roebuck's motion."[37] Napoleon, apparently agreeing with Slidell's assessment that Palmerston and his cronies in the British government started the rumors, suggested that he might "make a direct proposition to England for joint recognition," thus, effectively preventing Palmerston from misrepresenting the French position. Napoleon, however, left himself an exit by telling Slidell that he would ask the Cabinet's opinion on the matter and let him know in a day or two.[38] Two days later, Slidell learned through private contacts in the foreign ministry that the Cabinet had counseled the emperor against taking the lead in favor of recognition. It had agreed, however, with Napoleon that a communication should be made to the British Cabinet reaffirming French willingness to cooperate with Britain in recognizing the South.[39]

On June 20, as Slidell was receiving his unofficial information from his friend at the foreign ministry, Lindsay and Roebuck met with Napoleon. The two Englishmen and their Confederate friends were encouraged by what they now believed was an impending proposal by Napoleon for Great Britain to join France in recognizing the South. Roebuck and Lindsay urged Napoleon to invite England to join France in recognizing the Confederacy, but suggested that if they refused, France should act alone and reap all the benefits.[40] In reply, Napoleon told the unauthorized British diplomats that he was distressed over the affairs in the United States but was not prepared to take the lead in any recognition effort. The emperor cited his earlier initiative that was "immediately transmitted to the United States government" as a reason for not engaging in another initiative. He did point out that he had requested Baron Gros, who had replaced Flahault in London, to make clear to the British government that he would support any recognition proposal. He further instructed the two men to deny in Parliament that he had changed his views on the recognition of the Confederacy.[41]

Almost a week later, on June 26, Lord Clanricarde asked Russell in the House of Lords if the government was in possession of a recognition proposal. Russell flatly denied that Gros had delivered any proposal or suggestion of recognition. Mason quickly conveyed this disquieting information to Slidell, who at once visited his friend at the French Ministry of Foreign Affairs. He then reassured Mason that Baron Gros had indeed been instructed to remind Palmerston of France's willingness to join Britain in recognizing the Confederacy.[42] On the same day that Slidell wrote to Mason, Roebuck called on Baron Gros and inquired if he had received such a dispatch. Gros declined to discuss the matter in detail. Mason wrote Benjamin, that this settled nothing because all parties understood that Drouyn de Lhuys's communication to Gros would be informal.[43]

Slidell, Mason, and Roebuck were convinced that Napoleon's communication had reached Russell through Gros. On the day of the debate on Roebuck's motion in Parliament, Lord Campbell again asked Russell if he had received written or verbal communication from Napoleon indicating a desire to join Great Britain in intervention. Russell again denied he had received any communication. In fact, Russell added, Baron Gros had called on him earlier and told him he had received no instructions to approach Great Britain on the matter of recognition.[44] Unfortunately for an embarrassed Roebuck and Lindsay, the opening of their debate was clouded by Napoleon's apparent change of heart.[45]

Roebuck, nevertheless, introduced his motion on June 30 in favor of recognition, at which time he launched into a speech on the American question, urging Confederate recognition. Roebuck spoke of the recent interview with Napoleon and even hinted at the Palmerston ministry's attempt to undermine his motion by spreading inaccurate rumors, thus explaining the unauthorized diplomacy he and Lindsay were engaged in. Clearly, after Roebuck's speech and Russell's denial of any communication from France, the outcome of the debate was decided. Although several members of the House arose to back it, others, including a long-time supporter of the Confederacy, Lord Robert Montagu, objected to recognizing the Confederacy on the grounds that it would endanger Great Britain's neutral position.[46]

Finally, on July 2, William E. Forster asked British Undersecretary Layard if any communication had been received from the emperor. Layard denied any communication with France on the question of intervention. Spence, therefore, urged Roebuck to withdraw his motion because of strong opposition to it growing out of the failure of the French to support the Confederate initiative.[47] Lord Robert Cecil and Lindsay concurred in asking that Roebuck postpone a vote on his motion until news arrived of the outcome of Lee's invasion of Pennsylvania.

Throughout the debate, the Roebuck and Lindsay initiative was harshly criticized and their unofficial diplomatic mission was called into question. On July 13, Roebuck moved to discharge his motion, and Palmerston sarcastically attacked Roebuck's private diplomacy. Responding to Palmerston's biting comments, Lindsay corroborated Roebuck's account of the interview with Napoleon and pointed out that Palmerston had earlier made good use of private unofficial diplomats to obtain favorable commercial treaties.[48]

Even before the final exchange on July 13, the Southern lobby and the Confederate agents in London realized they were beaten. The failure of the Tories to step forward and support Roebuck's motion puzzled Mason. The Tories, Mason reported to Benjamin, believed that a defeat of the government in the House would bring on an election and that Palmerston's immense personal popularity might be challenged. The absence of Tory support and Roebuck's public embarrassment by Napoleon's withdrawal caused the defeat of the Confederate initiative. A discouraged Hotze wrote, "Now all hope of parliamentary action is passed [*sic*]." Most of the Confederates in Great Britain agreed with Hotze that "diplomatic means can now no longer avail, and everybody looks to Lee to conquer recognition."[49]

After receiving a letter from Roebuck outlining the interview with Napoleon, Slidell contacted Drouyn de Lhuys, Persigny, and his "friend." After lengthy discussions with his contacts in Paris, Slidell was confident that Roebuck's account was accurate. The evidence strongly suggests that Napoleon instructed Drouyn de Lhuys to communicate, informally through Gros, his willingness to cooperate with the British on the American question. The problem stems from an overly optimistic interpretation of Napoleon's intentions by Roebuck, Lindsay, Slidell, and Mason. Russell, like Thouvenel, and, to some extent, Seward, did not view unofficial communications as having ever been received unless acted upon. Confederate representatives should have understood this diplomatic technique and should have pursued a more cautious approach.

Slidell made his opinion on the Roebuck affair clear to Benjamin on July 6, when he wrote: "I suspect that M. Drouyn de Lhuys has not carried out in good faith the wishes of his sovereign; he is a man of timid temperament, fond of little dramatic finesse, and is very far from being as decided as the Emperor in his view of the policy to be pursued in our affairs." Slidell requested and received rather complete documentation and explanations from the French government by July 19. After reviewing the evidence, he again concluded that de Lhuys "has been not a little instrumental in producing the 'imbroglio.'"[50] Mason, too, informed Benjamin on July 10 that he believed that Drouyn de Lhuys had not carried out Napoleon's orders.[51]

A review of the telegrams forwarded by Drouyn de Lhuys to Gros that relate to the Roebuck initiative suggest that both cooperated in delaying implementation of Napoleon's instructions. Several telegrams instructed Gros to speak to Lord Palmerston "officially" on recognition. It appears, however, that Gros deliberately frustrated the process by delaying his approach to either Russell or Palmerston.[52]

By early August, the Confederate commissioners had no hope that Palmerston and Russell would join France in any initiative. The embarrassing failure of Roebuck's motion, coupled with the disastrous news from the battlefields of Vicksburg and Gettysburg, left few options for further diplomatic initiatives. The Roebuck fiasco and Russell's persistent refusal to receive Mason as the legitimate representative of the Confederate government in Great Britain were viewed in Richmond as intolerable.

The determination of the Palmerston government to acknowledge the legality of the Union naval blockade had already fueled the fires of anti-British feeling within the Confederacy. The newspapers throughout the South railed against the British government and urged Benjamin to break off diplomatic relations. Russell's and Palmerston's treatment of Mason and the Confederacy was an insult to Southerners that they could no longer abide. On August 4, Benjamin wrote Mason to leave London because the British government "has determined to decline the overtures made through you for establishing, by treaty, friendly relations between the two governments, and entertains no intention of receiving you as the accredited Minister of this government near the British Court."[53] In a personal note accompanying the official dispatch from Benjamin, Mason was assured that his efforts and ability were not in question and, in fact, if circumstances changed before the letter arrived, Mason was authorized to remain in place.[54]

On September 21, Mason informed Russell of his impending departure. The British foreign secretary delivered the final rebuff on September 25, replying to Mason that the reasons he had not been received as a representative of an "established state . . . are still in force and it is not necessary to repeat them."[55] With this final blow to his Southern honor, Mason left for Paris to join Slidell, where he expected to continue the diplomatic fight. Benjamin decided to appoint Mason "special commissioner to the Continent" and so notified the Virginian on November 15. In his capacity as commissioner to the Continent, Mason assumed a certain presence of command that irritated Slidell, who felt that he had been more effective than Mason. Mason also traveled extensively and frequently returned to Great Britain to join the propaganda efforts. His departure reduced his influence with Southern sympathizers in Britain, who must have felt abandoned by the representative in the cause they had actively supported with both influence and money.[56]

Chapter 12

The Burden of Southern Honor:
The Diplomatic Break with
Great Britain

Benjamin's instructions to Mason to leave England were in part a response to the increased demand for "satisfaction" within the Confederacy. While the Southern commissioners were being rudely treated in Great Britain, the Confederate government believed its treatment of British consuls residing and working within Southern territory was accommodating and courteous. The British consuls, under the direction of Lord Lyons, repeatedly attempted to protect British subjects from service in the Confederate army. By the summer of 1863, however, state governors throughout the South were desperate for able-bodied men to fill vacancies in local militia. The ranks of the local militia had been depleted by the demands of the Richmond government for replacements of soldiers lost in battle. Davis and Benjamin were under pressure from a Confederate Congress, influenced by an increasing resentment of Great Britain in the press, to demonstrate the Confederacy's commitment to the creation of a nation with or without British recognition.[1]

Mason's withdrawal publicly betrayed the Confederacy's British friends. Mason's retirement to the Continent validated the policy of British neutrality that was supported by the enemies of the Southern lobby. During the late summer of 1863, while Southern armies were scrambling to reorganize after the crushing defeats of Vicksburg and

Gettysburg, Lindsay, Spence, Gregory, and other Confederate supporters in Great Britain scrambled to reorganize the eroding support for Confederate recognition.[2] A desperate situation was rendered hopeless by the absence of a highly placed Confederate commissioner in London. Members of the Confederate lobby who had staked their reputations, fortunes, and political futures on the success of the Confederacy had now been abandoned and betrayed by their Southern friends.

The Erlanger loan, by now considered a barometer of Southern fortunes, dropped to 36 percent by late August and continued to drop to just below 30 percent after Mason's departure. The *Morning Star* declared the Confederate cause "past help, past hope."[3]

Henry Hotze remained in England and became the highest ranking Confederate agent continuing to reside in Britain. Hotze wrote Benjamin that Mason's departure failed to produce the "profound sensation expected." If the government in Richmond expected any substantial change in the British government's position because the Confederate government's main unofficial representative had decided to withdraw, they quickly discovered their error in judgment. Hotze included in his communication to Benjamin an editorial comment from the *Times* that expressed regret for offending the Confederates but pointed out that "the loss is theirs, while the relief to our government will be great." The *Times* editorial and the communication from Hotze validates Lindsay's earlier assessment of the consequences of Mason's withdrawal.[4]

Based on the repeated failure of previous Southern initiatives and the advice of both Mason and Slidell, a change in tactics was needed. The ultimate result, however, was a withdrawal from the major diplomatic field of battle by a beleaguered and demoralized Southern coalition in London. The misguided and ill-advised policy of pursuing independent action by Napoleon had no chance of success, given the realities of the political situation in Europe. Certainly, after the political shift in Italy and Napoleon's commitment to the Poles, France could not act independently of Great Britain without becoming vulnerable on the Continent.[5]

Members of the Confederate Congress, recognizing the problems created by foreign consuls residing in the Confederacy without proper credentials from the Richmond government, began in early 1862 to advocate the dismissal of any consuls unwilling to petition the Confederate government for appropriate credentials. Congressman Ethelbert Barksdale of Mississippi introduced and obtained passage of a resolution in the House demanding that the status of foreign representatives be clarified to protect the "sovereign integrity" of the Confederacy.[6] William Yancey, after returning from Great Britain, demanded that the Senate pass legislation invalidating the activities of foreign consuls who refused to obtain Confederate exequaturs. Yancey resented his earlier treatment by the British government and appears to have wanted similar treatment for the British representatives within the Confederacy.[7] By the summer of 1863, the mood in Richmond was in favor of Davis initiating some action against the British consuls that would reestablish the dignity of the Confederacy. On March 15, an editorial in the *Montgomery Advertiser* expressing Southern sentiment declared, "If England, France, and Spain and other nations, desire representatives in the Confederacy to look after their own commercial interest and the interest of their citizens, let them take an honorable course and recognize the Confederate States as a nation."[8] For a while longer, however, Davis and Benjamin continued to resist the pressure, hoping to achieve a diplomatic breakthrough in the British Parliament.

Henry Foote of Tennessee offered a resolution from the Foreign Affairs Committee requesting the names of all foreign consuls, including the sources of their exchequer. Foote was an outspoken adversary of Benjamin and Davis and seems to have sought through his resolution to embarrass the Davis administration.[9] The resolution also called for the publication of all correspondence from Confederate representatives abroad, except for those materials deemed too sensitive for the public, which would still need to be submitted to the Congress. Benjamin, however, refused to provide a list of Confederate agents or submit their correspondence to the Congress. He knew that the failed Confederate diplomatic initiatives would present an opportunity for the administration's critics to demand the withdrawal of Mason, Slidell, Mann, and all diplomatic representatives, thus completely humiliating Davis and the State Department.[10] Congressman Swann also of Tennessee then reintroduced into the Confederate House a resolution demanding the dismissal of foreign consuls unless they obtained their exchequers from the Confederacy. He also pressed Congress to demand the recall of Confederate commissioners from abroad.[11]

The two Tennesseans were ruthlessly ambitious and determined to create political problems for the Davis administration. Regardless of the motives, the resolutions reflected the general tone of the Southern press and embodied the deep hostility toward the British within the Confederacy.[12]

A series of diplomatic irritations finally led the Confederate government to expel the consuls, even as it ordered Mason's withdrawal from Great Britain.[13] The final collision between Benjamin and the British consuls occurred in October 1863. Earlier in the year, British Consul George Moore and British Vice Consul F. J. Cridland in Richmond were expelled for their persistent effort to extract British expatriates from the Confederate army. Benjamin pointed out to the consuls in his letter of February 20, 1863, when he asked them to submit to the authority of the Confederate State Department, that their negotiations with the Virginia governor on behalf of the British suspects exceeded the authority of "Her Majesty's Consul at the Port of Richmond."[14]

With this earlier incident in mind, Benjamin monitored a conflict that developed between Governor Joe E. Brown of Georgia and British Consul Alan Fullerton at Savannah. Fullerton was determined to prevent Brown from drafting into the Georgia militia a number of so-called British residents in Savannah. Brown, however, claimed the expatriates were long-time residents of Georgia and, as such, were required to perform the duties of any able-bodied male citizen. Fullerton's efforts were not limited to the prevention of enlistment, but extended to the protection of deserters who had previously volunteered. Many of these naturalized Georgians joined because of public pressure and the belief that the war would be over quickly.[15] Of course, public opinion was overwhelmingly on the side of the state and its governor. The patient and always-alert secretary of state waited for an appropriate opportunity to intervene in the conflict with the governor.[16]

A similar series of incidents developed between Governor Milledge L. Bonham of South Carolina and British Vice Consul H. R. Walker, the successor in Charleston to Robert Bunch. Eventually, the complete correspondence of Fullerton/Brown and Walker/Bonham was published. The perception throughout the Confederacy was to confirm the British government's arrogant disrespect for the Confederacy. Great Britain ignored the authority of the Richmond government and appointed consuls without the knowledge and consent of the Confederacy. The appointees often appeared to engage in treasonable activities openly supporting the Union war effort. Public anger increased when Fullerton and Walker publicly denied the right of the state or the Confederacy to conscript any British subject domiciled in the South, and further proceeded to advise any British citizen conscripted into the Confederate army to throw down his arms and retreat when asked to engage in battle with the Union army. Brown appealed to the Confederate secretary of state for support when he learned that Fullerton and Walker were acting on the precise instructions of Lord Russell.[17]

Davis could, and usually did, resist public opinion and acted deliberately after consultation with certain trusted advisors. Judah Benjamin was certainly as close to the president as any other person in the government. Davis decided, reluctantly, to allow Benjamin to publish in the October 3 *Charleston Mercury* his reply to Governor Brown's request for an opinion on the Walker correspondence. In his published reply to Walker's contention that British citizens were not subject to military service and should throw down their arms, Benjamin wrote that such action "does not meet with the approval of this department. While the Governor claims no military service from sojourners, those who have acquired residence in the Confederacy are bound by law to aid in its defense."[18] Undoubtedly, Benjamin wanted to expel all the British consuls, despite the diplomatic implications in Great Britain. Davis, however, required further convincing.

Fullerton's arrogant reply, and his defense that he was following John Russell's instructions, reached Benjamin on October 7. Fullerton and the other British consuls fell into Benjamin's trap and provided the most reluctant of the Confederate leadership with adequate provocation for their expulsion. President Davis was en route to Chattanooga and was unavailable for consultation.[19] Benjamin decided to take the responsibility for calling a meeting of the Cabinet. After a lengthy but orderly presentation of the facts, the secretary of state asked the Cabinet to approve a significant policy change in the absence of the president. The Cabinet unanimously directed Benjamin to expel not only Fullerton, but also all British consuls operating within the jurisdiction of the Confederacy.[20]

For Benjamin to call a meeting of the Cabinet was unprecedented, particularly because Benjamin did not always enjoy the confidence of the other Cabinet members. Nevertheless, the president ultimately supported the Cabinet's decision and "had no hesitation in directing that all consuls and consular agents of the British government be notified that they can no longer be permitted to exercise their functions or even to reside within the limits of the Confederacy."[21] The president was reluctant before Fullerton's self-incriminating letter to jeopardize future negotiations with England. Benjamin's actions— first in calling a Cabinet meeting, and second in initiating a major shift in Confederate foreign policy—suggests that the president was aware of and cooperated in Benjamin's strategy. There is no evidence to suggest the president authorized Benjamin to call the Cabinet meeting in his absence; but an informal understanding probably existed between Davis and his Cabinet about who was in charge in the president's absence. Nevertheless, Benjamin did patiently await the initiatives of the state governors before taking action against the British consuls. The evidence was overwhelming that the British officials were interfering directly with the execution of Confederate law and, at least from the Confederate perspective, were advising citizens to commit treasonous acts.[22]

In contrast to the British style, the French consuls, while very active in both commercial and extralegal activities, were deferential to the government in Richmond. These officials sought and obtained the cooperation of local officials and, in general, avoided unnecessary provocation.[23] A good example of the contrasting style between the British and French approach to the Confederate government is found in the actions of Alfred Paul, the French consul in Richmond, to obtain the so-called "Rothschild Tobacco."

The international trading house of Rothschild and Company joined the French state tobacco monopoly, Regie Imperiale, in the purchase of some 9,200 hogsheads of tobacco in March and April of 1861. The purchase and delivery of the tobacco to Richmond for shipment preceded the announcement of the Union blockade. Immediately after the blockade announcement, the House of Rothschild transferred the responsibility for shipment of its share (approximately 2,200 hogsheads) to the New York firm of August Belmont and Company. The Regie Imperiale instructed the French consul in Richmond to act on behalf of both parties owning the valuable commodity.

The Confederate government immediately moved to confiscate the tobacco on behalf of the newly formed government; but Paul, securing the services of competent Southern attorneys, managed to protect the title to the tobacco and the Confederate government allowed him to store all of it as a "neutral commodity."[24] Merciér used the tobacco to partially disguise his visit to Richmond in the spring of 1862 to see Benjamin. Throughout 1862, French commercial interests sought to find a legal way of shipping the tobacco through the blockade. Throughout the process, French officials remained respectful of the Confederate and U.S. laws—therein was the major part of the problem.[25]

In January of 1863, Drouyn de Lhuys instructed Paul to "try to obtain permission to send all of the tobacco to France."[26] Paul approached Benjamin and received reluctant permission to ship the tobacco through the Port of Richmond on the James River. He then traveled to Washington to secure permission to pass through the Union blockade. Gideon Welles refused to allow the shipment to leave Richmond, but granted permission for the tobacco to pass through the Port of Savannah. After consultations in Washington with Merciér, it was determined that the tobacco should remain in Richmond until a more convenient method of transportation could be arranged. Paul also pointed out to Merciér that he expected the Confederates to levy a substantial tax on the tobacco and that warehousing bills were mounting up.[27]

Merciér then approached Seward, while Paul returned to Richmond for discussions with Benjamin. The issue for Seward and Welles, of course, was the validity of the blockade, while Benjamin and the Confederate government were concerned about a foreign government (the United States) regulating its Southern port activities. In any case, the matter of the French tobacco in Richmond remained unresolved through the summer of 1863. The extremely high value of the 9,200 hogsheads of tobacco and the size of the vessel required for its shipment probably prevented any clandestine attempt at removing it from Richmond. French officials remained active, within the legal parameters of both governments, in their attempts to export the tobacco, but it remained in Richmond until after the war, despite repeated and complicated negotiations. The contrast between Paul's legal efforts during wartime in neutral commercial activities and those of British blockade runners and profiteers enabled the French consuls to remain in place within Confederate-controlled territory throughout the war. [28]

The final break with Great Britain signaled the end of any sustained diplomatic effort to obtain recognition from that source. This amounted to the complete abandonment of the King Cotton strategy. Henry Hotze and C. J. McRae, who had replaced Spencer as the chief purchasing agent, were constrained to confine their work to procurement of supplies and propaganda efforts. Slidell's advice to concentrate Confederate diplomacy in France now became the official policy of the Confederate government. The expulsion of the British consuls and Mason's withdrawal from London signaled the official acceptance in Richmond of Slidell's strategy.

Chapter 13

France, Mexico, and Frustrated Confederates

Beginning in October 1863 and continuing until the end of the Confederacy, the efforts of the Confederate State Department and its commissioners in Europe were devoted principally to obtaining an alliance with France. Slidell wrote Benjamin that the South's best hope would come from a "general war in Europe. The Lincoln government would encourage the fitting-out of vessels under the Russian flag to prey upon the commerce of France, and Great Britain would, in turn, open our ports and blockade those of the North."[1] Indeed, the situation in Europe was volatile and the outbreak of hostilities on the Continent remained a possibility until the collapse of the Confederacy. The Polish crisis, however, calmed down by November 1863.

The situation in France appeared favorable for a Confederate diplomatic initiative in early 1864. James Bulloch, forced out of England by a strict interpretation of the British neutrality law, brought the bulk of Confederate naval construction to French builders, particularly the Arman naval contractors. The Confederate Navy Department appointed Commodore Samuel Barron to command Confederate naval operations in Europe. Barron, whose family lived in South Carolina, had been a captain in the old navy before resigning to join the navy of Virginia. Later as a Commander in the Confederate navy, he commanded the CSS *Winslow* on August 27–28, 1862, at the fall of Fort Hatteras. He was a close friend of Stephen Mallory and shared the secretary of the navy's belief in naval power. Barron, now a flag officer, arrived in Paris in October, 1863, shortly after the British had taken the *Laird Rams* into custody. Despite the loss of the *Rams,* Barron took command of an ambitious construction program and was optimistic for the ultimate success of his newly authorized fleet.

When Barron arrived in Paris, four corvettes and two ironclads were under construction in France. The *Florida* was undergoing repair at the government dockyard in Brest. In addition, a successful recruiting effort provided the Confederate officer with sufficient officers and men to accommodate his needs. Shortly after his arrival, the *Georgia* put into Cherbourg and in November, the *Rappahannock* arrived in Calais. Barron had nine major warships under his command, counting those vessels under construction. No other Confederate officer could boast such a fleet. The energetic Confederate naval agents bombarded Slidell, and now Mason, with repeated requests for funding and diplomatic access to the French judicial and marine ministries.[2]

Confederate Secretary of the Navy Mallory, Matthew Maury, and Bulloch all believed that Confederate naval prospects were bright. They expected to get their ships to sea quickly and initiate action against the enemy merchant marine.[3] As long as the French government maintained its tolerant policy, they expected to put a formidable fleet to sea that might threaten northern coastal cities. They were not fully aware of the Union forces working to prevent Confederate naval success in France.[4]

On September 9, 1863, an employee of J. Voruz and Company, the French naval contractor building the Confederate corvettes, approached William Dayton with convincing proof that the ships were being built for the Confederate navy and not for neutral countries. The papers consisted of various financial agreements between Erlanger and Company and Arman and Company, the firm responsible for the construction of the ironclad rams in France. These documents detailed the purchases of armaments in violation of the French neutrality law.[5] Later, Dayton's contact produced a copy of the Bulloch-Arman ironclad contract, clearly proving that the ships were indeed destined for action against the United States. On September 22, Dayton presented copies of the incriminating papers to Drouyn de Lhuys and the French minister immediately began an investigation through the Ministry of Marine.[6]

The investigation proceeded slowly, probably because the ships were far from completion and the naval contractors possessed a great deal of influence, both with the Ministry of Marine and with the emperor. The emperor had previously assured Slidell that naval construction specifically for the Confederates, if properly arranged, would be tolerated. It was, therefore, important that the investigation proceed carefully and with tact. Dayton appreciated the circumstances and did not press Drouyn de Lhuys, who was generally friendly to the Union, to rush his discreet inquiries. On October 22, the French Ministry of Marine withdrew permission to arm the corvettes and in December, ordered Arman and Company to seek other buyers for the ironclad ships.[7]

In February 1864, the department detained the ironclads and in early May confiscated the corvettes. The decision to confiscate the corvettes provided the legal basis for the emperor's personal order to the builders to sell all such ships to neutral governments. One of the ill-fated Arman ships, the ironclad *Cheops,* was sold to Prussia on May 25, 1864. The *Sphinx* had already been sold to Denmark. The ships could not be delivered, however, because by the spring of 1864, Denmark and Prussia were belligerents and forbidden under French law to take delivery of warships. Dayton's strategy of allowing Drouyn de Lhuys to conduct and conclude his investigation of warships under construction without harassment or pressure was extraordinarily successful.[8]

The U.S. minister, however, persisted in his demands to prevent the rearmament and refurbishing of existing Confederate ships of war in French ports. Here he was much more aggressive and pursued "every rumor."[9] The USS *Kearsage* maintained a presence off the coast of France and was eventually joined, in June 1864, by the *Niagara, Sacramento,* and *Iroquois.* It was the duty of these ships to maintain a careful watch over the Confederate ships in the vicinity, including those under construction, until a decision as to their disposition was made by the French government.[10]

Confederate agents worked diligently, if somewhat belatedly, to devise a scheme to disguise the ultimate destination and ownership of the ships under construction. These schemes, often bordering on the bizarre, ultimately failed. The Confederate effort, although it had little hope for success once the Voruz papers were obtained, was not aided by Slidell's inept backstairs diplomacy. The Confederate diplomat naively believed that Napoleon would ultimately allow the escape of the Confederate vessels because of the emperor's previously stated Southern sympathies. Slidell also continued to receive assurances from numerous officials in the government that the emperor desired Confederate success.[11]

The chief Southern adversary and guiding force behind the successful effort to eliminate the Confederate ships was Drouyn de Lhuys. The French foreign minister believed that the invasion of Mexico had already overextended his country's military and economic capabilities. Like his predecessor, Edouard Thouvenel, Drouyn de Lhuys was committed to nonintervention. By late 1863, he was convinced that any clash with the United States would have disastrous effects on France's ability to maintain its security in Europe. He, therefore, implemented strategies that worked at cross-purposes to those of his sovereign.[12]

While Napoleon was committed to Southern recognition, Confederate naval construction in France, and the reestablishment of imperial rule in Mexico, the more practical Drouyn de Lhuys sought to maintain a balance of power in Europe. In a Cabinet meeting with the Empress Eugenie, presiding in the absence of Napoleon, Drouyn de Lhuys was able to gain full control over the Confederate ships in French ports; but even with Cabinet approval, he still needed to move carefully to overcome the emperor's personal policy toward the vessels.[13]

The fact that the Confederates decided to sell the ironclads by mid-February but retained the corvettes indicates they still believed, or at least hoped, that the emperor's personal wishes would prevail. Slidell felt the emperor's initiative and promises would ultimately survive the intrigues of Drouyn de Lhuys.[14]

In correspondence with his friend, Minister of Marine Prosper Chasseloup-Laupat, Drouyn de Lhuys suggested a direct relationship between the Confederate ships and the French commitment to Mexico. He emphasized the need to prevent antagonizing American officials in Washington until a satisfactory resolution to the Mexican situation could be developed. For example, in February 1864, as Maximilian was preparing to leave for Mexico, Drouyn de Lhuys asked the minister of marine to "avoid all acts which would in the eyes of the United States constitute serious unfounded complaints that would adversely affect the enterprise which we pursue at Mexico."[15] Eventually, the French foreign minister was able to convince Napoleon that the threat from the United States to his plans for Mexico was greater than any assistance or advantage to be gained by allowing the Confederate ships to escape. The emperor, therefore, ordered Arman and Company to sell the corvettes in May 1864.[16]

The prior decision of the Confederate leadership to sell the ironclads, while retaining ownership of the corvettes, provoked a confrontation between Slidell and Barron. Barron, acting on the advice of Bulloch, argued that the only hope of success for the Confederate navy was to launch all the ships as a united fighting force. The rams were the offensive heart of the fleet, while the corvettes were little more than raiders. Slidell believed the diplomatic opportunities presented by the selection of Maximilian as emperor of Mexico would be aided by a show of cooperation with Confederate sympathizers in the French government. Ultimately, Slidell's arguments prevailed within the group of Southern operatives.[17] Slidell, however, was not accustomed to the tenaciousness of Bulloch. Bulloch and Arman arrived at a secret agreement whereby two of the corvettes and one ram could be sold to other governments while their representatives pursued a scheme to secure the remaining vessels for the Confederacy. Unfortunately for the Confederacy, the result was a bizarre scheme to fabricate the sale of the ships to the pasha of Egypt, while secretly delivering the ships to the Confederate navy. The result was an embarrassing, highly publicized failure that produced resentment and animosity within the Confederate entourage in Europe. The effect, however, was anticlimactic because by the time the plot was exposed, Napoleon had accepted Drouyn de Lhuys's theory that conflict with the United States should be avoided in order to protect any hope of success in Mexico.[18]

Despite the commitment of the French Minister to neutrality and nonintervention, Slidell doggedly pursued diplomatic action to involve France in the Civil War. Benjamin wrote from Richmond a desperate plea for Slidell to approach the French once again on the matter of the "selfish policy of England" regarding the blockade. He requested that the French use their navy to open selected Confederate ports. In exchange, the Confederate secretary of state offered cotton for eight cents per pound. Slidell recognized the desperate tone of Benjamin's instructions and responded that "so long as the Polish question remains in its present uncertain condition, it will be a serious obstacle to our recognition."[19] Slidell's limited optimism stemmed from the expectation that Confederate support would soon be needed to sustain Napoleon's Mexican adventure. Slidell, hoping for a favorable declaration from the emperor in his speech to the Chambers on November 5, was disappointed when the emperor limited his foreign policy discussion to Indochina and Mexico. Still determined, Slidell quickly decided that the emperor's failure to mention the American Civil War was, perhaps, an intention not to show his new policy toward America in order to avoid outspoken objections. Slidell received unofficial confirmation that his assumptions were correct through Jean Francois Mocquard, Napoleon's private secretary. Mocquard reported that the emperor could not state his continued willingness to act in concert with Great Britain without making Great Britain appear responsible for the present condition of affairs in America. Any such inference would tend to separate the two governments, further complicating Continental affairs.[20]

In December 1863, Slidell once again decided to act without specific instructions from the Confederate secretary of state. After a visit with Drouyn de Lhuys on November 9, he concluded that France would not be forced into any military engagement in North America beyond their commitment to Mexico. Slidell also received information about the same time the emperor was trying to organize a congress of European powers in support of a legitimate emperor for Mexico. Slidell, sensing the probable failure of the emperor's efforts, decided to encourage the French to occupy Matamoras and release several blockade runners loaded with munitions for the Confederacy. He informed Benjamin on December 3 of his initiative.[21] Although the French did not immediately undertake an operation to capture Matamoras, Slidell was successful in obtaining the release of the munitions ships. He wrote Benjamin on December 15 that he expected the emperor to be so preoccupied with matters in Europe that "further success should not immediately be expected."[22]

Henry Hotze confirmed Slidell's view of the European situation when he wrote James Bulloch from London that "Europe is a powder magazine which the slightest spark can explode."[23] The Polish crisis had united Russia and France, creating an awkward situation for further Confederate diplomatic initiatives. Russia was the strongest defender of the Union cause in Europe, while France was the most sympathetic to the Confederacy. Napoleon's attempts to create a European congress further alienated and strained relations with Great Britain, while the Schleswig-Holstein question threatened to engulf Europe in a general war. Thus, there was little hope for Slidell's suggestion that the French move immediately on Matamoras in pursuit of a new strategy designed to create a Franco-Confederate alliance in Mexico, with the puppet regime of Maximilian as its cornerstone.[24]

It does not seem unreasonable, when removed from the context of Europe, that a policy of cooperation would benefit the desperate Confederacy and save the French initiative in Mexico. The success of the Confederacy would create a buffer between the United States and Maximilian's Mexico. It was more evident after the Union victory at Chattanooga and Grant's later offensive into Virginia, that without foreign intervention the Confederacy was doomed. A Union victory would present Napoleon and Maximilian with a formidable opponent determined to support the traditions of the Monroe Doctrine. If peace came to America based on the division of the Union, the Confederacy could ill afford to alienate the French in Mexico while still confronted by a vengeful and hostile United States to the North.

Given the immense French investment of men and money in Mexico and the obvious benefit to France of a Confederate success, the Southern diplomatic initiative to achieve a Franco-Confederate alliance is understandable. Unquestionably, such an alliance posed a danger for France, but the French commitment had already provoked a United States reaction. Napoleon must have realized that after the defeat of the Confederacy and the reconstruction of the Union, he would face the power of the United States without the support of any European ally.

Secretary of State Seward, ably assisted by William Dayton, conducted a brilliant diplomatic campaign to prevent the Confederates from using the Mexican issue effectively. Seward left no doubt that the United States disapproved of the French efforts to set up a monarchy in Mexico and repeatedly communicated, through Dayton to French officials, United States concerns over the violation of the Monroe Doctrine. In a forceful presentation to Drouyn de Lhuys on October 8, 1863, Dayton informed the French minister that the United States would not recognize Maximilian.[25] In April 1865, John Bigelow, who replaced Dayton after his death in December 1864, arrogantly repeated the U.S. demands. The French press raged against the Monroe Doctrine and the Juarez government, claiming that Juarez was "one of those ephemeral heros brought to power by the money and intrigues of the United States."[26]

When Maximilian accepted the Mexican crown in January 1864, he recognized that the security and, indeed, the survival of his regime, depended on a Confederate victory. He stated, "The creation of this new state, by aid of the support of France and England will be, in my opinion, an absolute necessity for the Mexican Empire, and cannot fail greatly to facilitate the test of the power guaranteeing the existence of the Empire."[27] The future emperor of Mexico believed that British and French recognition should precede his acceptance of the Mexican crown. The young Austrian's failure to insist on this condition before his acceptance and departure for Mexico may have been the fatal sin of omission. The newly crowned emperor departed for Mexico City aboard the Austrian frigate *Novara*, the same ship that would return three years later with his coffin.[28]

The Confederate government, for its part, understood how closely its interests were involved with Napoleon's Mexican venture and the government of Maximilian. On January 7, 1864, before Maximilian's final acceptance of the Mexican crown, Benjamin issued letters of accreditation to William Preston as Confederate diplomatic representative to Maximilian, with authorization to accord his government recognition. Preston was to make no move until he was certain of receiving a cordial reception; but once received and accredited as Confederate minister to Mexico, he was to cultivate the friendship of the marquis of Montholon, French minister to Mexico, and urge a French-Confederate military alliance to check Union aggression south of the Rio Grande. Preston was further to emphasize that "the future safety of the Mexican empire is inextricably bound to the safety and independence of the Confederacy. Mexico must indulge in no illusion on this point."[29]

Benjamin sent a copy of Preston's instructions to Slidell. By the time it arrived, Slidell was already convinced that Napoleon had decided against any alliance with the Confederacy and had, in fact, influenced Maximilian to refuse Slidell's invitation to meet before the archduke departed for Mexico. Maximilian had approached friends of Slidell's before his arrival in Paris, seeking an appointment to discuss open-recognition possibilities with the Confederacy. Despite repeated attempts to arrange an appointment with Maximilian, Slidell was unsuccessful.[30] It was now up to Preston to obtain an audience with Maximilian immediately upon his arrival in Mexico.[31]

Dudley Mann, however, unearthed evidence that "Louis Napoleon has enjoined upon Maximilian to hold no official relations with the Confederate government in France or Mexico." Mann received this information directly from King Leopold of Belgium. Confederate commissioners on both sides of the Atlantic warned Maximilian and Napoleon, indirectly through confidential sources, that they were committing a serious and irreparable mistake in allowing this opportunity for mutual recognition to pass. Slidell wrote Benjamin, "I have taken care, of course in no offensive tone, to let the leading Mexicans here understand that [Napoleon] makes a great mistake, both as regards his hope of avoiding difficulties with the North and his reliance upon the South to aid him in meeting them, for without the active friendship of the South, he will be entirely powerless to resist Northern aggression."[32]

Benjamin's decision to direct the Confederate diplomatic effort toward France and abandon any hope of obtaining British recognition and leadership of the European community favorable to the

Confederacy resulted in failure. By the spring of 1864, Union armies were moving toward Richmond and Sherman was well along on his march through Georgia. Confederate diplomats, much like Confederate generals in the field, resorted in the final days of the Confederacy to desperate attempts to salvage anything from a failing diplomacy in Europe.

Chapter 14

The Desperate End Game

By the summer of 1864, the Confederate government recognized that desperate diplomatic measures were required for the Confederacy to survive. The military situation was rapidly deteriorating. Sherman was on the outskirts of Atlanta and Grant was pushing Lee to the outer defenses of Richmond. The Confederacy was cut by Union control of the Mississippi, and Sherman was preparing to further separate the struggling nation. The military situation was hopeless, but the bloodletting continued as a proud people continued the fight. The only hope to salvage the Southern nation in any recognizable form was through a negotiated settlement. The Confederate commissioners in Europe had failed and the European powers were openly rejecting the possibility of intervention. Popular opinion on both sides of the conflict reflected a war weariness that produced a willingness to compromise in order to stop the carnage.[1]

Ironically, with victory in sight, Lincoln faced strong political opposition as the 1864 fall elections approached. The Republican Party nominated Lincoln at its convention in Baltimore in June. The platform was uncompromising in its demand for unconditional reunion and the abolition of slavery. The radicals within the Republican Party demanded the aggressive prosecution of the war in order to achieve the stated objectives of the platform. Lincoln and Seward, much like their Southern counterparts, recognized the long-term benefits of a negotiated settlement. Lincoln needed the support of moderate Republicans and Northern Democrats, first to win the election, and then to develop a Reconstruction policy that would enable the reunited states to heal their wounds. If the South returned willingly to the Union, their representatives in Washington would presumably support the moderate policies of Lincoln after the war ended.[2]

Davis and Benjamin, although they did not fully appreciate the sufficient fundamental differences that still existed to prevent any negotiated settlement, sought an opportunity to stop the killing. The first of the desperate Confederate maneuvers began in May of 1864. Confederate agents were pursuing uncoordinated activities in Canada. These included military operations such as the St. Albans raid across the border into Vermont, and the plots to free prisoners of war from prison camps in the Middle West. Confederate agents were also involved in a number of munitions purchases and political intrigues across the border designed to prevent Lincoln's re-nomination and subsequent reelection.[3] These intrigues took the form of peace overtures toward leading antiwar Democrats but the Confederate agents, operating with little direction from Richmond, were ineffective and generally antagonized potential supporters.[4]

Working for the Confederate cause in Canada were James P. Holcombe, a professor at the University of Virginia and a representative in the Confederate Congress; Clement C. Clay, formerly a U.S. Senator from Alabama; and Jacob Thompson, who had served as Buchanan's secretary of the interior before the war. But by far the most active of the Confederate agents was George N. Sanders, who returned to Canada after his frustrating failures in England. It was the secretive and adventuresome Sanders who first approached W. C. Jewett, a soldier of fortune from a prominent family in Portland, Maine, proposing that the two appoint themselves as liaisons between the two belligerents to arrange a cessation of hostilities. Sanders claimed that Jefferson Davis authorized him to negotiate a peace settlement with the full authority of the Confederate government, while Jewett claimed to have direct access to Lincoln. Thus began one of the strangest diplomatic episodes of the war.

On July 5, 1864, Jewett wrote to Horace Greeley informing him of Sanders's peace overture.[5] Greeley forwarded to Lincoln the Sanders/Jewett proposal on July 7, along with a detailed "plan of adjustment." Greeley suggested to Lincoln that Sanders and an appropriately sized party be granted safe conduct into the United States to negotiate with officials of the Union government. In addition, Greeley suggested that the president did not fully understand "how intently the people desire any peace consistent with the national integrity and honor."[6] Lincoln wrote Greeley on July 9 stating, "If you can find any person anywhere professing to have any proposition of Jefferson Davis, in writing, for peace, embracing the restoration of the Union and abandonment of slavery, whatever else it embraces, say to him he may come to me with you."[7] Greeley then engaged in an active correspondence with Sanders using Jewett as a go-between.

In a series of letters between Sanders and Greeley that began on July 10 and continued almost daily, Greeley attempted to arrange safe conduct for the Confederate representatives by giving assurances to Lincoln that the Confederates were duly empowered to represent Jefferson Davis. Greeley quickly recognized that Clay, Thompson, and Holcombe enjoyed the confidence of the Confederate government, while Sanders remained on the periphery, having suffered a loss of confidence as a result of his shady financial dealings in England. Greeley wrote the three legitimate Confederate agents residing at the Clifton House Hotel on the Canadian side of Niagara Falls on July 17. In his communication, Greeley stated that Sanders had informed him that the three men were "duly accredited from Richmond as the bearers of propositions looking to the establishment of peace."[8] The Confederates quickly responded the next day that they were in the "confidential employment" of the Confederate government, but were not "authorized" to negotiate with Washington.[9] Greeley, recognizing that he had overstated the authority of the Confederate envoys to Lincoln, asked the Confederates to await further instructions from Lincoln.

On July 20, Greeley received a short letter addressed to "whom it may concern" from Lincoln. This letter is important because it clearly states the conditions on which Lincoln was prepared to negotiate a cease-fire. He wrote, "Any proposition which embraces the restoration of peace, the integrity of the whole Union, the abandonment of slavery, and which comes by and with an authority that can control the army now at war against the United States, will be received and considered by the executive government of the United States, and will be met by liberal terms on substantial and collateral points, and the bearer or bearers thereof shall have safe conduct both ways."[10]

Greeley, accompanied by Major John Hay, one of Lincoln's personal secretaries, proceeded to deliver the communication to Professor Holcombe on July 20. The two men were met at Clifton House by Sanders, who was described by Hay as "a seedy looking Rebel, with grissled whiskers and a flavor of clo'."[11] Sanders led them to

Professor Holcombe's room, where Hay and Greeley presented the president's message. Holcombe said he would contact his colleagues and provide Greeley with a response by the next day.

The lengthy response to Lincoln's "to-whom-it-may-concern" letter was provided not to Greeley but to Jewett on July 20. The Confederates claimed to be concerned about "the most momentous decision ever submitted to human statesmanship," but said they failed to understand "[w]hat may be the explanation of this sudden and entire change in the views of the President, of this rude withdrawal of a courteous overture for negotiation."[12] The Confederate response, signed by Clay and Holcombe, was clearly an attempt to embarrass the president to create political difficulties in the forthcoming election.

Jewett received the letter and immediately provided the text to local newspapers for publication. The Lincoln administration quickly disavowed Jewett as a representative of the government, claiming he was, in fact, a Southern conspirator. Greeley had already returned to New York from Niagara Falls, leaving the matter in the hands of Jewett. Although Greeley's timely departure might suggest his participation in a "grand scheme" to embarrass the administration, it is more likely that he was caught up in a clumsy but sincere attempt to arrange a peaceful settlement for his war-torn country.[13]

Meanwhile, in one final desperate attempt to obtain European intervention, Benjamin and Davis decided to emancipate Southern slaves in exchange for European intervention. This surprising shift in the Confederate president's position first appeared in his message to Congress on November 7, 1864. His message called for the employment of slaves in government jobs, such as cooks, teamsters, and hospital attendants.[14] While this proposal was not very radical, since Congress had already authorized such activities several months earlier, the surprise was Davis's call for the government to purchase slaves rather than impress them into service. The president went on to say that, in exchange for loyal service, the government should "liberate the Negro on his discharge after service faithfully rendered."[15] Congressional reaction to President Davis's suggestion was generally negative and led Benjamin to suggest that the forthcoming diplomatic mission to Europe be top secret.

Benjamin, aware of the desperate situation confronting the Confederacy, convinced Davis that they should offer the Europeans emancipation and all of the government's cotton at a bargain price in exchange for recognition. Davis reluctantly agreed with his adviser and accepted the secretary of state's recommendation that he appoint Duncan F. Kenner, a long-time Louisiana friend and political associate of Benjamin, as a special commissioner to communicate the offer to the Europeans.[16]

Kenner had advocated emancipation as part of a package to obtain recognition as early as 1863. In the political aftermath of the Emancipation Proclamation, Kenner believed that slavery was a major obstacle to European recognition. He approached his old friend and colleague, Judah Benjamin, with the suggestion that Confederate commissioners engage the Europeans in discussions to determine an acceptable position to them. Although Benjamin tended to agree with Kenner's enlightened position, President Davis had traditionally opposed emancipation. Before they could undertake any initiative involving emancipation of the slaves, Kenner and Benjamin had to convince Davis that slavery's preservation was hopeless. Davis, however, pointed out that the Confederate constitution, in Article 1, Section 9, explicitly prohibited Congress from passing any law "denying or impairing the right of property in Negro slaves."[17] Davis was well aware that the right to slave property was a right guaranteed by each state and was one of the fundamental reasons the Southern states decided to secede. Kenner, therefore, decided in 1863 not to propose to Congress his idea of emancipation in exchange for European recognition. If slavery was a major stumbling block in the path of recognition, 1863 would have been the time to remove it before military defeat was obvious.

By late 1864, the desperate military situation confronting the Confederacy called for more troops and supplies to turn back the Union army. The only probable source was in Europe. With public opinion, as demonstrated in newspaper editorials throughout the South, now supporting the use of slaves in the defense of the remaining Confederate territory, Benjamin was able to convince the president to offer total emancipation in exchange for European recognition.[18] Davis decided that the political and legal consequences of this decision required not only secrecy, but a person with political influence and good judgment to carry the message to the Europeans.

The obvious choice was Kenner, who had served faithfully in the Confederate Congress and who was one of the wealthiest men in the South. The Louisiana lawyer and planter was a former partner of both Benjamin and John Slidell and owned 473 slaves at the outbreak of hostilities. Davis met with Kenner in late December to discuss what turned out to be the last desperate Confederate diplomatic initiative to gain recognition.[19]

While Kenner was willing to accept the mission, he was well aware that his old friends Slidell and Mason held strong feelings with re-

gard to slavery and never allowed any serious discussion of emancipation to enter previous diplomatic overtures. Kenner, therefore, insisted that the president, through the secretary of state, give him
authority to overrule, if necessary, the Confederate commissioners
residing in Europe. On December 27, Benjamin wrote detailed instructions to Mason and Slidell and entrusted the dispatches to Kenner
for personal delivery. The instructions included Kenner's requested
authority as well as an outline of both the emancipation proposal and
specific instructions from the recently appointed secretary of the treasury, George A. Trenholm, about how to obtain the Confederacy's
cotton.[20]

On January 12, Kenner left Richmond by train for Wilmington,
North Carolina, the Confederacy's last open port on the East Coast,
to board a blockade runner for his escape to Europe. Unfortunately,
by the time he arrived at Wilmington, the city was under attack and
the Confederate fortifications at Fort Fisher were being bombarded.
Kenner was forced to return to Richmond. Determined to complete
his mission, he slipped through Union lines and traveled in disguise
to New York, where he boarded a passenger ship to England. His
escape in the frigid winter across the Potomac was hazardous and
risky, but with the aid of old friends from his prewar associations, he
made good his escape.[21]

On February 21, 1865, after ten days on the rough and bitterly
cold North Atlantic, the *America,* with Kenner aboard, docked in
Southampton. The Southern agent left immediately for London to
meet Mason, only to discover the Virginian was in Paris meeting with
Slidell. Recognizing that time was of the essence, Kenner sent telegrams to Dudley Mann in Brussels, as well as to Mason and Slidell, to
meet him in Paris to discuss his mission.[22] The newly appointed Confederate diplomat explained his plan to Slidell, Mason, and Mann at
Slidell's office in the Paris Grand Hotel. As Kenner had expected,
Slidell, and particularly Mason, were reluctant to endorse emancipation. Mann, however, recognized the necessity of such overtures and
supported the concept. Kenner was unable to convince Mason to
cooperate without showing him his written authority from Benjamin.[23]

The experienced European diplomats convinced Kenner that the
best strategy would be to approach Lord Palmerston in London first,
because the French had repeatedly expressed a willingness to follow
the British lead. Accepting this advice, Kenner returned to London
with Mason to request an interview with Palmerston. Although
Kenner and Mason arrived in London on March 3, Mason continued to delay the negotiations, arguing that the time was not right

for such a proposal because the war news was so negative. News that Charleston had been evacuated and Columbia burned arrived during the first week of March. While Mason continued to await further developments, Slidell approached the French emperor on the afternoon of March 4.[24] Napoleon once again told Slidell of his sympathy for the Southern cause but refused to take any initiative. When Slidell raised the issue of emancipation, the emperor replied that although the English might have been deterred by the question of slavery, the issue had never influenced his decision concerning the Confederacy.[25]

Finally, on the morning of March 14, Mason, unaccompanied by Kenner, went to see Palmerston. Although instructed to communicate the emancipation proposal, Mason did not plainly introduce the subject. Because of his personal belief that the British refusal to recognize the Confederacy stemmed from a purely economic motivation and had little to do with the slavery issue, he only made oblique references to the South's willingness to abolish slavery. Finally, Palmerston responded by denying that slavery was the issue preventing recognition. The prime minister told Mason that it was the South's failure to achieve military success that prevented British recognition and that sadly for his cause, "nothing could be done to prevent the death of the Confederacy."[26]

Within a week, Richmond fell, and on April 9, the surrender of Lee's army at the Appomattox Court House confirmed the hopelessness of the Kenner mission. Kenner petitioned the U.S. government on June 20, 1865, at the legation in Paris to take the oath of allegiance prescribed by President Andrew Johnson in his Amnesty Proclamation. Unlike many of the Confederates residing in Europe, Kenner returned in August to Ashland, his Louisiana plantation.[27]

The Kenner mission was doomed to failure from its conception because it was not the institution of slavery that prevented the Europeans from recognizing the Confederacy. It was the absence of any threat to the vital interests of the Continental powers that prevented recognition or intervention. Both Napoleon and Palmerston, the leading policymakers of their respective nations, explained to Slidell and Mason, even as the Confederacy was collapsing, that slavery was not their main concern.[28]

Late in 1864, while Kenner was accomplishing his dramatic escape from the crumbling Confederacy to pursue the last foreign Confederate diplomatic initiative, Davis decided to pursue peace negotiations directly with the Lincoln administration. The fall of Fort Fisher had convinced many congressmen and Senator Robert M. T. Hunter that "we cannot carry on the war any longer" and should "make terms with the enemy, on the basis of the old Union."[29] Alexander Stephens called the loss of Fort Fisher "one of the greatest disasters that had befallen our cause from the beginning of the war."[30] With the Union armies on the outskirts of Richmond, the survival of the Confederacy was at stake.

With the mood in Richmond favorably disposed to peace negotiations as a result of the rapidly deteriorating military situation, Davis decided to act on a proposal of Francis Preston Blair. Blair, an old Jacksonian Democrat, knew Davis well from prewar politics within the Democratic Party, and approached Davis with a proposal for North-South reunification. Blair's idea involved a joint action by the North and South to expel the French from Mexico. The proposed military convention would temporarily suspend hostilities between the North and South and allow both governments to direct their full military power against the French threat. During this "reunited period," statesmen could negotiate the outstanding sectional problems and extend the temporary truce to a permanent peace.[31]

Blair had badgered Lincoln for some time to endorse his Mexican proposal. Lincoln, however, wanted nothing to do with Blair's proposed military adventure but allowed Blair to pursue a peace conference. Blair obtained from Lincoln a safe-conduct pass enabling him to pass safely through the lines to meet with Davis in Richmond.

Davis, for his part, expected little change in Lincoln's previously stated conditions for settlement. The demand for "unconditional submission" outlined in the Niagara Falls correspondence was unacceptable to the South. The Confederate president, however, saw an opportunity to encourage and stiffen Southern resistance by publicly articulating Lincoln's demands while demonstrating his government's willingness to negotiate to obtain peace. Davis again failed to accept the realities of the military situation and believed, along with other die-hards, that the South could fight on.[32] With these thoughts in mind, Davis authorized Blair to communicate to Lincoln that he was ready to "enter into conference with a view to secure peace to two countries." Lincoln quickly responded that he was ready to receive the Southern overtures "with the view of securing peace to the people of one common country."[33]

Davis's communication and Lincoln's response define the fundamental reason that peace could not be obtained through negotiation. The key phrase in Davis's letter is "two countries." Lincoln, on the other hand, defines the fundamental difference when he includes the phrase "securing peace to the people of one common country."[34]

Clearly, reunion is implied in Lincoln's offer to entertain Southern representatives, while Davis expresses the South's continued commitment to separation. Although the Southern commissioners would ultimately raise the issue of military intervention in Mexico, Davis apparently did not expect this issue to form the basis for negotiations. Blair was by no means the first to suggest that external threats to the "old United States" could form a basis for uniting against a common adversary. The strategy was never accepted with sufficient enthusiasm by either side to provide a basis for settlement. It was the desperate situation and the impending collapse of the Confederacy that made Blair's proposal appear as a viable option.[35]

Davis decided to appoint three commissioners who were prominent advocates of a negotiated peace to conduct the negotiations for the Confederacy. He probably believed that the negotiations were determined to fail and that this would embarrass and discredit the leading advocates of a negotiated peace, who also spearheaded Davis's political opposition. The commission was made up of Vice President Alexander Stephens, Robert M. T. Hunter, now serving as president of the Senate, and John A. Campbell, assistant secretary of war. Campbell, a former Supreme Court justice, had represented the Confederacy in Washington during the winter of 1860–61 at the height of the secession crisis. At that time, too, he had advocated a negotiated settlement. Even though Campbell had resigned his position on the U.S. Supreme Court, he was branded in the South as a traitor to his section and his talents were underutilized by the Confederacy throughout the war. Hunter's political ambitions and opposition to the president led to his resignation as secretary of state to pursue a career in the Senate, where he opposed the policies of Davis, even though he was committed, because of his ambitions to become president, to separation from the Union. The basis of Stephens's opposition to the president was the issue of states' rights. He continued to oppose the "centralizing" policies of the Davis administration, despite the military necessity that required their adoption.

The three Confederate commissioners were scheduled to meet with Secretary of State William H. Seward at Hampton Roads. Lincoln decided at the last minute, however, to join Seward at the conference. The face-to-face meeting, lasting approximately four hours, took place on February 3, 1865, on the Union steamer *River Queen*. Lincoln's earlier instruction to Seward contained the basis for Union negotiations and included "(1) the restoration of the national authority throughout *all* the states; (2) no rescinding by the executive of the United States on the slavery question; (3) no cessation of hostilities short of an end to the war and the disbanding of all forces hostile to the settlement."[36]

Each of the Confederate representatives pursued a part of the Southern agenda. First, Stephens feebly pursued the Blair suggestion of a military intervention in Mexico. It was quickly rejected by Lincoln, who explained that Blair acted without any official authorization to introduce such a proposal. Next, Hunter pursued the idea of an armistice and introduced the constitutional arguments for separation of the Union. Lincoln rejected the idea of an armistice and said the only means of stopping the war was the complete surrender of all Confederate armed forces. Hunter continued by suggesting to Lincoln that even Charles I had entered into agreements with rebels against his government during the English civil war. Lincoln replied, "I do not profess to be posted in history, and all I can distinctly recollect about the case of Charles I, is, that he lost his head."[37]

It remained for the moderate Judge Campbell to pursue what at first appeared to be reasonable and obtainable Southern objectives. He questioned Lincoln and Seward about their plans for punishing Rebel leaders and confiscating property, particularly property in slaves. Lincoln promised generous treatment based on his power to use the "presidential pardon." On the question of emancipation, Lincoln suggested the possibility of compensating owners to the amount of $400 million, provided the Southern states would ratify the Thirteenth Amendment. Seward, entering the conversation, suggested that the Southern representatives' return to Washington might create gradual emancipation and delay the effects of the Thirteenth Amendment while ensuring partial compensation for emancipated slaves.[38]

Campbell, demonstrating his knowledge of constitutional law, then asked Seward who would decide the issue of emancipation if the Thirteenth Amendment was defeated in the Senate after a return of the Southern constituency. Seward responded that the decision would remain for the Supreme Court.[39] Lincoln stood by his wartime actions against slavery and said that no slave freed by these acts could ever be re-enslaved. Campbell then asked which slaves had been freed by Union action, and a heated discussion followed. Ultimately, Lincoln remained resolute in his commitment to emancipate the slaves, but willing to negotiate favorable conditions to obtain post-war Southern cooperation.[40]

It is reasonable to assume that both Lincoln and Seward were prepared to accept a generous peace settlement that did not necessarily include immediate universal emancipation. The accounts of both Stephens and Hunter suggest that the two Northerners were prepared to support the liberal use of the presidential pardon and compensation for emancipated slaves as a means to reconstruct the Union. The one issue remaining clear throughout the evidence is Lincoln's and Seward's commitment to reconstruction of the Union, while the Southerners persisted in their demands for two separate nations. Campbell's account, probably more accurate than the later recollections of Stephens and Hunter, suggests that both Lincoln and Seward were firmly committed to universal emancipation and to the Thirteenth Amendment. In any case, it is clear that Lincoln was prepared to arrange generous terms and possibly gradual emancipation that would have allowed the South to avoid the complete loss of substantial capital investments in slave property and allow for "face-saving" grounds to surrender the Confederate army.[41]

Ultimately the proposal the three Confederate representatives brought back to Richmond was simply to surrender the South's military forces unconditionally to prevent further bloodshed. In exchange for immediate surrender, Southerners received Lincoln's and Seward's commitments to the liberal use of the presidential pardon and protection against the confiscation of property. The protection of property rights did not extend, however, to slavery. After preparing their report and presenting it to President Davis, the three commissioners were pressured by Davis to include such phrases as "degrading submission" and "humiliating surrender." The three Southern participants at the Hampton Roads conference, aware that Davis wanted to discredit the whole idea of surrender and negotiations, unanimously refused to include the inflammatory phrases requested.

Davis decided to include the objectionable phrases in a message to Congress on February 6 that accompanied the report of the commissioners. He told the Confederate Congress that the South must fight on and never submit to the "disgrace of surrender." Referring to the Northern president as "His Majesty Abraham I," Davis went on to suggest that Southern armies would "compel the Yankees, in less than twelve months, to petition us for peace on our own terms."[42] Although Davis received editorial support for his speech throughout the South, most informed Southerners recognized that the end was near. It is unfortunate for the South that this final opportunity for a diplomatic settlement was lost. While the goal of two nations was not attainable, it is likely that a surrender of the armed forces would have produced support in the North for moderate reconstruction.

When the combined news of the failed Hampton Roads conference and the military disasters in Virginia and South Carolina reached Europe, any hope that the Kenner mission would succeed was lost.

Amazingly, the Confederates were prepared to accept emancipation in exchange for European support, while refusing to make similar concessions on the slavery issue to their Northern adversaries. The Union officials were prepared, at least unofficially, to negotiate concessions from late 1864 to obtain peace. Lincoln was involved in a fight for his political life in the fall of 1864, but the Confederacy failed to capitalize on the diplomatic opportunities presented by the war-weary opposition to the president. Any negotiated separation was unobtainable, but a well-designed strategy presenting a peace alternative originating in the South would have prevented the destruction and devastation of large areas of the South by an often vindictive Union army.[43]

Davis and Benjamin realized the hopelessness of their military situation, as evidenced by the Kenner mission to obtain European intervention at any cost. Yet, these desperate men were prepared to allow the insincerity of negotiations at Niagara Falls and to send Confederate commissioners to Hampton Roads with the preconceived notion that they would fail. The Confederate leadership, by this point, believed the cost in blood and treasure was too high to allow any surrender of their commitment to a separate nation.

Chapter 15

The Legacy of Failure

Ultimately, the dream of Southerners to create an independent nation was lost on the battlefield, at places like Shiloh, Gettysburg, and Chattanooga. Despite the dramatic impact of sporadic Confederate victories, diplomats were burdened with battlefield news that indicated the inability of the Southern army and navy to defend their territorial integrity. A successful diplomatic strategy that obtained either European recognition or a negotiated settlement with the Union would have ensured the existence of the Confederacy as a sovereign, independent nation. Although slavery was not the reason Southern diplomats failed, it did contribute to their burden. The existence of a sovereign nation that allowed slavery was accepted, as in Brazil for example; but to recognize a new nation tolerating slavery was quite a different matter.[1]

Confederate diplomatic failure resulted from a number of complex and interconnected reasons, not the least of which was an overreliance on economic leverage. From the early initiatives of Yancey to the desperate attempts of Slidell just before the end, the misguided commitment to King Cotton diplomacy burdened the Confederate diplomatic effort. Although cotton textile manufacturing was an important component of the European economy, other economic activity compensated for the reduction in textile output. Increased naval construction, munitions sales, and a substantial increase in the shipping business sustained the economies of Great Britain and France. Southerners failed to recognize the difference between the integrated and diverse economies of Europe and their own economy that depended on agriculture to sustain it. Hence, the Europeans were prepared to allow the battlefield to determine if and when Confederate independence would be recognized.

The Confederate State Department under Judah Benjamin eventually recognized that withholding cotton to create an artificial shortage created more domestic hardship than diplomatic influence. Even though Benjamin initiated a change in strategy when he proposed to the French an exchange of cotton for direct intervention, the reliance on the power of cotton persisted. Europeans were convinced that the South could sustain itself in a defensive war, and that even without outside intervention, the American Civil War would ultimately produce two separate nations. The two new nations would be noticeably weaker than one united nation, providing more opportunity for the European powers to expand their economic influence in the Western Hemisphere. Confederate diplomatic initiatives failed to recognize the economic realities or take into account the preconceived notions of Europe's leadership.[2]

The political situation in Europe, including Napoleon's move into Mexico, created both an opportunity and an obstacle for Confederate operatives in France. Napoleon's sympathetic attitude to the South was overcome by the realities of European politics requiring the cooperation of the British in any recognition or intervention response. Jefferson Davis and the Confederate leadership feared French expansion and reentry into the Western Hemisphere. The result was an inconsistent and poorly conceived strategy to form a military alliance with the French in Mexico. Any military arrangement with the French was out of the question because the Confederacy was too weak to make any substantial military contribution to the French effort in Mexico. Certainly when compared to the risk of a French war with the North, the South had little to offer in exchange for French support. The Southern people, although committed to slavery and racial labor control, remained concerned with any European return to the Western Hemisphere, much as their brothers to the North. Southern nationalism existed, but only within a greater sense of Americanism. Once slavery was doomed, Southerners returned to the old Union and accepted their role in the reunited states of America.

During the independence movement, Mason and Slidell were continually burdened by a well-conceived and directed Union diplomatic effort led by the relentless William H. Seward. Ably assisted by Adams in London and Dayton in Paris, the U.S. secretary of state consistently dictated the parameters of the diplomatic debate. The Confederates frequently found their initiatives defeated before they could get underway. Seward effectively identified the vulnerability of Canada to U.S. military operations and bluffed and maneuvered the British and French ministers in Washington. Both Lyons and Mercier believed that the South would ultimately be successful in separating from the Union, but continually counseled caution and delay because of Seward's belligerent and aggressive diplomatic tactics.[3]

The European powers thus decided to leave the American war to the Americans. Their decision to remain neutral was not based on any high moral commitment. The lofty platitudes of the antislavery advocates were quickly overwhelmed by the forces of enlightened self-interest. The French had little moral hesitation in their effort to exploit Mexico. The British frequently demonstrated a willingness to use force in India and other colonies. The issue of slavery allowed European liberals and opponents of Southern recognition to take the moral high ground. However, it was the almost universal commitment to imperial objectives and a balance of power that deterred the Europeans. Great Britain was already a giant imperial power and had shunned a deeper involvement in South and Central America because of the expense and requirements of further territorial acquisitions. Napoleon, although favorably disposed to the Confederate cause, was persuaded not to act except jointly with the British. Moreover, any encouragement from the British to intervene in the American conflict was perceived by Napoleon as an attempt to overextend and weaken France on the Continent. Both French foreign ministers, Thouvenel and Drouyn de Lhuys, were committed to nonintervention. They felt France was vulnerable because of the political situation on the Continent.

Confederate diplomats operating in this atmosphere of power politics, with its global implications, were poorly equipped by experience and training to deal with the world of realpolitik. There was little chance that the Confederates could overcome the reluctance of the British. The Palmerston government and the loyal opposition led by Disraeli both appreciated the high cost of involvement. The British minister of war, George Cornwall Lewis, was convinced that any involvement in the American Civil War would be a terrible mistake. It was clear to Palmerston that any military undertaking in the United States would weaken Great Britain's ability to influence Continental politics by separating its resources. Seward, although probably not

comprehending completely the international scene, was in possession of an established worldwide diplomatic apparatus and was more
effective than his Confederate opponents in reinforcing the conservative thinking of European leadership. Seward also emphasized the
differences between French and British interests in order to prevent
any joint action against the United States.[4]

The outcome of the American Civil War was often in doubt, because both sides possessed military advantages and both governments
were responsible to their respective electorates. The American Union,
to a large extent, is indebted to the power politics of Europe for its
existence. Assistance from France had ensured the success of the
American Revolution. The French Revolution and Napoleonic Wars
allowed the United States to secure its territory and mature as a sovereign nation without the threat of European power. The commitment of the Europeans during the 1820s and 1830s to the realignment of the Colonial map allowed the United States to increase its
hegemony in the Western Hemisphere. Hence, the failure of the
Confederate diplomats to secure the support of a European power,
as their forefathers did during the American Revolution, contributed
substantially to the preservation of the Union.

The Confederate diplomatic effort focused on the overriding objective of recognition and accompanying intervention. The Confederate approach to this goal reflected the ideological foundations of
the people who seceded from the Union. Their commitment to reactionary and counterrevolutionary values is evidenced in their commitment to a caste social system and a desire to preserve the "virtuous" rural plantation lifestyle. Their belief in aristocracy and traditional
republican values forced them to resist the sweeping tide of liberal-
ism and the new market economy produced by the industrial revolution of the nineteenth century. Confederate diplomats often spoke of
free and open trade with the Europeans as an inducement to recognition, but paradoxically, they continued to rely on economic coercion
anchored on an artificially created cotton shortage.[5]

In many ways, the Southern Americans who sought to create a
new nation wanted to preserve traditional American Southern values
and prevent the power of a centralizing government from encroaching on those values. Much like the Union, the Confederate war aims
changed substantially as the war progressed. The original commitment to slavery gradually subsided and by 1864, many Confederate
leaders strongly advocated the end of slavery and a body of federal
laws to control a black underclass. The commitment to states' rights
quickly subsided because of the centralizing needs of the war effort.

The Confederate constitution provided the State Department with the power to negotiate treaties with foreign nations and conduct an active diplomacy in pursuit of Confederate interest abroad. Southern states relinquished, after the lessons of government under the Articles of Confederation, sufficient power to a federalized, constitutional government to engage in a massive military and diplomatic effort.[6]

Confederate diplomacy failed to overcome a host of burdens in order to achieve its ultimate objective of European recognition or intervention. Further, the Confederate State Department bungled opportunities to negotiate favorable terms to either coexist with the old Union or end the war. Diplomatic failure contributed, as much as any other element, to Confederate defeat and reflected the values of a people committed to the traditions of a dying past.

Notes

Abbreviations

In citing works in the notes, short titles have generally been used. Works frequently cited have been identified by the following abbreviations:

A.M.A.E., E.U.	Archives du Ministere des Affaires, Etats-Unis, Paris.
FRUS	Dept. of State. *Papers Relating to the Foreign Affairs (Relations) of the United States, 1861–1865.* 15 vols. Washington, D.C.: Government Printing Office, 1862–66. Reprint, New York: Kraus Corp., 1965.
Hansard's	*Hansard's Parliamentary Debates.* Edited by Thomas C. Hansard. 3d ser., 356 vols. London: Wyman, 1830–91. (Copy Special Collection, Univ. of Tennessee, Knoxville, Tenn.)
Index	Papers and correspondence of Henry Hotze (including complete collection of *Index*). R. W. Woodruff Library, Emory Univ., Atlanta, Ga.

ORA   Dept. of the Army. *Official Records of the Union
               and Confederate Armies in the War of the Rebel-
               lion.* Washington, D.C.: Government Printing
               Office, 1894–1927.
ORN   Dept. of the Navy. *Official Records of the Union
               and Confederate Navies in the War of the Rebel-
               lion* and index. 30 vols. Series 1, vols. 1–27; Se-
               ries 2, vols. 1–3. Washington, D.C.: Government
               Printing Office, 1894–1927.
Times   London *Times.*

Preface

1.   Frank L. Owsley, *King Cotton Diplomacy: Foreign Relations of the Confederate States of America* (Chicago: Univ. of Chicago Press, 1st ed. 1936, 2d ed., 1959); Brian Jenkins, *Britain and the War for the Union,* 2 vols. (Montreal and London: McGill-Queen's Univ. Press, 1973); Norman B. Ferris, *Desperate Diplomacy: William H. Seward's Foreign Policy, 1861* (Knoxville: Univ. of Tennessee Press, 1976) and *The Trent Affair: A Diplomatic Crisis* (Knoxville: Univ. of Tennessee Press, 1977); Howard Jones, *Union in Peril: The Crisis over British Intervention in the Civil War* (Chapel Hill and London: Univ. of North Carolina Press, 1992); Frank J. Merli, *Great Britain and the Confederate Navy, 1861–1865* (Bloomington: Indiana Univ. Press, 1970); Douglas B. Ball, *Financial Failure and Confederate Defeat* (Champaign: Univ. of Illinois Press, 1991).

Introduction

1.   Richard E. Beringer, Herman Hattaway, Archer Jones, and William N. Still Jr., *Why the South Lost the Civil War* (Athens: Univ. of Georgia Press, 1986); Richard N. Current, "God and the Strongest Battalions," in *Why the North Won the Civil War,* ed. David Donald (Baton Rouge: Louisiana State Univ. Press, 1960; reprint, New York: Collier Books, 1963), 15–32.

2.   Richard E. Beringer, Herman Hattaway, Archer Jones, and William M. Still Jr., *The Elements of Confederate Defeat: Nationalism, War Aims, and Religion* (Athens: Univ. of Georgia Press, 1986), ch. 2; Drew G. Faust, *The Creation of Confederate Nationalism: Ideology and Identity in the Civil War South* (Baton Rouge: Louisiana State Univ. Press, 1988), introduction.

3.   Norman Graebner, "Northern Diplomacy and European Neutrality," in *Why the North Won the Civil War,* ed. David Donald (Baton Rouge: Louisiana State Univ. Press, 1960; reprint, New York: Collier Books, 1963), 55–78; Ferris, *Desperate Diplomacy;* Owsley, *King Cotton Diplomacy.*

4.   Owsley, *King Cotton Diplomacy;* Howard Jones, *Union in Peril;* Jenkins, *Britain and the War;* David P. Crook, *The North, the South, and the Powers* (New York: John Wiley & Sons, 1974); Ferris, *Desperate Diplomacy.*

5.   Gavin Wright, *Old South, New South: Revolution in Southern Economy Since the Civil War* (New York: Basic Books, 1986), 22–30; Owsley, *King Cotton Diplomacy,* ch. 1.

6.   Owsley, *King Cotton Diplomacy;* Lynn M. Case and Warren F. Spencer, *The*

United States and France: Civil War Diplomacy (Philadelphia: Univ. of Pennsylvania Press, 1970).

1. The Diplomacy of Secession

1. David M. Potter, *The Impending Crisis, 1848–1861* (New York: Harper & Row, 1976), 524–63; Emory M. Thomas, *The Confederate Nation* (New York: Harper & Row, 1979), 167–88; E. Merton Coulter, *The Confederate States of America, 1861–1865* (Baton Rouge: Louisiana State Univ. Press, 1950), 84–99.

2. William C. Davis, *Jefferson Davis: The Man and His Hour* (New York: Harper Collins, 1991), 224–27; Clement Eaton, *Jefferson Davis* (New York: The Free Press, 1977), 47–56; Varina H. Davis, *Jefferson Davis: A Memoir by His Wife*, 2 vols. (New York, 1890), 1: 56–71. Jefferson Davis wrote most of this two volume memoir expecting it to be an autobiography, but his wife completed the work after his death in 1889. Burton J. Hendrick, *Statesmen of the Lost Cause: Jefferson Davis and His Cabinet* (New York: Literary Guild, 1939), 263.

3. William Davis, *Jefferson Davis*, 193–95.

4. Ibid., 222–25; Eaton, *Jefferson Davis*, 82–88.

5. Eric Foner, "Politics, Ideology, and the Origins of the American Civil War," in *Politics and Ideology in the Age of the Civil War* (New York: Oxford Univ. Press, 1980), 34–57.

6. James L. Roark, *Masters without Slaves: Southern Planters in the Civil War and Reconstruction* (New York: W. W. Norton & Co., 1977), 24–32; Emory M. Thomas, *The Confederacy as a Revolutionary Experience* (Englewood Cliffs, N.J.: Prentice Hall, 1971; reprint, Columbia: Univ. of South Carolina Press, 1991).

7. Coulter, *The Confederate States*, 19–26.

8. Allan Nevins, *Ordeal of the Union, 1847–1857*, vol. 1, *The Ordeal of the Union: The War for the Union* (New York: Charles Scribner's Sons, 1947), 38; James M. McPherson, *Battle Cry of Freedom: The Civil War Era* (New York: Oxford Univ. Press, 1988), 202–17.

9. Michael F. Holt, "James Buchanan, 1857–1861," in *Responses of the Presidents to Charges of Misconduct*, ed. C. Vann Woodward (New York: Basic Books, 1974), 86–96; Allan Nevins, *The Emergence of Lincoln, 1857–1861*, vol. 3, *The Ordeal of the Union: The War for the Union* (New York: Charles Scribner's Sons, 1950), 196–200, 372–75.

10. David Herbert Donald, *Lincoln* (New York: Simon & Schuster, 1995).

11. James G. Randall, *Lincoln the President: Springfield to Bull Run*, 4 vols. (New York: Dodd, Mead & Co., 1956), 1: 288–91; Glyndon G. Van Deusen, *William H. Seward* (New York: Oxford Univ. Press, 1967).

2. The Failure of Diplomacy Produces War

1. Clement Eaton, *A History of the Southern Confederacy* (New York: Macmillan, 1954).

2. James M. Matthews, ed., *The Statutes at Large of the Provisional Government of the Confederate States of America*, 3 vols. (Richmond, Va.: R. M. Smith, 1864), 36–38; Confederate States, *Journal of the Congress of the Confederate States of America, 1861–1865*, 6 vols. (Washington, D.C.: Government Printing Office, 1904–5; reprint, New York: Kraus, 1968), 5: 404–7; E. Merton Coulter, "The Effects of Secession upon the Commerce of the Mississippi Valley," *Mississippi Valley Historical Review* 3 (1916–17): 280.

3.   Coulter, *The Confederate States,* 120–21; Emory Thomas, *The Confederate Nation,* 72–80; Jefferson Davis, *The Rise and Fall of the Confederate Government,* 2 vols. (New York: D. Appleton, 1881).

4.   James D. Richardson, ed., *Compilations of Messages and Papers of Jefferson Davis and the Confederacy,* 2 vols. (Nashville: U.S. Publishing Co., 1905; reprint, New York: Chelsea House, 1966), 1: 318–691. In addition to the instructions from Davis to the Washington commissioners, many documents regarding the seizing of forts and arsenals throughout the Confederacy are included; Rembert W. Patrick, *Jefferson Davis and His Cabinet* (Baton Rouge: Louisiana Univ. Press, 1944), 27–45.

5.   Richard N. Current, *Lincoln and the First Shot* (Philadelphia and New York: J. B. Lippincott Co., 1963), 142–43. The distance and inaccessibility of Key West allowed the naval station there to remain under Union control throughout the war.

6.   Nevins, *The Emergence of Lincoln,* 3: 380–83.

7.   Martin J. Crawford to Robert Toombs, Mar. 3, 1861, Robert Toombs, Papers, Univ. of South Carolina Library (hereafter cited as Toombs Papers).

8.   Phillip Shaw Paludan, *The Presidency of Abraham Lincoln* (Lawrence: Univ. Press of Kansas, 1994), 32–35; Eric Foner, "Politics," 42–44.

9.   Benjamin P. Thomas, *Abraham Lincoln* (New York: Alfred A. Knopf, 1952), 230–34.

10.   Donald, *Lincoln,* 208–10; Paludan, *The Presidency of Abraham Lincoln,* 60–62.

11.   Donald, *Lincoln,* 289–93.

12.   Henry Cleveland, *Alexander H. Stephens, in Public and Private, with Letters and Speeches, Before, During and Since the War* (Philadelphia, 1866), 152; McPherson, *Battle Cry of Freedom,* 264–67.

13.   Potter, *The Impending Crisis,* 573.

14.   Van Deusen, *William H. Seward,* 278, 599.

15.   Ibid., 563; Current, *Lincoln and the First Shot,* 63–74.

16.   Although North Carolina was not adjacent to the border, its belated secession associated it with the upper-South border states.

17.   McPherson, *Battle Cry of Freedom,* 277–79.

18.   Charles Lewis Wagandt, *The Mighty Revolution: Negro Emancipation in Maryland, 1862–1864* (Baltimore: Johns Hopkins Univ. Press, 1964), 17.

19.   Van Deusen, *William H. Seward,* 278. Van Deusen points out that Seward's political ally and friend, Thurlow Weed, claimed later that the President "had told three different men he would surrender Sumter if by so doing, he could keep Virginia in the Union."

20.   James D. Richardson, ed., *Compilations of Messages and Papers of the Confederacy, Including Diplomatic Correspondence, 1861–1865,* 2 vols. (Nashville: U.S. Publishing Co., 1905), 1: 96; Paludan, *The Presidency of Abraham Lincoln,* 89–93; Donald, *Lincoln,* 296–301; Coulter, *The Confederate States,* 37–39.

21.   Emory Thomas, *The Confederate Nation,* 81; Potter, *The Impending Crisis,* 575–76.

22.   William Howard Russell, *William Howard Russell's Civil War Private Diary and Letters, 1861–1862,* ed. Martin Crawford (Athens: Univ. of Georgia Press, 1990), 26–27. This remark was made privately at a dinner party on Mar. 27 at Seward's home, or at a dinner on Mar. 28 with the President and his Cabinet, which Seward's daughter and son attended; also see Frederick W. Seward, ed., *Seward at Washington as Senator and Secretary of State: A Memoir of His Life with Selections from His Letters, 1861–1862,* 2 vols. (New York: Derby & Miller, 1891).

23.   Cleveland, *Alexander H. Stephens,* 154.

24.   Richardson, *Messages and Papers of the Confederacy*, 1: 63–64. In February, the Confederate Congress had passed secret resolutions declaring that "immediate steps should be taken to obtain possession of Forts Sumter and Pickens . . . either by negotiation or force"; Paludan, *The Presidency of Abraham Lincoln*, 38.

25.   Forsyth to secretary of war, Mar. 4, 1861, *ORA*, ser. 1, vol. 1: 283.

26.   Crawford to Toombs, Mar. 16, 1861, *ORA*, ser. 2, vol. 2: 258–60 (all references to *ORA* are to ser. 1 unless otherwise noted).

27.   Jefferson Davis, *The Rise and Fall*, 1: 311.

28.   Eaton, *Jefferson Davis*, 1365–67; McPherson, *Battle Cry of Freedom*.

29.   Forsyth to Walker, Apr. 6, 1861, *ORA*, vol. 1: 583; Crawford to Toombs, Apr. 8, 1861, *ORA*, vol. 1: 588.

30.   Current, *Lincoln and the First Shot*; Roy Meredith, *The Storm Over Sumter* (New York: Simon & Schuster, 1957); W. A. Swanberg, *First Blood: The Story of Fort Sumter* (New York: Charles Scribner's Sons, 1957). These historians present slightly different views and interpretations of the facts surrounding the Sumter crisis and the opening engagement of the war.

31.   Wagandt, *The Mighty Revolution*. Wagandt's book focuses on emancipation and the status of blacks in Maryland, but he provides an overview of Lincoln's strategy and methods to prevent Maryland from seceding and joining the Confederacy; Coulter, *The Confederate States*, 55–61; Paludan, *The Presidency of Abraham Lincoln*, 13–14, 18–19.

3. The Burden of Cotton

1.   Norman Rich, *Great Power Diplomacy, 1814–1914* (New York: McGraw-Hill, 1995), 158–62.

2.   Wilbur Devereux Jones, *The American Problem in British Diplomacy, 1841–1861* (Athens: Univ. of Georgia Press, 1974), 126; Kenneth Bourne, *Britain and the Balance of Power in North America, 1815–1908* (London: Longmans, Green & Co., 1967), 75–205. Both these studies provide an excellent overview of Anglo-American relations in the late antebellum period and place this period in broad historical perspective.

3.   Russell, *Russell's Civil War Private Diary*, introduction. In his introductory essay to this collection from the British correspondent's diary, Crawford explains the influence of the London *Times* on British popular opinion.

4.   David P. Crook, *Diplomacy during the American Civil War* (New York: John Wiley & Sons, 1975), 15–26; A. R. Tyrner-Tyrnauer, *Lincoln and the Emperors* (New York: Harcourt, Brace & World, 1962); Henry Kissinger, *Diplomacy* (New York: Alfred A. Knopf, 1993). Chapter 3 gives a discussion of European politics and diplomacy during this period.

5.   The phrase "King Cotton" was first articulated by David Christy in his famous *Cotton Is King: Or Slavery in the Light of Political Economy* (Cincinnati, 1855).

6.   Emory Thomas, *The Confederate Nation*, xi; Louis M. Sears, *John Slidell* (Durham, N.C.: Duke Univ. Press, 1925), 9–11; Eli N. Evans, *Judah P. Benjamin, the Jewish Confederate* (New York: Free Press, 1988), introduction. Ironically, a number of prominent leaders in the Confederate government, including members of the Cabinet, were born outside the Confederate states, either in Europe or the northern sections of America.

7.   Faust, *The Creation of Confederate Nationalism*, 80–81. Also see Frank L. Owsley's "Defeatism in the Confederacy," *North Carolina Historical Review* 3 (July

1926): 446–56, and Owsley's *States Rights in the Confederacy* (Chicago: Univ. of Chicago Press, 1925).

8.   Warren F. Spencer, *The Confederate Navy in Europe* (Tuscaloosa: Univ. of Alabama Press, 1983), 3–6; Tom Henderson Wells, *The Confederate Navy: A Study in Organization* (Tuscaloosa: Univ. of Alabama Press, 1971), 150–57; Beringer, Hattaway, Jones, and Still, *Why the South Lost*, 17–22; McPherson, *Battle Cry of Freedom*, 324–31.

9.   Ferris, *Desperate Diplomacy*, introduction. Ferris emphasizes the calculated risk undertaken by Seward immediately after secession that was both desperate and brilliant in its conception, enabling Union diplomats to seize the diplomatic initiative.

10.   *Punch*, 40, no. 134 (Mar. 30, 1861).

11.   Howard Russell, *William Howard Russell, My Diary North and South*, ed. Eugene H. Berwanger (Philadelphia: Temple Univ. Press, 1988), 70.

12.   Owsley, *King Cotton Diplomacy*, 38–44; Robert W. Fogel and Stanley L. Engerman, *Time on the Cross: The Economics of American Negro Slavery* (Boston: Little, Brown, 1974), 74–90.

13.   Eugene A. Brady, "A Reconsideration of the Lancashire 'Cotton Famine,'" *Agricultural History* 37 (July 1963): 156–62; Robert H. Holt, "Long Live the King?" *Agricultural History* 37 (July 1963): 166–69; Case and Spencer, *The United States and France*, 258–85; Emory Thomas, *The Confederate Nation*, 174–77.

14.   Owsley, *King Cotton Diplomacy*, 3–14; Henry Blumenthal, "Confederate Diplomacy: Popular Notions and International Realities," *Journal of Southern History* 32 (1966): 151–71.

15.   Wright, *Old South, New South*, ch. 1.

16.   Varina Davis, *Jefferson Davis*, 2: 160.

17.   Russell, *My Diary*, 70.

18.   For example, see the London *Times*, May 30 and July 10, 1861; also, Edwards to Russell in *Russell's Civil War Private Diary*, 12: 21.

19.   Russell, *My Diary*, 51.

20.   Robert Barnwell to Alexander Stephens, Feb. 9, 1861, Rhett to Robert Toombs, Feb. 13, 1861, in Richardson's *Messages and Papers of the Confederacy*, 1: 30–31.

21.   Eaton, *Jefferson Davis*, 164–67. "Cooperatists" were a group of leaders who believed that cooperation with the secessionists, temporarily, would allow time to convince the moderates to join the Unionists and return to the Union.

22.   Laura A. White, *Robert Barnwell Rhett: Father of Secession* (New York: Century Co., 1931; reprint, Gloucester: P. Smith Publishers, 1965), 195; Jefferson Davis, *The Rise and Fall*, 1: 241–42; Patrick, *Jefferson Davis and His Cabinet*, 50–52; William Davis, *Jefferson Davis*, 327–35. William Davis provides a general overview of the Rhett-Davis dispute.

23.   Wilfred Buck Yearns, *The Confederate Congress* (Athens: Univ. of Georgia Press, 1960), 165; Blumenthal, "Confederate Diplomacy," discusses possible alternatives to the cotton strategy.

24.   John W. DuBose, *The Life and Times of William Lowndes Yancey*, 2 vols. (reprint, New York: Peter Smith, 1942), 2: 600.

25.   Confederate States, *Journal of the Congress*, 1: 252–53, 257; White, *Robert Barnwell Rhett*, 263.

26.   Eaton, *Jefferson Davis*, 171–73.

27.   Yearns, *The Confederate Congress*, 166; Patrick, *Jefferson Davis and His Cabinet*, 221; Ball, *Financial Failure*, 16–17, 88–89.

28.   *Atlanta Southern Confederacy* (July 18, 1861).

29.   Owsley, *King Cotton Diplomacy*, 1–48.

30.   Evans, *Judah P. Benjamin*, 157–61.

31.   Bunch to Russell, Great Britain, Foreign Office, *British and Foreign State Papers*, 116 vols. (Kue, England: Public Records Office, 1812–1925), letterbox no. 9, pt. 1, vol. 78; Owsley, *King Cotton Diplomacy*, 29–32.

32.   Matthews, *Statutes at Large*. See also James M. Matthews, ed., *Public Laws of the Confederate States of America*, 1st Cong., sess. 1–4; 2d Congress, 1st sess. (Richmond, Va., 1862–64).

33.   The London *Economist* (Oct. 12, 1861; Mar. 15, 1862; May 3, 1862). Quotes extensively from the official British Board of Trade figures.

34.   Owsley, *King Cotton Diplomacy*, 145–49. Owsley quotes John Watts on the cotton famine and provides statistical data on the cotton shortage and the hardships it caused factory workers in Lancashire. Owsley quotes extensively from the 16th annual report of the Poor Board Log and reprints a table provided in the London *Economist* by Watts on Mar. 11, 1865, showing the numbers of unemployed in the British textile districts.

35.   DuBose, *William Lowndes Yancey*, 508–14; Coulter, *The Confederate States*, 19–32; Emory Thomas, *The Confederate Nation*, 307–22; Nevins, *The Emergence of Lincoln*, 3: 390–98; McPherson, *Battle Cry of Freedom*, 251–54.

36.   Yancey, Rost, and Mann to Earl Russell, London, Aug. 14, 1861, William Yancey, Papers, State of Alabama Historical Archives, Montgomery (hereafter cited as Yancey Papers); DuBose, *William Lowndes Yancey*, 2: 538.

37.   William B. McCash, *Thomas R. R. Cobb: The Making of a Southern Nationalist* (Macon, Ga.: Mercer Univ. Press), 84.

38.   Spencer B. King, ed., *The War-Time Journal of a Georgia Girl* (Macon, Ga.: The Ardivan Press, 1960), 31.

39.   Noble E. Cunningham Jr., *In Pursuit of Reason: The Life of Thomas Jefferson* (Baton Rouge: Louisiana State Univ. Press, 1987; reprint, New York: Ballantine Books, 1988), 311–18; Charles Sellers, *The Market Revolution* (New York: Oxford Univ. Press, 1991), 37–41; Lance Banning, *The Jeffersonian Persuasion: Evolution of a Party Ideology* (Ithaca, N.Y.: Cornell Univ. Press, 1978), 280.

40.   William Davis, *Jefferson Davis*, 308–13.

41.   Crook, *The North, the South*, 81–83; Eaton, *Jefferson Davis*, 171.

4. Poorly Chosen Diplomats Produce Poor Diplomacy

1.   Jefferson Davis to Howell Cobb, Feb. 24, 1861, Richardson, *Messages and Papers of Jefferson Davis*, 1: 57.

2.   Toombs to Yancey and Rost, Mar. 16, 1861, *ORN*, ser. 2, vol. 3: 191–95; Confederate States, *The Papers of John Pickett*, Records of the Confederate States of America, Library of Congress, Washington, D.C. (hereafter referred to as Pickett Papers; references to document numbers are provided wherever possible); Owsley, *King Cotton Diplomacy*, 51–56.

3.   Pickett Papers.

4.   Ferris, *Desperate Diplomacy*; Ephraim Douglass Adams, *Great Britain and the American Civil War*, 2 vols. (New York: Russell & Russell, 1924); Howard Jones, *Union in Peril*; Van Deusen, *William H. Seward*.

5.   Bunch to Russell, Mar. 21, 1861, Charles F. Adams Jr., "The British Proclamation of May, 1861," *Proceedings of the Massachusetts Historical Society* 48 (Jan. 1915): 208–10.

6. McPherson, *Battle Cry of Freedom,* 387–90.

7. Paul Pecquet De Bellet, *The Diplomacy of the Confederate Cabinet of Richmond and Its Agents Abroad: Being Memorandum Notes Taken in Paris during the Rebellion of the Southern States from 1861 to 1865,* ed. William Stanley Hoole (Tuscaloosa, Ala.: Confederate Publishers, 1963), 55–68. This quote is attributed to Du Bellet and included in the edited collection contained in this volume.

8. Hendrick, *Statesmen of the Lost Cause,* 107, 140–52.

9. Van Deusen, *William H. Seward;* Frederick William Seward, *Reminiscences of a War-Time Statesman and Diplomat, 1830–1915* (New York: Putnam's, 1916); W. Stanley Hoole, ed., "Notes and Documents: William L. Yancey's European Diary, March–June, 1861," *Alabama Review* 25 (Apr. 1972): 134–42.

10. Crook, *Diplomacy,* 29. Crook quotes Mann but fails to identify the person to whom Mann made this remark.

11. Paludan, *The Presidency of Abraham Lincoln.* See chapter 2 for a discussion of civil rights.

12. J. Preston Moore, "Lincoln and the Escape of the Confederate Commissioner," *Illinois State Historical Journal* 57: 23–27. Mann reported this quotation.

13. Crook, *Diplomacy,* 26–29; Case and Spencer, *The United States and France;* Ferris, *Desperate Diplomacy;* Owsley, *King Cotton Diplomacy;* Howard Jones, *Union in Peril,* 32–33.

14. Yancey and Mann to Toombs, no. 1, *ORN,* ser. 2, vol. 3: 214.

15. Ibid., Yancey and Mann to Toombs, May 21, 1861, ser. 2, 3: 214–16; Yancey, Rost, Mann to Toombs, June 1, 1861, ser. 2, 3: 219–21.

16. Yancey and Mann to Toombs, June 1, 1861, Pickett Papers; *ORN,* ser. 2, vol. 3: 214–16, 219–21; Adams, *Great Britain,* 1: 86–88.

17. Ibid. These sources, taken together, provide a complete account of the interview from the Confederate perspective. A full discussion of this informal meeting is provided by Owsley, *King Cotton Diplomacy,* 55–59.

18. Yancey, Rost, and Mann to Toombs, June 1, 1861, *ORN,* ser. 2, vol. 3: 219–21.

19. Russell to Lyons, May 11, 1861, *British Foreign Office Dispatches* (American), vol. 755, no. 128.

20. Yancey, Rost, and Mann to Toombs, June 1, 1861, *ORN,* ser. 2, vol. 3: 219–21.

21. Thomas Wodehouse Legh Newton, *Lord Lyons: A Record of British Diplomacy,* 2 vols. (London: Edward Arnold, 1913).

22. Merciér to Thouvenel, Washington, Jan. 20, 1861, *A.M.A.E.,* E.U., 21: 32–35.

23. Ibid.; Merciér to Thouvenel, Washington, Feb. 11, 1861, *A.M.A.E.,* E.U., 23: 60. Although this remark by Lyons was included in a dispatch before the passage of the bill, the legislative debate suggested its imminent passage and probably resulted from Lyons's frustrated attempts to influence legislators to vote against the tariff. See also Van Deusen, *William H. Seward,* 271; Henry Blumenthal, *A Reappraisal of Franco-American Relations, 1830–1871* (Chapel Hill: Univ. of North Carolina Press, 1959), 123. Both Van Deusen and Blumenthal flatly state that Merciér recommended to his home government that the Confederacy be recognized.

24. Daniel B. Carroll, *Henri Merciér and the American Civil War* (Princeton, N.J.: Princeton Univ. Press, 1971), 57–61; Crook, *Diplomacy,* 51–52; Howard Jones, *Union in Peril,* 74–76. Carroll disagrees with the conclusions of Van Deusen and Blumenthal, and argues that Merciér only wanted Confederate recognition if circumstances re-

quired it. Crook concludes that Merciér only wanted to recognize the Confederacy if the North would allow the South to exist within a "customs union." Jones suggests that Merciér favored Confederate recognition, but only if the British agreed.

25.   Norman E. Saul, *Distant Friends: The United States and Russia, 1763–1867* (Lawrence: Univ. Press of Kansas, 1991), 264–78; Tyrner-Tyrnauer, *Lincoln and the Emperors*, 46–57.

26.   Howard Jones, *Union in Peril*, 12–17; Ferris, *Desperate Diplomacy*, 194–98.

27.   Ferris, *Desperate Diplomacy*.

28.   Adams, *Great Britain*, 1: 86; Russell to Lyons, May 6, 1861, *British Foreign Office Dispatches* (American), vol. 755, no. 121; London *Gazette*, May 14, 1861.

29.   Cowley [First Earl of Cowley, Henry Richard Charles Wellesley] to Russell, May 7, 1861, *British and Foreign State Papers*, vol. 1390, no. 677; Dallas to Seward, *FRUS*. Russell informed American Minister Dallas on May 1 that France and England would act together with regard to the American problem, but refused to commit as to what that action would be.

30.   W. L. Yancey and A. W. Mann to Toombs, May 21, 1861, Pickett Papers; *ORN*, ser. 2, vol. 3: 216. The two Confederate commissioners wrote that "England is not averse to a disintegration of the United States."

31.   Adams, *Great Britain*, 1: 111–12; Adams to Seward, May 17, 1861, *FRUS*; Jenkins, *Britain and the War*, 1: 109.

32.   Yancey, Rost, and Mann to Toombs, no. 2, June 1, 1861, Pickett Papers; *ORN*, ser. 2, vol. 3: 219–21.

33.   Charles F. Adams Jr., "The British Proclamation of May 1861," *Proceedings of the Massachusetts Historical Society* 48 (Jan. 1915): 190–241; *ORN*, ser. 2, vol. 3: 219–21.

34.   Both of these quotations appear in Norman Graebner's article, "Northern Diplomacy and European Neutrality," in *Why the North Won*, 55–78; Frank L. Owsley, "America and the Freedom of the Seas, 1861–1865," in *Essays in Honor of William E. Dodd*, ed. Avery Craven (Chicago: Univ. of Chicago Press, 1935), 194–256.

35.   Jenkins, *Britain and the War*, 1: 258.

36.   Ferris, *Desperate Diplomacy*; Case and Spencer, *The United States and France*; Edward A. Trescot, "The Confederacy and the Declaration of Paris," *American Historical Review* 23 (July 18, 1918): 826–35. This is an interesting contemporary account by an underutilized Confederate patriot.

37.   Reports from Yancey, Mann, and Rost to Toombs, June 1, 1861, *ORN*, ser. 2, vol. 3: 214–16, 219–21. These reports include accounts of the interview. Case and Spencer, *The United States and France*, 147–49.

38.   Yancey and Mann to Toombs, July 15, 1861, Pickett Papers; Yancey and Mann to Toombs, Aug. 1, 1862, *ORN*, ser. 2, vol. 3: 221–25, 229–30.

39.   Jenkins, *Britain and the War*, 1: 88–89; Norman B. Ferris, "Tempestuous Mission, 1861–1862, the Early Diplomatic Career of Charles Francis Adams" (Ph.D. diss., Emory Univ., 1962); Seward to Adams, July 9, 1861, *FRUS*.

40.   Yancey and Rost to Toombs, June 10, 1861, *ORN*, ser. 2, vol. 3: 221.

41.   Ibid., Yancey to Toombs, July 15, 1861, ser. 2, vol. 3: 221–25.

42.   Ibid.

43.   Case and Spencer, *The United States and France*, 77–125.

44.   McPherson, *Battle Cry of Freedom*, 312–17.

45.   Jasper L. Ridley, *Lord Palmerston* (London: E. P. Dutton & Co., 1971), 551.

46.   Quoted in Howard Jones, *Union in Peril*, 57.

47.   Adams, *Great Britain*, 1: 179.

48. Entries of Aug. 6 and Sept. 10, 1861, Charles Francis Adams Jr., Papers, Massachusetts Historical Society, Boston (hereafter cited as Adams Diary).

49. Owsley, *King Cotton Diplomacy,* 217; Case and Spencer, *The United States and France,* 165–67.

50. Yancey Papers, box 43; DuBose, *William Lowndes Yancey,* 2: 63.

51. Yancey, Rost, and Mann to Russell, Aug. 14, 1861, *ORN,* ser. 2, vol. 3: 238–47.

52. Ibid. The idea of a slave rebellion and race war impressed Russell probably more than anyone realized at the time. He later used this point in the "Blockade Defeat" speech in the House of Lords in the winter of 1862.

53. Ibid., Hunter to Yancey, Rost, and Mann, July 29, 1861, 3: 227–29.

54. Ibid., Russell to Yancey, Rost, and Mann, Aug. 24, 1861, 3: 247–48; James Murray Mason, Papers, Library of Congress, Washington, D.C. (hereafter referred to as Mason Papers). This communication is included in the papers of James M. Mason along with some other letters from Russell to the Confederate commission, which were apparently left with Mason after he took charge in London.

55. Merli, *Great Britain,* see especially chapter 2.

56. Adams, *Great Britain,* 1: 137–39; Howard Jones, *Union in Peril,* 50–51; Case and Spencer, *The United States and France,* 69–71; Brian Jenkins, "Frank Lawley and the Confederacy," *Civil War History* 23 (June 1977): 144–60.

57. *ORN,* ser. 4, vol. 1: 542–46.

58. Kenny A. Franks, "The Implementation of the Confederate Treaties with the Five Civilized Tribes: A Breakdown of Relations," *Journal of the West* (1973): 439–54; Emory Thomas, *The Confederate Nation,* 188–89.

59. William L. Shea and Earl J. Hess, *Pea Ridge: Civil War Campaign in the West* (Chapel Hill: Univ. of North Carolina Press, 1992), 143–46.

60. Toombs to Pickett, May 17, 1861, Pickett Papers; *ORN,* ser. 2, vol. 3: 202–7. John Pickett, after a diplomatic career of frustrating failures, ensured his place in American history when, after the war, he managed to obtain most of the Confederate State Department correspondence. He smuggled the documents into Canada and kept them secure in his possession until he ultimately sold the so-called "Pickett Papers" to the U.S. government.

61. Owsley, *King Cotton Diplomacy,* 88–119; Pickett to Toombs, June 15, 1861, Pickett Papers.

62. Ronnie C. Tyler, *Santiago, Vidaurri, and the Southern Confederacy* (Austin: Univ. of Texas Press, 1973); LeRoy P. Graf, "The Economic History of the Lower Rio Grande Valley, 1820–1875" (Ph.D. diss., Harvard Univ., 1972).

5. Interrupted Momentum and Disrupted Strategy

1. Yancey and Rost to Hunter, Oct. 5, 1861, *ORN,* ser. 2, vol. 3.

2. Carroll, *Henri Mercier,* 93–95.

3. Seward to Adams, Apr. 10, 1861; Seward to Dayton, Apr. 22, 1861, *FRUS.* These papers also contain a circular of Mar. 9, 1861.

4. Adams, *Great Britain,* 166–68; Milledge Bonham Jr., *The British Consuls in the Confederacy,* Columbia University Studies in History, Economics and Public Law (New York: Longmans, Green & Co., 1911; reprint, AMS Press, 1967), 24.

5. Jenkins, *Britain and the War,* 1: 148–52. Jenkins provides several examples of the use of British consuls in residence as the primary source of information on Confederate activities, including political and military activity.

6.   Lyons to Russell, dispatch no. 433 and 438, Aug. 19, 1861, *British Foreign Office Dispatches,* 115/255; *ORA,* ser. 2, vol. 2: 123, 1006, 1049, and 1056.

7.   Ferris, *Desperate Diplomacy,* 99–116; Adams, *Great Britain,* 1: 184–96; Jenkins, *Britain and the War,* 1: 136–39; Case and Spencer, *The United States and France,* 116–17; Howard Jones, *Union in Peril,* 61–65.

8.   Eugene H. Berwanger, *The British Foreign Service and the American Civil War* (Lexington: Univ. Press of Kentucky, 1994), 36–54.

9.   Seward to Adams, Aug. 17, 1861, *FRUS,* no. 63; Bonham, *British Consuls,* 26–28.

10.   Adams Diary, Sept. 2, 1861.

11.   Adams to Seward, Sept. 9, 1861, no. 41, *FRUS.*

12.   Ibid.; Case and Spencer, *The United States and France,* 113–20.

13.   Lyons to Bunch, July 5, 1861, *British and Foreign State Papers,* dispatch no. 5, 767; Jenkins, *Britain and the War,* 1: 138.

14.   Norman B. Ferris, "Transatlantic Misconception: William H. Seward and the Declaration of Paris Negotiations of 1861," in *Rank and File: Civil War Essays in Honor of Bell I. Wiley,* eds. James I. Robertson Jr. and Richard M. McMurry (San Rafael, Calif.: Presidio Press, 1976), 55–78.

15.   Trescot, "The Confederacy."

16.   Edward A. Trescot, Papers, South Carolina Archives, Columbia (hereafter cited as Trescot Papers).

17.   Jenkins, *Britain and the War,* 1: 138.

18.   Trescot, "The Confederacy."

19.   Patrick, *Jefferson Davis and His Cabinet,* 97.

20.   Donald R. McVeigh, "Charles James Faulkner in the Civil War," *West Virginia History* 12 (Jan. 1951): 129–41. Faulkner was Buchanan's Minister to France, but was quickly recalled at the outbreak of the secession crisis. Even though he was a competent and efficient diplomat, he was relegated to a staff position under General Thomas "Stonewall" Jackson. His diplomatic expertise was never requested by Davis or the Confederate State Department; Gillard Hunt, "April 1908," *American Historical Review* 23 (Oct. 1918): 309.

21.   Matthews, *Statutes at Large,* 213. Matthews has edited in three volumes most of the important resolutions, bills, amendments, reports, communications, correspondence, and petitions of the Confederate Congress. The originals are in the manuscript division of the Library of Congress, Washington, D.C. Also refer to personal notes on the Declaration of Paris in the Trescot Papers, Library of Congress, later published in the Gillard Hunt article "April 1908."

22.   Trescot to Hunter, Aug. 3, 1861, R. M. T. Hunter, Papers, Hunter-Garnett Collection, Univ. of Virginia, Charlottesville (hereafter cited as Hunter Papers).

23.   Toombs to Stephens, July 5, 1861, Toombs Papers; White, *Robert Barnwell Rhett,* 209–10.

24.   Henry H. Simms, *Life of Robert M. T. Hunter* (Westport, Conn.: Greenwood Press, 1935), 93–98.

25.   Berwanger, *British Foreign Service.*

26.   Adams, *Great Britain,* 192–94; Bonham, *British Consuls,* 45; Bunch to Lyons, Oct. 31, 1861, "Correspondence on the withdrawal of Bunch's Exchequer," from Great Britain, *Hansard's,* doc. no. 22, 25: 862, pp. 40–43.

27.   Russell to Adams, enclosed with correspondence from Adams to Seward, Nov. 29, 1861, *FRUS;* Russell to Adams, Dec. 9, 1861, "Correspondence on the withdrawal of Bunch's Exchequer," *Hansard's,* doc. no. 26.

28. Thouvenel to Merciér, Paris, Oct. 3, 1861, *A.M.A.E.*, E.U.; Carroll, *Henri Merciér*, 290–96.

29. Ferris, *The Trent Affair.*

30. Yancey to Hunter, Yancey Papers.

31. Matthews, *Statutes at Large*, 98–99; Yearns, *The Confederate Congress*, 162–70. Congress confirmed the appointment of Mason and Slidell, but a significant number of Congressmen from the cotton states argued no further unofficial diplomats should be sent to Europe until King Cotton forced the recognition of the Confederacy.

32. Hunter to Mason, Sept. 23, 1861, *ORN*, ser. 2, vol. 3: 257–64; Hunter to Slidell, Sept. 23, 1861, Pickett Papers. The instructions from Hunter to each of the Confederate diplomats are contained in these dispatches.

33. Sears, *John Slidell*, 170–72. Overtures were made to Slidell by the Davis administration to join the first diplomatic mission to Europe, but he refused, probably because of his hostility toward Dudley Mann.

34. The London *Times*, Dec. 9, 1861.

35. Slidell to Eustis, Aug. 4, 1861, George Eustis, Papers, Library of Congress, Washington, D.C. In this handwritten note to his secretary, Slidell points out to Eustis the expectation of a "protracted stay in France."

36. Case and Spencer, *The United States and France*, 192–95.

37. Stephen Russell Mallory, Papers, Library of Congress, Washington, D.C., 1: 9 (hereafter cited as Mallory Papers).

38. Hendrick, *Statesmen of the Lost Cause*, 125–31.

39. *The Charleston Mercury*, Oct. 29, 1861.

40. Mary Boykin Chestnut, *A Diary from Dixie*, ed. Ben Ames Williams (Cambridge: Harvard Univ. Press, 1980), 123–24.

41. Cobden is quoted by Jenkins in *Britain and the War*, 1: 192.

42. Hunter to Mason, Sept. 23, 1861, Mason Papers, box 30, letter 275; Simms, *Life of Robert M. T. Hunter.*

43. Mason Papers.

44. Virginia Mason, *The Public Life and Diplomatic Correspondence of James M. Mason: With Some Personal History by His Daughter*, 2 vols. (Roanoke, Va.: Stone Printing, 1903).

45. Ferris, *The Trent Affair*; Stuart L. Bernath, *Squall Across the Atlantic: American Civil War Prize Cases and Diplomacy* (Berkeley: Univ. of California Press, 1970).

46. A copy of this telegram is contained in the Mason Papers.

47. Mason to Hunter, *ORN*, ser. 2, vol. 3: 276–77.

48. Virginia Mason, *Public Life.*

49. Mason to Davis, Oct. 11, 1861, *ORN*, ser. 2, vol. 3: 281–82.

50. Whiting to Seward, Oct. 25–26, 1861, *ORN*, ser. 2, vol. 3: 282. U.S. Consul Whiting at Nassau informed Seward that he had "learned from good authority that the steamer *Theodora* is, in fact, the Charleston packet *Gordon* and that the ship is on its way to Havana with a large number of passengers." Apparently, the Consul was not aware that Mason and Slidell were passengers because he took over two weeks to forward the information.

51. Virginia Mason, *Public Life*, 199–213.

52. Gideon Welles, *Diary of Gideon Welles, Secretary of the Navy under Lincoln and Johnson*, 3 vols., ed. Howard K. Beale (New York: Norton, 1960), 2: 187; Welles to DuPont, *ORN*, ser. 1, vol. 1: 114–17.

53. James P. Baxter, "The British Government and Neutral Rights, 1861–1865,"

American Historical Review 34 (Oct. 1928): 9–29; Adams, *Great Britain,* 1: 210; Welles, *Diary of Gideon Welles.*

54. Ferris, *The Trent Affair,* 10–11.

55. Diary entry Nov. 16, 1861, Charles Wilkes, Papers (Diary), Library of Congress, Washington, D.C.

56. Ibid. Nov. 8, 1861.

57. Bernath, *Squall Across the Atlantic.*

58. Jenkins, *Britain and the War,* 1: 197.

59. Charles F. Adams Jr., "The *Trent* Affair," *Proceedings of the Massachusetts Historical Society* 46 (Nov. 1911): 49.

60. The diary of Thomas Bragg, Nov. 26, 1861, Southern Historical Collection, as quoted by Jenkins, *Britain and the War,* 1: 198.

61. Richardson, *Messages and Papers of the Confederacy,* 1: 43.

62. Crook, *The North, the South,* 144–47; Jenkins, *Britain and the War,* 1: 199; Robin W. Winks, *Canada and the United States: The Civil War Years* (Baltimore: Johns Hopkins Univ. Press, 1960), 99–102.

63. Lyons to Russell, Nov. 22, 1861, *British Foreign Office Dispatches,* 30/22/35.

64. Alice O'Rourke, "The Law Officers of the Crown and the *Trent* Affair," *Mid-America* 54, no. 3 (1972): 157–71.

65. Russell to Lyons, Dec. 1, 1861, Lyons Papers, quoted by Jenkins, *Britain and the War,* 1: 213.

66. Norman Ferris, "The Prince Consort, the *Times,* and the *Trent* Affair," *Civil War History* 6 (1960): 152–56.

67. Russell to Lyons, Dec. 1, 1861, and Dec. 6, 1861, *British and Foreign State Papers,* 5: 758; Ferris, "The Prince Consort."

68. Case and Spencer, *The United States and France,* 188–89. Case and Spencer argue that the French note supporting the British position, received in Washington on Christmas Day, made the difference to the Lincoln Cabinet in deciding to comply with British demands.

69. Adams to Seward, Dec. 3, 1861, *FRUS*; John Bigelow, *Retrospections of an Active Life,* 5 vols. (New York: The Baker & Taylor Co., 1909), 1: 385–89.

70. Margaret Clapp, *Forgotten First Citizen: John Bigelow* (Boston: Little, Brown, 1947); V. H. Cohen, "Charles Sumner and the *Trent* Affair," *Journal of Southern History* 22 (1956): 205–19.

71. Donald, *Lincoln,* 320–23; Paludan, *The Presidency of Abraham Lincoln,* 91–93.

72. Case and Spencer, *The United States and France,* 247–50. The Confederate conspiracy argument is presented by Case and Spencer using only circumstantial evidence. An adequate circumstantial case can be constructed to refute the conspiracy position. In any case, no hard evidence exists to support the position of Case and Spencer.

73. Mason, *Public Life,* 1: 187.

6. A New Initiative in Europe

1. Benjamin Moran, Papers, Library of Congress, Washington, D.C., (hereafter cited as Moran Papers), Feb. 7, 8, 10, 1862. Although pro-Union, Moran strongly believed that recognition would remain a prominent issue until the Union achieved decisive military victory on the battlefield. He reacted to Yancey's demands, however, by declaring them "remarkable" for their "flat imprudence."

2.   Mason Papers, Feb. 5, 1861. Personal notes in Mason's handwriting; Slidell to Hunter, Feb. 11, 1861, *ORN*, ser. 2, vol. 3: 336–42; Mason to Hunter, Feb. 7, 1861, Pickett Papers.

3.   Hunter to Mason, Sept. 20, 1861, Hunter to Slidell, Sept. 23, 1861, *ORN*, ser. 2, vol. 3: 257–73.

4.   Mason and Slidell arrived in London on Jan. 29, 1862, according to the London *Times* of Jan. 30, 1862.

5.   Case and Spencer, *The United States and France*, 251–56.

6.   Russell to Lyons, London, Dec. 20, 1861, *British Foreign Office Dispatches*, 5/758/487.

7.   Case and Spencer, *The United States and France*, 251–52. These newspaper quotes appear to identify the pro-Southern atmosphere in France.

8.   Dayton to Seward, Paris, Jan. 27, 1862, *FRUS*, vol. 51, no. 109.

9.   Frederick Seward, *Seward at Washington*, 2: 55–56.

10.   Dayton to Seward, *FRUS* no. 109, Paris, Jan. 27, 1862. The long interview is detailed in this correspondence; Frederick Seward, *Seward at Washington*, 2: 56–57; Case and Spencer, *The United States and France*, 255–58.

11.   Adams, *Great Britain*, 1: 253.

12.   Merciér to Thouvenel, Washington, July 15, 1861, and July 21, 1861, *A.M.A.E., E.U.*, 24: 393–401, 124: 453–59; Bray Hammond, "The North's Empty Purse, 1861–1862," *American Historical Review* 67, no. 1 (1961): 1–18.

13.   Seward to Dayton, Jan. 20, 1862, *FRUS*.

14.   Warren F. Spencer. "Edouard Drouyn de Lhuys and the Foreign Policy of the Second French Empire" (Ph.D. diss., Univ. of Pennsylvania, 1955, 63–67).

15.   Dayton to Seward, Paris, Jan. 27, 1862, *FRUS*, vol. 51, no. 109.

16.   Hersh Lauterpacht, *Recognition in International Law* (Cambridge: Cambridge Univ. Press, 1947), 117–23; Bourne, *Britain and the Balance of Power*.

17.   Simms, *Life of Robert M. T. Hunter*.

18.   Slidell to R. M. T. Hunter, Paris, Feb. 11, 1862, *ORN*, ser. 2, vol. 3: 336–38. Slidell relays Rost's conclusions to Hunter in this dispatch.

19.   Dayton to Seward, Paris, Mar. 25, 1862, *FRUS*, 51, no. 109; Weed to Seward, Paris, Apr. 15, 1862, Seward Papers quoted in Case and Spencer, *The United States and France*, 288.

20.   Dayton to Seward, dispatch no. 109, *FRUS*, Jan. 27, 1862. In his report to Seward, Dayton, alluding to his private sources, said "I thought the meeting would settle the character of the address and I felt it important . . . to go as far . . . upon the points herein before stated." Dayton's sources are not revealed in either his private notes and papers or the official correspondence. It is obvious that Dayton's contacts were highly placed and furnished him with confidential information. His close working relationship with the French government has traditionally been underestimated.

21.   The *Moniteur* (Jan. 28, 1862). The entire text of the Emperor's speech was printed in this semiofficial newspaper the day after the speech.

22.   John Bigelow to Seward, Paris, Jan. 28, 1882, *FRUS*.

23.   The *Moniteur*, Jan. 30, 1862.

24.   Case and Spencer, *The United States and France*, 254–56; Henry Blumenthal, *France and the United States: Their Diplomatic Relations, 1789–1914* (Chapel Hill: Univ. of North Carolina Press, 1970), 74–105. Blumenthal provides a detailed account of the political situation in Europe during the time of the American Civil War.

25.   Baxter, "The British Government."

26. Jenkins, *Britain and the War*, 1: 246; Owsley, *King Cotton Diplomacy*, 230–35; Case and Spencer, *The United States and France*, 261–62; Crook, *Diplomacy*, 176–78.

27. Charles F. Adams to Seward, London, July 10, 1862, *FRUS*; Moran Papers, July 19, 1862; Graebner, "Northern Diplomacy and European Neutrality," in *Why the North Won*.

28. Slidell to Benjamin, Paris, Oct. 28, 1862, *ORN*, ser. 2, vol. 3: 574–78; Slidell to Mason, Aug. 17, 1862, Mason Papers; Owsley, *King Cotton Diplomacy*, 237. Owsley believed that the French made numerous informal, as well as formal, overtures to the British throughout 1861 and 1862 to recognize the South.

29. Mason to Hunter, Pickett Papers, Feb. 7, 1861; *ORN*, ser. 2, vol. 3: 330–32; Howard Jones, *Union in Peril*, 131–36.

30. Gregory to Mason, Mason Papers, Feb. 7, 1862.

31. Mason to Hunter, dispatch no. 2, *ORN*, ser. 2, vol. 3: 330–32.

32. Mason to Hunter, Feb. 22, 1862, dispatch no. 4, Pickett Papers; notes of Mason on the Russell interview, Feb. 8, 1862, Mason Papers; Russell to Mason, Feb. 8, 1862, Mason to Russell, Feb. 17, 1862, *ORN*, ser. 2, vol. 3: 342–46.

33. Russell to Mason, Feb. 20, *ORN*, ser. 2, vol. 3: 343. Mason misread Russell, who later favored intervention during the full Cabinet debate.

34. Howard Jones, *Union in Peril*, 126.

35. Lindsay to Russell, Feb. 5, 1862, Mason Papers. A complete copy of Lindsay's letter was forwarded to Mason.

36. Spence to Mason, Feb. 20, 1862, Mason Papers.

37. Ibid., Slidell to Mason, Feb. 12, 1862.

38. Ibid., Mason to Slidell, Feb. 15, 1862.

39. Norman Graebner, "European Intervention and the Crisis of 1862," *Journal of Illinois State Historical Society* 69 (Feb. 1976): 35–45.

40. Russell to Lyons, Feb. 15, 1862, London, Russell Papers, quoted in Howard Jones, *Union in Peril*, 123.

41. Russell to Lyons, Feb. 15, 1862, Russell Papers, quoted by Jenkins, *Britain and the War*, 1: 242; London *Times*, (Feb. 20, 1862); Mason to Hunter, *ORN*, ser. 2, vol. 3: 379–84, quotes in part from the *Times* report.

42. Crook, *Diplomacy*, 172–77; Owsley, *King Cotton Diplomacy*, 244–47. It would be difficult for Britain to reverse its long-standing tradition that justified the closing of Dunkirk in 1713, the bombardment of Copenhagen, and the seizure of the Danish fleet in a power struggle in 1807, even though the Paris Declaration was an expedient way to appease European allies in 1856.

43. Mason to Slidell, Feb. 27, 1862, Mason Papers.

44. Robert Blake, *Disraeli* (New York and London: St. Martin's Press, 1967), 426–51. Blake points to the revival of Disraeli as a leader in the political opposition to Palmerston and discusses the political implications of the debate on the American question.

45. Jenkins, *Britain and the War*, 1: 253.

46. Crook, *Diplomacy*, 177. Crook suggests that Disraeli's advisor on foreign affairs, Ralph Earle, was against any discussion of recognition and suggested that little political advantage was to be gained by the opposition party.

47. *Hansard's*, Commons, 3d ser., 165 (1862): 1148–1231; Brian Jenkins, *Sir William Gregory of Coole: The Biography of an Anglo-Irishman* (Gerrards Cross, Buckinghamshire: C. Smythe, 1986); William H. Gregory, Family Collection, R. W. Woodruff Library, Emory Univ., Atlanta, Ga.

48. Owsley, *King Cotton Diplomacy,* 246; *Hansard's,* Commons, 3d ser., 165 (1862): 1238.

49. *Hansard's,* Commons, 3d ser., 165 (1862): 113–14.

50. Ibid., 165: 1231–33; Owsley, *King Cotton Diplomacy,* 247.

51. *Hansard's,* Commons, 3d ser., 165 (1862): 113–14; Joseph M. Hernon Jr., "British Sympathies in the American Civil War: A Reconsideration," in *Journal of Southern History* 33 (Aug. 1967): 356–67.

52. *Hansard's,* Commons, 3d ser., 165 (1862): 1148–1231.

53. Crook, *Diplomacy,* 180.

54. Ibid. Spence is quoted by Crook.

55. Adams to Seward, Mar. 13, 1862, *FRUS,* 75; The *Economist,* Mar. 29, 1862.

56. *Hansard's,* Lords, 3d ser., 165 (1862): 1238–43; Douglas A. Lorimer, "The Role of Anti-Slavery Sentiment in English Reactions to the American Civil War," *Historical Journal* 19 (June 1976): 405–20.

57. Owsley, *King Cotton Diplomacy,* 248–49. Owsley states, "Russell alluded to the Negro question, by implication, at least on economic grounds." If a slave insurrection occurred, according to Owsley, the British (Russell) felt that cotton production would be completely destroyed and the cotton supply indefinitely interrupted. Russell did not articulate, either in his speech or in related communications, specifically to any "economic factor." The implication is possibly more Owsley's than Russell's.

58. Hotze to Hunter, *ORN,* ser. 2, vol. 3: 352–54.

59. Ibid.; Hotze to Hunter, no. 4, Feb. 28, 1862, Pickett Papers.

60. Hotze to Hunter, no. 5, Mar. 11, 1862, Pickett Papers.

61. Ibid., Mason to Hunter, no. 6, Mar. 11, 1862; *ORN,* ser. 2, vol. 3: 358–60.

62. William P. Roberts, "James Dunwoody Bulloch and the Confederate Navy," *North Carolina Historical Review* 24, no. 3 (1947): 315–66.

63. Slidell to Benjamin, Paris, Apr. 14, 1862, *ORN,* ser. 2, vol. 3: 393–95; Adams, *Great Britain,* 1: 289–92. Adams provides a summary of Lindsay's interview with Napoleon III.

64. Cowley to Russell, Paris, Apr. 13, 1862, *British Foreign Office Dispatches,* 30/ 22.

65. Case and Spencer, *The United States and France,* 269.

66. Slidell memorandum to Benjamin, Paris, Apr. 14, 1862, *ORN,* ser. 2, vol. 3: 393–95; Adams, *Great Britain,* 1: 289–92. Slidell felt that Thouvenel, hearing of Lindsay's interview with Rouher and somewhat annoyed, immediately communicated the information to the Emperor. Slidell again points out the pro-Union sentiments of Thouvenel.

67. Case and Spencer, *The United States and France,* 270. Case and Spencer believe that Napoleon missed this point of contradiction between war supplies and the demands for humanitarian response.

68. Adams, *Great Britain,* 1: 289. Adams reproduces the complete text of Lindsay's first interview with Napoleon.

69. Slidell to Benjamin, Paris, May 15, 1862, *ORN,* ser. 2, vol. 3: 419.

70. Cowley to Russell, Paris, Apr. 13, 1862, *British Foreign Office Dispatches,* 30/22.

71. Slidell memorandum, Paris, Apr. 14, 1862, *ORN,* ser. 2, vol. 3: 293–95; Adams, *Great Britain,* 1: 289–92; Case and Spencer, *The United States and France,* 271.

72. Cowley to Russell, Paris, Apr. 13, 1862, *British Foreign Office Dispatches,* 30/22.

73. Cowley to Russell, Apr. 15, 1862, quoted in Case and Spencer, *The United States and France,* 271.

74. Ibid., Thouvenel to Flahault, Paris, Apr. 14, 1862, 272.

75. Russell to Cowley, Apr. 15, 1862, *British Foreign Office Dispatches,* 27/1422/402; Case and Spencer, *The United States and France,* 272.

76. Slidell to Benjamin, Paris, Apr. 18, 1862, *ORN,* ser. 2, vol. 3: 295–96. There is no supporting evidence for this extraordinary claim by Lindsay, although the Confederates continued to claim a secret deal had been made between the Russell-Palmerston government and the Seward-Lincoln administration.

77. Case and Spencer, *The United States and France,* 273.

78. Slidell to Benjamin, Paris, Apr. 18, 1862, *ORN,* ser. 2, vol. 3: 295–96.

79. Flahault to Thouvenel, London, Apr. 16, 1862, quoted in Case and Spencer, *The United States and France,* 273.

80. Ibid., quotes Napoleon III to Cowley, Paris, Apr. 20, 1862, 274; Cowley to Russell, Apr. 22, 1862, *British Foreign Office Dispatches,* 30/22, enclosure with correspondence.

81. Hotze to Secretary of State, London, Apr. 25, 1862, *ORN,* ser. 2, vol. 3: 299, 400.

82. Flahault to Thouvenel, London, May 11, 1862, telegram enclosure, Russell to Cowley, *British Foreign Office Dispatches,* 27/1423/528.

83. Thouvenel to Merciér, Paris, May 15, 1862, quoted in Case and Spencer, *The United States and France,* 274.

84. Slidell to Benjamin, Paris, May 15, 1862, *ORN,* ser. 2, vol. 3: 419.

85. Cowley to Russell, Paris, May 13, 1862, *British Foreign Office Dispatches,* 30/22.

7. Benjamin Takes Control of the State Department

1. McPherson, *Battle Cry of Freedom,* 282; Emory M. Thomas, *The Confederate State of Richmond: A Biography of a City* (Athens: Univ. of Georgia Press, 1971), 98.

2. Evans, *Judah P. Benjamin,* 120–23; Robert Douthat Meade, *Judah P. Benjamin and the American Civil War* (New York: Oxford Univ. Press, 1943), 148–49; Patrick, *Jefferson Davis and His Cabinet,* 11.

3. Bell I. Wiley, *Confederate Women* (Westport, Conn.: Greenwood Press, 1975), 7.

4. Howell Cobb to M. Cobb, Mar. 20, 1862, Howell Cobb, Papers, Univ. of Georgia Library, Athens.

5. Patrick, *Jefferson Davis and His Cabinet,* 182–83.

6. Evans, *Judah P. Benjamin,* 185–93; Emory Thomas, *The Confederate Nation,* 148–50.

7. Benjamin to Slidell, May 11, 1862, Pickett Papers; *ORN,* ser. 2, vol. 3. A number of dispatches written during April and May did not reach Slidell until July 5, 1862.

8. Evans, *Judah P. Benjamin,* 172–75; Meade, *Judah P. Benjamin,* 266–67.

9. Quoted in Jenkins, *Britain and the War,* 2: 8.

10. Coulter, *The Confederate States,* 381; Mallory to Bulloch, May 9, 1861, *ORN,* ser. 2, vol. 2: 64–65; James Dunwoody Bulloch, *The Secret Service of the Confederate States in Europe: Or How the Confederate Cruisers Were Equipped,* 2 vols. (New York: R. Bentley & Son, 1884; reprint, Franklin, 1972), 1: 46; Spencer, *The Confederate Navy in Europe,* 55–57; Merli, *Great Britain,* 17. Mallory's position had changed little from his original assessment that a Confederate navy required European support.

11. Merli, *Great Britain,* 100–116. Merli provides a good overview of the relationship between Confederate diplomats and Bulloch.

12.   Caleb Huse, *The Supplies for the Confederate Army: How They Were Obtained and How Paid For, A Fragment of History* (Boston: Marvin, 1904); Richard I. Lester, *Confederate Finance and Purchasing in Great Britain* (Charlottesville: Univ. Press of Virginia, 1975), 149–53.

13.   Spencer, *The Confederate Navy in Europe*; Richard Todd, *Confederate Finance* (Athens: Univ. of Georgia Press, 1954); Wells, *The Confederate Navy*.

14.   Adams, *Great Britain*, 1: 281–92; Carroll, *Henri Merciér*, 146–79; Case and Spencer, *The United States and France*, 272–85.

15.   Carroll, *Henri Merciér*, 146–49. Merciér's biographer explains in detail the genesis of the idea of the trip to Richmond and provides the most complete published translation of the relevant Merciér correspondence on the matter.

16.   Baron Edouard de Stoeckl, Papers, Library of Congress, Washington, D.C. (microfilm, Middle Tennessee State Univ., Murfreesboro); Carroll, *Henri Merciér*, 153.

17.   Blumenthal, *A Reappraisal*, 141–42.

18.   Carroll, *Henri Merciér*, 163–73; Van Deusen, *William H. Seward*, 363.

19.   Senator L. T. Wigfall of Texas challenged Stephen Douglas in one of the last debates in the U.S. Senate before Sumter. James L. Orr of South Carolina was once Speaker of the U.S. House of Representatives and now served as chairman of the Confederate Committee on Foreign Affairs. Clement C. Clay of Alabama owed his position to the success and social status of his wife, a famous author and actress.

20.   Merciér to Thouvenel, dispatch no. 97, Apr. 28, 1862, Washington; *A.M.A.E.*, E.U., vol. 127.

21.   Ibid.

22.   Benjamin's report of the interview to the president, *ORN*, ser. 2, vol. 3: 461–67. This statement is included in Benjamin's June 19 communication to Slidell, but is not included in exactly this blunt way in any of Merciér's communications to Thouvenel or Seward, although Benjamin's response was reported by Merciér.

23.   Merciér to Thouvenel, Apr. 28, 1862, *A.M.A.E.*, E.U., vol. 127.

24.   Owsley, *King Cotton Diplomacy*, 285; Carroll, *Henri Merciér*, 162–65.

25.   Merciér to Thouvenel, Washington, Apr. 28, 1862, *A.M.A.E.*, E.U., 127: 50–79.

26.   Dayton to Seward, Paris, May 22, 1862, *FRUS*, 51: 341–42; undated hand-written draft of Dayton's notes of his interview with Thouvenel and his proposed report to Seward in William L. Dayton, Papers, Firestone Library, Princeton, N.J. (hereafter cited as Dayton Papers); Van Deusen, *William H. Seward*, 367–69. These dispatches provide the basis for the slightly different conclusions reached by Carroll and Van Deusen.

27.   Case and Spencer, *The United States and France*, 279–81. Case and Spencer provide an extended translation of Merciér's communication to Thouvenel detailing the interview with Benjamin.

28.   Merciér to Thouvenel, Washington, May 6, 1862, *A.M.A.E.*, E.U., 127: 85–105.

29.   Owsley, *King Cotton Diplomacy*, 286–87; Adams, *Great Britain*, 1: 297–99.

30.   Benjamin to Slidell, May 11, 1862, Benjamin to Slidell, June 6, 1862, *ORN*, ser. 3, vol. 2; Carroll, *Henri Merciér*, 165. In the several dispatches forwarded to Thouvenel mentioning the interview with Benjamin and other Confederate leaders, Carroll points out that several separate meetings between Merciér and Benjamin took place. Benjamin, in reporting to Slidell, mentions only one meeting. The reason the number of meetings is important is to determine the extent of discussions involving a new cotton strategy.

31. Merciér to Thouvenel, Washington, May 6, 1862, *A.M.A.E,* E.U., 127: 85–105.

32. Carroll, *Henri Merciér,* 166. Merciér's biographer concludes that this plan, like many of Merciér's suggestions for peace, was firmly planted in the future, not the present.

33. Francis Leigh Williams, *Matthew Fontaine Maury: Scientist of the Sea* (New Brunswick, N.J.: Rutgers Univ. Press, 1963), 330; Patricia Jahns, *Matthew Fontaine Maury and Joseph Henry: Scientists of the Civil War* (New York: Hastings House, 1961), 190–98.

34. Matthew Fontaine Maury, Papers, Library of Congress, Washington, D.C.

35. Merciér to Thouvenel, May 28, Washington, *A.M.A.E.,* E.U., 127: 364.

36. Howard Jones, *Union in Peril,* 117–19.

37. Merciér to Thouvenel, undated correspondence in 1862 volume of *A.M.A.E.,* E.U., 122–24; Case and Spencer, *The United States and France,* 275–85. This is the most complete account of the Richmond visit.

38. *New York Times,* May 6, 1862.

39. Benjamin to Slidell, no. 5, July 19, 1862, Pickett Papers; *ORN,* ser. 3, vol. 2: 461–67; *New York Times,* May 6, 1862.

40. Thouvenel to Merciér, Paris, May 21, 1862, 127: 176–81; Thouvenel to Merciér, May 15, 1862, 127: 171–73; Merciér to Thouvenel, Washington, Apr. 28, 1862, 127: 167–68, *A.M.A.E.,* E.U.; Carroll, *Henri Merciér,* 175. Carroll points out the inconsistencies in the various accounts sent by Merciér. Merciér probably was responding to a superior that was displeased with his actions, although Carroll does not reach this conclusion.

41. Slidell to Mason, May 14, 1862, Mason Papers.

42. Ibid., Mason to Slidell, May 17.

43. Ibid., Slidell to Mason, May 16, Paris; Owsley, *King Cotton,* 292–95.

44. *Index,* May 1, 1862.

45. *The Economist,* May 3, 1862.

46. Case and Spencer, *The United States and France,* 283.

47. Henry Hotze Collection, Library of Congress, Washington, D.C.

48. Mobile *Daily Register,* May 11, 1887, Henry Hotze obituary.

49. *Index.*

50. Charles P. Cullop, *Confederate Propaganda in Europe: 1861–1865* (Coral Gables: Univ. of Miami Press, 1969), 19.

51. Hotze to Joel White, Sept. 14, 1861, *ORN,* ser. 4, vol. 1: 611–12. This letter contains details of the delays and frustrations Hotze experienced in his passage through Union and Canadian territory.

52. Hunter to Hotze, Nov. 14, 1861, *ORN,* ser. 2, vol. 2: 117.

53. Hotze to Hunter, Mar. 24, 1862, *ORN,* ser. 2, vol. 2: 371; Apr. 25, 1862, 3: 400–401; Stephen B. Oates, "Henry Hotze: Confederate Agent Abroad," *Historian* 27 (Feb. 1965): 131–54.

54. *Index.*

55. Case and Spencer, *The United States and France,* 281.

8. Will the Emperor Help Obtain Recognition?

1. Evans, *Judah P. Benjamin,* 186–95.

2. Seward to Adams, dispatch no. 289, July 7, 1862, 124; dispatch no. 372, Oct. 12, 1862, 211–12; Seward to Dayton, dispatch no. 166, June 20, 1862, 351, *FRUS.*

These dispatches contain an overview of the military sentiment in the United States at the end of the summer campaign, and the outlook for a major battle on Union soil.

3. Cullop, *Confederate Propaganda,* 7–8.

4. Owsley, *King Cotton Diplomacy,* 294–95.

5. Dudley to Seward, May 10, 1862, United States, Dept. of State, *Dispatches from United States Ministers to Great Britain, 1792–1870* (Washington, D.C.: National Archives).

6. Adams Diary, 1: 140.

7. Benjamin to Mason, Apr. 8, 1862, *ORN,* ser. 2, vol. 3: 373.

8. Pickett Papers. Benjamin's memo to Mallory with a request for the secretary of navy's response regarding the disrupted communications with diplomatic agents in Europe.

9. Merli, *Great Britain,* 246.

10. Meade, *Judah P. Benjamin,* 246.

11. State Dept. Ledger Book, Pickett Papers. Each page of the ledger book is signed by Washington and is kept in a meticulously neat handwriting. Ball, *Financial Failure,* 186; Charles S. Davis, *Colin J. McRae: Confederate Financial Agent* (Tuscaloosa, Ala.: Confederate Publishing Co., 1961), 94. DeLeon received far more financial assistance than Hotze and achieved less.

12. L. Q. Washington, "The Confederate State Department," *The Independent* (Sept. 1901). This article is an invaluable source of information about the organization of the State Department written by its chief clerk.

13. Edmund Kirke, "Our Visit to Richmond," *Atlantic Monthly* (Sept. 1864).

14. Earl Schenck Miers, ed., *John B. Jones: A Rebel War Clerk's Diary, 1866* (New York: Sagamore Press, 1958; reprint, Baton Rouge: Louisiana State Univ. Press, 1993), 282; Meade, *Judah P. Benjamin,* 245.

15. Slidell to Benjamin, June 23, 1862, in Meade, *Judah P. Benjamin,* 2: 259–60.

16. *Index,* July 10, 1862.

17. *Morning Star,* July 9, 1862.

18. Spence to Mason, July 11, 1862, Mason Papers.

19. Jenkins, *Britain and the War,* 2: 95.

20. Adams to Seward, July 17, 1862, *FRUS,* 139–40; Adams Diary, 1: 167–69.

21. Moran to Dudley, June 17, 1862, quoted from The Dudley Papers, Huntington Library, quoted in Jenkins, *Britain and the War,* 2: 96. Jenkins stated, "Adams expected little to come of Lindsay's motion." This statement by Jenkins is extraordinary in light of the evidence and, indeed, of Jenkins's narrative.

22. Moran Papers, 2: 1040–44.

23. *Hansard's,* 3d series, (1862): 511–78.

24. Merciér to Thouvenel, July 11, 1862, *FRUS,* France, vol. 128, exhibit 107.

25. Case and Spencer, *The United States and France,* 388.

26. Slidell to Benjamin, July 25, 1862, Pickett Papers; *ORN,* ser. 2, vol. 3: 479–81; Adams, *Great Britain,* 2: 19; Owsley, *King Cotton Diplomacy,* 310–14.

27. Case and Spencer, *The United States and France,* 305–7.

28. Slidell to Benjamin, July 25, 1862, Pickett Papers; *ORN,* ser. 2, vol. 3: 479–87.

29. Ibid.

30. Ibid. The interview is described in a memorandum attached to this communication, more specifically identified as no. 10.

31. Ibid.

32. Case and Spencer, *The United States and France,* 323.

33. Ibid. Slidell to Mason, July 16 and 18, 1862, Mason Papers. In these dis-

patches to Mason, Slidell discusses his Mexican proposal and informs Mason of his intention to make the proposal in the appropriate situation during his interview.

34. Owsley, *King Cotton Diplomacy*, 312–14.

35. Ibid.

36. Slidell to Benjamin, July 25, 1862, *ORN*, ser. 2, vol. 3: 482.

37. Slidell to Benjamin, Pickett Papers, no. 10, July 25, 1862. The interview is described in detail in a memorandum enclosed with this dispatch. Slidell's report to Benjamin is contained in *ORN*, ser. 2, vol. 3: 479–87. All of the above quotations are contained in Slidell's memorandum. For a full discussion, see Owsley, *King Cotton Diplomacy*, 312–13, and Case and Spencer, *The United States and France*, 303–6.

38. Evans, *Judah P. Benjamin*, 185–90.

39. Slidell to Benjamin, Paris, July 25, 1862, Pickett Papers. At some point, Slidell's explanation for omitting any mention of the Mexican or cotton proposal was appended to the memorandum.

40. Owsley, *King Cotton Diplomacy*, 317.

41. Slidell to Benjamin, Paris, July 25, 1862, *ORN*, ser. 2, vol. 3: 479–81.

42. Thouvenel to Flahault, Paris, July 26, 1862, quoted in Case and Spencer, *The United States and France*, 311; Spencer, "Edouard Drouyn de Lhuys," 47. Spencer suggests on page 3 of his dissertation that both the French Foreign Ministers, Thouvenel and Drouyn de Lhuys, were sympathetic to the Union during the Civil War.

43. Slidell to Benjamin, Paris, Aug. 20, 1862, *ORN*, ser. 2, vol. 3: 518–20.

44. Slidell to Benjamin, Aug. 20, *ORN*, ser. 2, vol. 3: 518–20, dispatch no. 10.

45. Richardson, *Messages and Papers of the Confederacy*, 2: 315.

46. Russell had refused Mason's request for an interview in early August.

9. The Lost Diplomatic Opportunity of 1862

1. Crook, *The North, the South*, 221–22; Frank Merli and Theodore A. Wilson, "The British Cabinet and the Confederacy," *Maryland Historical Magazine* 65 (fall 1970): 239–62; Howard Jones, *Union in Peril*, 136–41.

2. Russell to Gladstone, Sept. 11, 1862, William E. Gladstone, Papers and Correspondence, British National Library (hereafter cited as Gladstone Papers).

3. The battle of Murfreesboro, Tennessee, should not be confused with the subsequent battle of Stone's River fought in and around the Tennessee town that resulted in a Union victory and the withdrawal of Bragg's army south toward Chattanooga.

4. Paludan, *The Presidency of Abraham Lincoln*, 130–35.

5. Russell to Palmerston, Sept. 14, 1862, quoted in Adams, *Great Britain*, 2: 38. Russell was in Europe accompanying Queen Victoria on a visit to her uncle, King Leopold of Belgium.

6. Russell to Cowley, Sept. 16, 1862, Henry Richard Charles Wellesley Cowley, Papers, Public Records Office, British Museum, London (hereafter cited as Cowley Papers).

7. Ibid., Palmerston to Russell, Sept. 14, 1862, and Cowley to Russell, Sept. 18, 1862, 2: 38–39.

8. Case and Spencer, *The United States and France*, 336.

9. Dayton to Seward, Paris, Sept. 17, 1862, *FRUS*, French, vol. 55; Case and Spencer, *The United States and France*, 336.

10. Graebner, "European Intervention."

11. Mason to Slidell, Sept. 10, 1862; Slidell to Mason, Sept. 12, 1862, Mason Papers.

12.   Slidell to Benjamin, no. 13, enclosing memorandum Sept. 13, 1862, *ORN,* ser. 2, vol. 3: 525–27; Case and Spencer, *The United States and France,* 344–46.

13.   Slidell to Benjamin, Sept. 29, 1862, no. 15, Pickett Papers; *ORN,* ser. 2, vol. 3: 546–48.

14.   Slidell to Mason, Oct. 2, 1862, Mason Papers, enclosing parts of the letters from Shaftesbury.

15.   Slidell to Benjamin, Oct. 9, 1862, no. 19, Pickett Papers.

16.   Case and Spencer, *The United States and France,* 342–46.

17.   Slidell to Mason, Oct. 17, 1862, Mason Papers.

18.   Owsley, *King Cotton Diplomacy,* 278, 436.

19.   Slidell to Benjamin, Oct. 28, 1862, no. 19, Pickett Papers.

20.   Case and Spencer, *The United States and France,* 349–52.

21.   Russell to Cowley, Sept. 22, 1862, Cowley Papers, vol. 4; Palmerston to Russell, Sept. 23, quoted in Adams, *Great Britain,* 2: 39.

22.   Palmerston to Russell, Sept. 27, 1862, quoted in Bigelow, *Retrospections,* 1: 550–51.

23.   *FRUS,* French 1862–63, 165–68; Charles F. Adams Jr., "Crisis in Downing Street," *Proceedings of the Massachusetts Historical Society* (May 1914): 372–424.

24.   Mason to Benjamin, Sept. 18, 1862, Pickett Papers, exhibit no. 17, *ORN,* ser. 2, vol. 3: 533.

25.   Palmerston to Gladstone, Sept. 24, 1862, quoted in Palmerston's *Gladstone and Palmerston, Being the Correspondence of Lord Palmerston with Mr. Gladstone, 1861– 1865,* ed. Phillip Guedalla (Convent Garden, England: Victor Gollancz, 1928), 232– 33. Palmerston's letter to Gladstone is printed in its entirety. See also Adams, *Great Britain,* 2: 41.

26.   Gladstone to Palmerston, Sept. 25, 1862, quoted in Palmerston, *Gladstone and Palmerston,* 233–36.

27.   Granville to Palmerston, Sept. 27, 1862, quoted in Owsley, *King Cotton Diplomacy,* 346–47.

28.   Adams, *Great Britain,* 2: 47; Robert L. Reid, ed., "William E. Gladstone's 'Insincere Neutrality' during the Civil War," *Civil War History* 15, no. 4 (1969): 293– 307; London *Times,* Oct. 8, 1862.

29.   Adams, *Great Britain,* 2: 48; Gladstone Papers, vol. 7. A memo to members of the Cabinet dated Sept. 20, 1862, outlines Gladstone's position.

30.   Lord Palmerston (Henry John Temple), Papers, British Library, London (hereafter cited as Palmerston Papers); also quoted in Adams, *Great Britain,* 2: 49. Russell attached a copy of the Emancipation Proclamation, Seward's circular letter of Sept. 22, and a copy of Lincoln's answer published in the *National Intelligencia,* responding to the Chicago abolitionists.

31.   Merli and Wilson, "British Cabinet"; Adams, *Great Britain,* 2: 52.

32.   Howard Jones, *Union in Peril,* 186–97. Jones gives Lewis considerable credit for sustaining the policy of neutrality within the British Cabinet. Edward E. Ellsworth, "Anglo-American Affairs in October of 1862," *Lincoln Herald* 66 (summer 1964): 89–96.

33.   Palmerston to Russell, Nov. 2, 1862, Great Britain, Foreign Office, *British and Foreign State Papers.*

34.   Ibid., Russell to Palmerston, Nov. 3; Lewis memorandum, Russell Papers; Owsley, *King Cotton Diplomacy,* 355; Adams, *Great Britain,* 2: 61–62; Howard Jones, *Union in Peril,* 188–91.

35. Mason to Benjamin, Nov. 7, 1862, no. 20, Pickett Papers; *ORN*, ser. 2, vol. 3: 600–601.

36. Mason to Benjamin, Nov. 8, 1862, Pickett Papers; *ORN*, includes a copy of the letter to Slidell.

37. Russell to Cowley, Nov. 13, 1862, *Hansard's*, Lords, 29 (1863); "Dispatch Respecting the Civil War in North America," London *Times*, Nov. 15, 1862; Gerald Carson, "God Bless the Russians," in *Timeline* 3, no. 4 (1986): 2–17.

38. Owsley, *King Cotton Diplomacy*, 357.

39. Slidell to Mason, Nov. 14, 1862, Mason Papers; E. A. Adamov, ed., "Documents Relating to Russian Policy during the American Civil War," *Journal of Modern History* 2 (1930): 603–11.

40. Slidell to Mason, Nov. 16, 1862, Mason Papers.

41. Ibid., Lindsay to Mason, Nov. 20, 1862.

42. Slidell to Benjamin, Nov. 29, 1862, no. 29, Pickett Papers; *ORN*, ser. 2, vol. 3: 612–13; Bigelow, *Retrospections*, 1: 574.

43. Howard Jones, *Union in Peril*, 224–30.

44. John Hope Franklin, *The Emancipation Proclamation* (Garden City, N.J.: Doubleday, 1963), 22–26.

45. Sadie D. St. Clair, "Slavery as a Diplomatic Factor in Anglo-American Relations during the Civil War," *Journal of Negro History* 30 (July 1945): 260–75; Harral E. Landry, "Slavery and the Slave Trade in Atlantic Diplomacy, 1850–1861," *Journal of Southern History* 27 (1961): 184–207; Kinley J. Brauer, "The Slavery Problem in the Diplomacy of the American Civil War," *Pacific Historical Review* 46 (Aug. 1977): 439–69.

46. Beringer, Hattaway, Jones, and Still, *Why the South Lost*. These authors conclude that the resources and leadership, if not the same, were equally balanced and suggest the South suffered a "loss of will" that resulted in their defeat.

10. The Diplomacy of Finance and the Erlanger Loan

1. Benjamin to Forstall, Pickett Papers, Jan. 17, 1862; Benjamin to Isaac, Campbell, and Company, Mar. 27, 1862, *ORA*, ser. 4, vol. 1: 1007–8.

2. Ball, *Financial Failure*, 160–65; Owsley, *King Cotton Diplomacy*, 362–63.

3. Spencer, *The Confederate Navy in Europe*, 89–90.

4. John C. Schwab, *The Confederate States of America, 1861–1865: A Financial and Industrial History of the South during the Civil War* (New York: Charles Scribner's Sons, 1901), 35–36.

5. Mason to Slidell, no. 16, Sept. 18, 1862, Pickett Papers; *ORN*, ser. 2, vol. 3: 529–32.

6. Mason to Benjamin, undated handwritten dispatch, Pickett Papers; *ORN*, ser. 2, vol. 3. Reference is made to a dispatch in the index under G. N. Sanders, but a separate dispatch is not included and the reference is probably to Mason's undated communication.

7. Ibid., Benjamin to Mason, Oct. 28, 1862; *ORN*, ser. 2, vol. 3: 581–82.

8. Owsley, *King Cotton Diplomacy*, 365–66; Richard I. Lester, "Confederate Fiscal and Procurement Activity in Great Britain during the Civil War," *Military Collector and History* 27, no. 4 (1975): 163–65; M. Foster Farley, "Confederate Financier George Trenholm: 'The Manners of a Prince,'" *Civil War Times Illustrated* 21, no. 8 (1982): 18–25.

9.   Benjamin to Mason, Oct. 28, 1862, Mason Papers. Reference is made to "Major Ferguson's having in his hands a substantial number of bonds that he requested Spence liquidate."

10.   Owsley, *King Cotton Diplomacy*, 366.

11.   Mason to Benjamin, no. 22, Dec. 10, 1862, Pickett Papers.

12.   Ibid., Benjamin to Mason, no. 12, Jan. 15, 1863; *ORN*, ser. 2, vol. 3: 648–51; Farley, "Confederate Financier."

13.   Owsley, *King Cotton Diplomacy*, 368; Ball, *Financial Failure*, 170–71.

14.   Lester, *Confederate Finance*, 21–22.

15.   Samuel B. Thompson, *Confederate Purchasing Operations Abroad* (Chapel Hill: Univ. of North Carolina Press, 1935), 14; Lester, *Confederate Finance*, 10. Caleb Huse was the chief purchasing agent for the Confederate War Department. He was extremely capable and hard working and enjoyed a close relationship with the Confederate banking house Fraser, Trenholm and Company.

16.   Slidell to Mason, Sept. 26, 1862, Mason Papers.

17.   *ORN*, ser. 4, vol. 2: 244–45, 478–82, 497–98, 525–27, 535–47.

18.   Slidell to Benjamin, no. 18, Oct. 28, 1862, Pickett Papers; *ORN*, ser. 2, vol. 3: 568–72. The contract is completely disclosed in this dispatch from Slidell to Benjamin but the earlier communications from Huse and Slidell to Mason are in the Mason Papers. A full account is also provided by Owsley, *King Cotton Diplomacy*, 370–72; Adams, *Great Britain*, 2: 158–63; and Lester, *Confederate Finance*, 27–57.

19.   Slidell to Benjamin, no. 18, Oct. 28, Pickett Papers; Judith F. Gentry, "A Confederate Success in Europe: The Erlanger Loan," *Journal of Southern History* 36, no. 2 (May 1970): 157–88. Gentry supports Slidell's conclusion that the political implications far outweigh the financial return received from the loan proceeds.

20.   Schenck, *John B. Jones*. There is no hard evidence that Huse personally profited from any munitions sales. It is more likely that the shady Crenshaw accused Huse to deflect any suspicion from his dealings with suppliers. Although neither allegation can be proved, the evidence is clear that the suppliers often kept two sets of books and double-charged the Confederate agents.

21.   Mason to Benjamin, no. 19, Nov. 4, 1862, Pickett Papers; *ORN*, ser. 2, vol. 3: 590–93.

22.   Richardson, *Messages and Papers of the Confederacy*, 2: 539; Lester, *Confederate Finance*, 30. Lester offers the suggestion that Vicompte de Saint Roman was Erlanger's chief representative in the Richmond group. This conclusion probably results from the frequent mention of Saint Roman in the Mason Papers in connection with conversations with Baron Erlanger in London. There is no reason to doubt the traditional acceptance of Beer as the chief Erlanger representative in Richmond.

23.   Richardson, *Messages and Papers of the Confederacy*, 2: 361–63; Lester, *Confederate Finance*, 29. Lester states that the Erlanger papers he examined clearly place Emile Erlanger in Paris at this time, therefore rejecting earlier suggestions by Schwab in *Confederate States of America* and Ernest A. Smith in *The History of the Confederate Treasury*, both published in 1901, that Erlanger visited America and actually went to Richmond. The conclusion of Schwab and Smith is further amplified by Allan Foreman in an article "A Bit of Secret Service History," *The Magazine of American History* 12, 1884, 223–31.

24.   Richardson, *Messages and Papers of the Confederacy*, 2: 405–8.

25.   Ibid., 2: 407; Lester, *Confederate Finance*, 30.

26.   Gentry, "A Confederate Success"; Lester, *Confederate Finance*, 31.

27.   Ibid.; *ORN*, ser. 2, vol. 3: 648–51.

28. Baroness Slidell Erlanger to Baron Emile Erlanger, Feb. 13, 1863, Erlanger Papers, quoted in Lester, *Confederate Finance,* 31.

29. Ibid., 23. Lester provides the most complete examination of the events based on his private collection of the papers of Baron Emile Erlanger, originals of which are housed in London and used by Lester in his original research for *Confederate Finance.* It has often been reported that Slidell's daughter married Erlanger's son, but in fact she married Emile Erlanger himself, and the couple apparently enjoyed a happy life together. Mathilde frequently traveled with Erlanger on extended business trips away from home and they corresponded regularly. They were married in 1862, and their private correspondence, included in the Erlanger Papers, covers the period from 1862 to 1898.

30. *The Economist,* Feb. 7, 1863.

31. Mason Papers.

32. *ORN,* ser. 2, vol. 3: 675–77. There appears to be a discrepancy between the debts owed and the agreed-upon price of 2.3 million pounds of cotton. Again, the question remains of what happened to this excess.

33. Erlanger to John Slidell, Mar. 16, 1863, from the Erlanger Papers quoted in Lester, *Confederate Finance,* 34.

34. Ibid., Erlanger to John Slidell, Mar. 18, 1863.

35. Slidell to Benjamin, Mar. 21, 1863, quoted in Richardson, *Messages and Papers of the Confederacy,* 541–43.

36. Owsley, *King Cotton Diplomacy,* 160–63.

37. Ibid., 169.

38. Clapp, *Forgotten First Citizen,* 185.

39. De Bellet, *Diplomacy of the Confederate Cabinet;* Slidell to Benjamin, no. 50, Dec. 6, 1863, Pickett Papers.

40. Cullop, *Confederate Propaganda,* 76–84. Cullop provides a thorough discussion of DeLeon's mission to Europe and seeks to explain the number of frustrating failures that confronted the South Carolina journalist. Cullop suggests that DeLeon did meet with modest success, despite his personality difficulties.

41. Josiah Gorgas, *The Civil War Diary of General Josiah Gorgas,* ed. Frank E. Vandiver (Tuscaloosa: Univ. of Alabama Press, 1947), 27.

42. Spence to Mason, Apr.–May 1863 (see especially May 9); Mason to Slidell, May 14, 1863, Mason Papers.

43. The articles of agreement between Mason and Erlanger, Apr. 7, 1863, Erlanger Papers, quoted by Lester, *Confederate Finance.* This agreement is witnessed by J. H. Schroder of London. The presence of Schroder's signature suggests the cooperation that existed between Erlanger and Schroder. These articles are also in *ORN,* ser. 2, vol. 3: 735–38.

44. Mason to Benjamin, no. 34, Apr. 27, 1863, Mason Papers.

45. Ball, *Financial Failure,* 78–79, 284–85.

11. The Burden of Multiparty Diplomacy

1. Mason to Slidell, Dec. 11, 1862, no. 23, Pickett Papers; *ORN,* ser. 2, vol. 3: 618–19.

2. Slidell to Hunter, Mar. 26, 1862, quoted in Richardson, *Messages and Papers of Jefferson Davis,* 2: 207–8; Virginia Mason, *Public Life,* 2: 63–68.

3. Owsley, *King Cotton Diplomacy,* 435.

4. Benjamin to Mason, Oct. 31, 1862, Mason to Benjamin, Jan. 14, 1863, Pickett Papers; *ORN,* ser. 2, vol. 3: 584–88, 643–45.

5. Jenkins, *Britain and the War*, 1: 313.

6. Davis's speech is printed in its entirety in the appendix, Confederate States, *Journal of the Congress*, 2: 908–12.

7. Richardson, *Messages and Papers of Jefferson Davis*, 1: 345–48. Message of the president to the 4th session of the First Confederate Congress.

8. Owsley, *King Cotton Diplomacy*, 431–32; Jenkins, *Britain and the War*, 2: 315–16.

9. Harriet Chappell Owsley, "Henry Shelton Sanford and the Federal Surveillance Abroad, 1861–1865," *Mississippi Valley Historical Review* 48, no. 2 (1961–62): 211–28; Dayton Papers, reel 2; Joseph A. Fry, *Henry S. Sanford: Diplomacy and Business in Nineteenth-Century America* (Reno: Univ. of Nevada Press, 1982), 96.

10. Mann to Benjamin, Jan. 5, 1863, no. 36, Mann to Benjamin, Feb. 10, 1863, no. 39, Pickett Papers; *ORN*, ser. 2, vol. 3: 689–90; Slidell to Mason, Feb. 11, 1863, Mason Papers.

11. Drouyn de Lhuys to Merciér, no. 1, Jan. 9, 1863, *A.M.A.E.*, E.U., vol. 129, quoted in Owsley, *King Cotton Diplomacy*, 439; Case and Spencer, *The United States and France*, 413–14, 507–9.

12. Case and Spencer, *The United States and France*, 400–406.

13. London *Times*, Jan. 13–14, 1863; *Index*, Jan. 15, 1863.

14. *Index*, Jan. 17, 1863.

15. Slidell to Benjamin, Jan. 21, 1863, no. 24, Pickett Papers; *ORN*, ser. 2, vol. 3: 666–68; Slidell to Mason, Jan. 21, 1862, Mason Papers.

16. Seward to Dayton, Feb. 6, 1863, no. 297, Dayton to Seward, no. 283, Mar. 6, 1863, *FRUS*; Dayton to Dudley, Mar. 3, Dayton Papers, reel 2. Dayton softened Seward's language while stating the U.S. position.

17. Paul H. Reuter, "United States–French Relations Regarding French Intervention in Mexico: From the Tripartite Treaty to Queretaro," *Southern Quarterly* 6, no. 4 (1968): 469–89.

18. Norman Rich, *Great Power Diplomacy*, 165.

19. Slidell to Hunter, Mar. 10, 1862, Pickett Papers; *ORN*, ser. 2, vol. 3: 356–58.

20. Owsley, *King Cotton Diplomacy*, 432–33.

21. Russell to Mason, *ORN*, ser. 2, vol. 3: 688–89.

22. Russell to Lyons, Feb. 14, 1863, quoted in Adams, *Great Britain*, 2: 155.

23. *Hansard's*, Lords, 3d. ser., 169 (1863).

24. Mason Papers, Mar. 18, 1863; Brian Jenkins, "William Gregory: Champion of the Confederacy," *History Today* 28, no. 5 (1978): 322–30.

25. Rich, *Great Power Diplomacy*, 161–63; Crook, *The North, the South*, 284–88.

26. Case and Spencer, *The United States and France*, 398–401.

27. Jenkins, "William Gregory."

28. *Morning Star*, quoted in Jenkins, *Britain and the War*, 2: 308.

29. Jenkins, *Britain and the War*, 2: 309.

30. DeLeon received a large sum of money from the Confederate government to conduct a propaganda campaign in France but was not as successful as Hotze in London. He was an experienced journalist and had served the U.S. government as a diplomat in Egypt before the war. It was this diplomatic experience that encouraged him to render unsolicited advice to Slidell and ultimately to allow sensitive communications to fall into the hands of the Union.

31. DeLeon to McHenry, June 22, 1863, Edouard DeLeon, Papers, Library of Congress, Washington, D.C.

32.   Case and Spencer, *The United States and France*, 398–426. See this chapter for the best outline of the events from a French perspective.

33.   Bigelow, *Retrospections*, 2: 26; Lindsay Papers quoted in Jenkins, *Britain and the War*, 2: 310.

34.   Sears, *John Slidell*, 146.

35.   *ORN*, ser. 2, vol. 3: 812–14; Slidell's note dated June 8 was not delivered by Persigny until June 12. Case and Spencer, *The United States and France*, 408.

36.   Jenkins, *Britain and the War*, 2: 309–13.

37.   *ORN*, ser. 2, vol. 3: 812–14.

38.   Ibid. The entire account of the meeting is contained in Slidell's memorandum. Unfortunately, no other record of this meeting confirms or denies Slidell's account.

39.   Note from a "friend" to Slidell, Paris, June 19, 1863, enclosed with dispatch from Slidell to Benjamin, Paris, June 21, 1862, Pickett Papers, no. 18.

40.   Lindsay to Mason, memo of meeting with Napoleon, Mason Papers; Owsley, *King Cotton Diplomacy*, 449. Owsley repeatedly identifies Slidell's "friend" as M. Cintrat at the Foreign Office. There is only one specific reference to this official, and Owsley assumes that Slidell has only one friend at the Ministry. He associates Cintrat frequently with the term "friend" or "my friend."

41.   Case and Spencer, *The United States and France*, 412; Owsley, *King Cotton Diplomacy*, 449.

42.   Slidell to Mason, June 29, 1863, Mason Papers.

43.   Mason to Benjamin, July 2, 1863, no. 41, Pickett Papers.

44.   *Hansard's*, 3d ser., 171 (1863): 1719.

45.   Jenkins, *Britain and the War*, 310–11. This is the best account of the debate in Parliament.

46.   Ibid., 314–15.

47.   Spence to Mason, July 3, 1863, Mason Papers; *Hansard's*, Commons, 3d ser., 171 (1863): 1782; Owsley, *King Cotton Diplomacy*, 455–58.

48.   *Hansard's*, 3d ser., 172 (1863): 661–73. Palmerston had used Lindsay to negotiate commercial treaties with France on an unofficial basis several years earlier.

49.   Mason to Jefferson Davis, Oct. 2, 1863, Mason Papers. Mason used the absence of Tory support as a rationalization to Davis in this later communication. Hotze to Benjamin, July 11, 1863, Pickett Papers; Oates, "Henry Hotze."

50.   Slidell to Benjamin, July 6, 1863, no. 40, and July 19, 1863, no. 42, Pickett Papers; *ORN*, ser. 2, vol. 3: 845–46.

51.   Ibid. Mason to Benjamin, July 10, 1863, no. 42.

52.   Edouard Drouyn de Lhuys to Baron Gros, July 1, 1863, *A.M.A.E.*, E.U., vol. 725, quoted in Owsley, *King Cotton Diplomacy*, 460–61. Spencer, "Edouard Drouyn de Lhuys," 136–42. The entire text of this telegram is quoted in French by Owsley.

53.   Benjamin to Mason, June 16, 1863, no. 24, Pickett Papers; *ORN*, ser. 2, vol. 3: 786.

54.   Benjamin to Mason, Aug. 4, 1863, no. 30, Pickett Papers; Benjamin to Mason, Aug. 4, 1863, Mason Papers. The personal note of commendation, including the authorization to use his own discretion, is in Benjamin's handwriting and is transcribed in *ORN*, ser. 2, vol. 3: 852–53.

55.   Mason to Benjamin, Oct. 19, 1863, Pickett Papers; *ORN*, ser. 2, vol. 3: 934–35.

56.   Owsley, *King Cotton Diplomacy*, 466.

12. The Burden of Southern Honor

1.   Yearns, *The Confederate Congress,* 163; Emory Thomas, *The Confederate Nation,* 187.

2.   Benjamin to Mason, Oct. 16, 1862, Pickett Papers; Mason to Slidell, Nov. 6, 1862, Mason Papers; Jenkins, *Britain and the War,* 2: 317–20. Jenkins provides an excellent overview of a number of organizations formed for the purpose of pursuing intervention. One such organization, the Society for Promoting the Cessation of Hostilities in America, was led by Rev. Francis Tremlett, while its activities were directed from behind the scenes by Matthew Fontaine Maury. The responsibility for the supervision of continued Confederate activity in England fell to Maury and Hotze. These men continued to work with James Spence, who organized Southern Clubs in Lancashire, Ipswitch, and Glasgow. These organizations denounced and often spoke at labor rallies denouncing the insincerity of the Union Emancipation Proclamation. The remnants of an organized campaign in support of the Confederate cause did not end with Mason's withdrawal, but support rapidly faded without the presence of an official designated commissioner.

3.   *Morning Star,* Aug. 24, 1863.

4.   Hotze to Benjamin, Sept. 26, 1863, *ORN,* ser. 2, vol. 3: 914; *London Times,* Sept. 23, 1863. The *Times* editorial was attached to the original communication but is not reprinted in the *ORN.* The entire editorial, however, is in the Sept. 23, 1863, newspaper.

5.   Norman Rich, *Great Power Diplomacy,* 158–61; Jenkins, *Britain and the War,* 2: 317–20; Crook, *The North, the South,* 284–87, 316–18; Laurence J. Orzell, "A 'Favorable Interval': the Polish Insurrection in the United States and France, 1863," in *Civil War History* 24, no. 4 (1978): 332–50.

6.   Confederate States, *Journal of the Congress,* 5: 47.

7.   Yancey to Barksdale, Nov. 17, 1862, Yancey Papers; Confederate States, *Journal of the Congress,* 2: 142; Austin L. Venable, "The Public Career of William Lowndes Yancey," in *Alabama Review* 16 (1963): 200–212.

8.   *The Montgomery Advertiser,* Mar. 15, 1863; Berwanger, *British Foreign Service.*

9.   Confederate States, *Journal of the Congress,* 5: 333.

10.   Owsley, *King Cotton Diplomacy,* 469; Evans, *Judah P. Benjamin,* 164–67.

11.   Coulter, *The Confederate States,* 143.

12.   Ibid., 192.

13.   Bonham, *British Consuls,* 220. Bonham provides numerous quotations from newspapers and journals and describes in detail several episodes illustrating the conflicting interest of the consuls and the Confederacy.

14.   Owsley, *King Cotton Diplomacy,* 473; Berwanger, *British Foreign Service.*

15.   Ella Lonn, *Foreigners in the Confederacy* (Chapel Hill: Univ. of North Carolina Press, 1940), 97–108.

16.   Bonham, *British Consuls,* 130–31; Robert H. Welborn, "The British Consulate in Georgia, 1824–1981," *Proceedings and Papers of the Georgia Association of History* (1982): 105–11; Newton, *Lord Lyons,* 2: 82–83, 121.

17.   Bonham, *British Consuls,* 232; Owsley, *King Cotton Diplomacy,* 494.

18.   *The Charleston Mercury,* Oct. 3, 1863, quoted in Bonham, *British Consuls,* 132.

19.   In addition to his extraordinarily strong friendship with Benjamin, Davis enjoyed a friendship with General Braxton Bragg. After the Battle of Chickamauga, Bragg was faced with a near mutiny from his staff officers. Bragg's army still had the Union

troops bottled up in Chattanooga, but the General needed the support of the president to survive a crisis in his command.

20. *ORN,* ser. 2, vol. 3: 853–54; Evans, *Judah P. Benjamin,* 236–37; Meade, *Judah P. Benjamin,* 293–94; Owsley, *King Cotton Diplomacy,* 492.

21. Walker to Russell, no. 139, Oct. 15, 1863, quoted in Bonham, *British Consuls,* 232.

22. Hoole, ed., *Diplomacy of the Confederate Cabinet at Richmond and Its Agents Abroad* (Tuscaloosa: Univ. of Alabama Press, 1963), 184–89.

23. Carroll, *Henri Merciér,* 330–34.

24. Warren F. Spencer, "French Tobacco in Richmond," *Virginia Magazine of History and Biography* 7 (1963): 187–92; Meade, *Judah P. Benjamin,* 104–6; Sears, *John Slidell,* 87. Spencer provides the best account of the court action and the legal issues raised.

25. Case and Spencer, *The United States and France,* 524–28.

26. Drouyn De Lhuys to Merciér, Jan. 8, 1863, quoted in Carroll, Henri Merciér, 336.

27. Bingham Duncan, "Franco-American Tobacco Diplomacy," *Maryland Historical Magazine* 51 (Dec. 1956): 273–301.

28. Case and Spencer, *The United States and France,* 528–40. Spencer, writing this portion of the book, provides a thorough account of the events and their long-term implications on the body of international law relating to the storage and shipment of neutral goods. See also Milledge L. Bonham Jr., *The French Consuls in the Confederate States: Studies in Southern History and Politics* (New York: Columbia Univ. Press, 1915).

13. France, Mexico, and Frustrated Confederates

1. Slidell to Benjamin, Aug. 5, 1863, *ORN,* ser. 2, vol. 3: 855–57; Rich, *Great Power Diplomacy,* 156–65.

2. Spencer, *The Confederate Navy in Europe,* 170; Merli, *Great Britain,* 223–25; Edward Boykin, *Sea Devil of the Confederacy: The Story of the Florida and Her Captain, John Newland Maffitt* (New York: Funk & Wagnalls, 1959), 229–33. See also Wilbur Devereux Jones, *The Confederate Rams at Birkenhead: A Chapter in Anglo-American Relations* (Tuscaloosa, Ala.: Confederate Publishers, 1961).

3. Philip Van Dorn Stern, *When the Guns Roared: World Aspects of the American Civil War* (New York: Doubleday & Co., 1965), 249–50.

4. Case and Spencer, *The United States and France,* 446–49.

5. Dayton to Seward, Paris, Sept. 24, 1863, Oct. 8, 1863, *FRUS,* no. 350, 360; Dayton Papers. A handwritten draft of this dispatch is included in Dayton's papers.

6. John Bigelow, *France and the Confederate Navy, 1862–1865* (New York: Harper, 1888; reprint, 1968), 195.

7. Drouyn de Lhuys to Merciér, Paris, Oct. 22, 1863, *A.M.A.E.,* E.U., no. 130, 217–18; Dayton to Seward, Oct. 23, 1863, *FRUS,* no. 54, 368.

8. Case and Spencer, *The United States and France,* 495–99. Spencer provides a careful analysis of Dayton's successful diplomatic efforts to prevent the construction and delivery of the Confederate ships. Serge Gavronsky, *The French Liberal Opposition and the American Civil War* (New York: Humanities Press, 1968), 228–34. The author suggests that the motives for the employee of Vorus and Company were grounded in the French liberal opposition to the war and identifies the liberal leadership supporting the Union diplomatic effort to neutralize Confederate naval agents in France.

Merli, *Great Britain,* 213–14. Merli provides a discussion of Bulloch's actions in shifting Confederate naval construction to France.

9.   Spencer, *The Confederate Navy in Europe,* 172.

10.   These ships were placed at the disposal of Dayton, whose intelligence as to Confederate activities proved timely and accurate.

11.   Bulloch, *The Secret Service,* 2: 216–21; Case and Spencer, *The United States and France.* For the full story of this failed Confederate naval initiative, see pages 462–97.

12.   Case and Spencer, *The United States and France,* 440–67, 547–55.

13.   Spencer, "Edouard Drouyn de Lhuys." Spencer provides a careful and thoughtful examination of the motives of Drouyn de Lhuys and describes him as a French patriot pursuing the interest of his country, notwithstanding the threat to his career.

14.   Kathryn A. Hanna, "The Role of the South in the French Intervention in Mexico," *Journal of Southern History* 20 (1954): 3–21.

15.   Ibid.

16.   Dayton to Seward, May 16, 1864, Paris, *FRUS,* 467; John Bigelow, Papers, New York Public Library, folder no. 3; Bulloch, *The Secret Service,* 2: 47; Roberts, "James Dunwoody Bulloch."

17.   Slidell to Benjamin, Feb. 16, 1864, Bulloch to Mallory, Feb. 18, 1864, *ORN,* ser. 3, vol. 2.; Roberts, "James Dunwoody Bulloch."

18.   Reuter, "United States–French Relations."

19.   Benjamin to Slidell, Sept. 2, 1863, Slidell to Benjamin, Oct. 25, 1863, *ORN,* ser. 2, vol. 3: 837–39, 882–89.

20.   Case and Spencer, *The United States and France,* 441–42.

21.   Slidell to Benjamin, Dec. 3, 1863, *ORN,* ser. 2, vol. 3: 960–73.

22.   Ibid., Slidell to Benjamin, Dec. 15, 1863, ser. 2, vol. 3: 976–78.

23.   Bulloch, *The Secret Service,* 1: 52.

24.   Hanna, "The Role of the South"; Jim Daddysman, "British Neutrality and the Matamoros Trade: A Step Toward Anglo-American Rapprochement," in *Journal of the West Virginia Historical Association* 9, no. 1 (1985): 1–12.

25.   Dayton to Seward, dispatch no. 361, Oct. 9, 1863, *FRUS.*

26.   Gavronsky, *French Liberal Opposition,* 172. The author provides numerous quotes from newspapers and periodicals of the day and chronicles the debate in *Corps legislatif.*

27.   Rich, *Great Power Diplomacy,* 178.

28.   Ibid., 181; Nancy Nichols Barker, "France, Austria, and the Mexican Venture," *French Historical Studies* 3 (1963): 224–45.

29.   *ORN,* ser. 2, vol. 3: 988–90.

30.   Slidell to Benjamin, Mar. 16, 1864, Pickett Papers, no. 58, *ORN,* ser. 2, vol. 3: 1063–65.

31.   Ibid., Quintero to Benjamin, Feb. 4, 1863.

32.   Ibid., Slidell to Benjamin, Mar. 16, 1864; *ORN,* ser. 2, vol. 3: 1063–65.

14. The Desperate End Game

1.   McPherson, *Battle Cry of Freedom,* 817–24; Benjamin to Slidell, June 23, 1864, *ORN,* ser. 2, vol. 3. In this dispatch, Benjamin accused Napoleon III of openly rejecting the Southern cause. Benjamin claimed Napoleon was deliberately devious and led the Confederates on to protect his Mexican mission.

2.   James G. Randall and Richard N. Current, *Lincoln the President: The Last Full*

Measure (New York: Dodd, Mead, 1955), 99; Ludwell H. Johnson III, "Lincoln's Solution to the Problem of Peace Terms, 1864–1865," *Journal of Southern History* 34 (1968): 581–86. Johnson discusses in detail the advantages that would have accrued to Lincoln if an agreement could have been reached for the Southern states to return to the Union. He also discusses the political aspects of the Niagara Falls and Hampton Roads conferences.

3. Winks, *Canada and the United States*, 278, 310–11. Winks provides detail of both Confederate and Union operations in Canada throughout the war, emphasizing the military and intelligence activities.

4. Harland Holt Horner, *Lincoln and Greeley* (Champaign: Univ. of Illinois Press, 1953), 295–98; McPherson, *Battle Cry of Freedom*, 822–23.

5. Henry J. Raymond, *The Life, Public Service, and State Papers of Abraham Lincoln* (New York: J. C. Derby and N. C. Miller, 1863), 571. The tone of this letter suggests that Greeley and Jewett had already corresponded unofficially regarding the Southerner's proposal. See Warren F. Spencer, "The Jewett-Greeley Affair: A Private Scheme for French Mediation in the American Civil War," *New York History* 51, no. 3 (Apr. 1970): 238–68. Spencer declares that the French became involved in this complex matter as a third-party mediator.

6. John G. Nicolay and John Hay, *Abraham Lincoln: A History*, 10 vols. (New York: The Century Company, 1890), 7: 372–74; Horner, *Lincoln and Greeley*, 299. Horner makes clear that Greeley opposed Lincoln's reelection, although he compromised his opposition publicly throughout Lincoln's first term and supported the duly-elected government while working vigorously as part of the loyal opposition.

7. Lincoln to Greeley, July 9, 1864, as quoted in Lincoln's *The Complete Works of Abraham Lincoln*, 12 vols., ed. John G. Nicolay and John Hay (New York: The Lamb Publishing Co., 1894; reprint, 1905), 10: 154.

8. Edward Chase Kirkland, *The Peacemakers of 1864* (New York: Macmillan, 1927; reprint, AMS Press, 1969), 75. Kirkland quotes Greeley to Jewett.

9. Nicolay and Hay, *Lincoln: A History*, 9: 190; Kirkland, *The Peacemakers of 1864*.

10. Lincoln, *Complete Works*, 10: 161.

11. Nicolay and Hay, *Lincoln: A History*, 7: 372–74.

12. Welles, *Diary of Gideon Welles*, 1: 359–63.

13. Horner, *Lincoln and Greeley*, 302–17. The entire text of the Clay/Holcombe letter is reprinted, along with a news release repudiating Jewett. Horner also includes most of the relevant correspondence of the whole Niagara Falls fiasco.

14. Richardson, *Messages and Papers of Jefferson Davis*, 2: 437; Jefferson Davis, *The Rise and Fall*, 2: 186–87.

15. Henry W. Allen to James A. Sedon, Sept. 26, 1864, *ORA*, ser. 1, vol. 41: 774; Robert F. Durden, *The Gray and the Black: The Confederate Debate on Emancipation* (Baton Rouge: Louisiana State Univ. Press, 1972), 29–30, 74–75.

16. Owsley, *King Cotton Diplomacy*, 530–41; James M. Callahan, *Diplomatic History of the Southern Confederacy* (Baltimore: Johns Hopkins Univ. Press, 1901; reprint, New York: Frederick Ungar, 1964), 246–47; Craig A. Bauer, "The Last Effort: The Secret Mission of the Confederate Diplomat, Duncan F. Kenner," *Louisiana History* 22, no. 1 (winter 1981): 67–95.

17. Pickett Papers. A copy of the Confederate Constitution is contained in the first folio of these papers. Also see Durden, *The Gray and the Black*, 3.

18. Craig A. Bauer, *A Leader among Peers: The Life and Times of Duncan Farrar Kenner* (Lafayette: Center for Louisiana Studies, Univ. of Southwestern Louisiana,

1993). This is the most recent study of the life of Kenner; see also Bauer, "The Last Effort," specifically p. 73.

19.   Planter account books, Duncan F. Kenner, Papers, Library of Congress, Washington, D.C.; Owsley, *King Cotton Diplomacy*, 534; Durden, *The Gray and the Black*, 76–81. Durden provides several Southern newspapers advocating the use of slaves in the army and suggesting emancipation, if necessary, to remove any European opposition to intervention.

20.   Benjamin to Slidell, Benjamin to Mason, Dec. 27, 1864, *ORN*, ser. 2, vol. 3: 1253–56; George A. Trenholm, Papers, Library of Congress Washington, D.C.; Emory Thomas, *The Confederate Nation*, 286; Coulter, *The Confederate States*, 169. Trenholm was secretary of treasury from July 1864 until the end of the Confederacy.

21.   Bauer, "The Last Effort," 77–79. Bauer provides a detailed account of Kenner's escape and identifies the old friends and acquaintances who hid the Southerner and provided him with false documents.

22.   Owsley, *King Cotton Diplomacy*, 536; Bauer, "The Last Effort," 87.

23.   Owsley, *King Cotton Diplomacy*, 558, 565; William W. Henry, "Kenner's Mission to Europe," *William and Mary Quarterly* 25 (July 1916): 9–12.

24.   Mason to Slidell, Mar. 4, 1865, Slidell to Mason, Mar. 5–6, 1865, Mason Papers; Owsley, *King Cotton Diplomacy*, 538.

25.   Slidell to Mason, Mar. 6, 1865, Mason to Benjamin, Mar. 31, 1865, Mason Papers; Case and Spencer, *The United States and France*, 565.

26.   Mason to Benjamin, Mar. 31, 1865, Mason Papers; *ORN*, ser. 2, vol. 3: 1276–78; Owsley, *King Cotton Diplomacy*, 539–40.

27.   Bauer, "The Last Effort," 94.

28.   Crook, *The North, the South*, 356–57.

29.   Gorgas, *Civil War Diary*, 166; Miers, *John B. Jones*, 440.

30.   Alexander Hamilton Stephens, *Memoirs: A Constitutional View of the Late War Between the States: Its Causes, Character, and Results*, 2 vols. (Philadelphia: National Publishing Co., 1868), 2: 619; Miers, *John B. Jones*, 389.

31.   John A. Campbell, *Reminisces and Documents Relating to the Civil War during the Year 1865* (Baltimore: John Murray & Co., 1887), 12; Stephens, *Memoirs*, 2: 589, 622; R. M. T. Hunter, "The Peace Commission of 1865," *Southern Historical Society Papers* 3 (Apr. 1877): 168–76. All three Confederate representatives at the Hampton Roads conference provide a summary of the Blair proposal as it was outlined to them before their departure for the conference with Lincoln and Seward.

32.   Paul J. Zingg, "John Archibald Campbell and the Hampton Roads Conference—Quixote Diplomacy, 1865," *Alabama Historical Quarterly* (spring 1974): 27; McPherson, *Battle Cry of Freedom*, 824. McPherson details a proposal in the Confederate Congress to make Robert E. Lee a dictator.

33.   Abraham Lincoln, *The Collected Works of Abraham Lincoln*, 9 vols., ed. Roy P. Basler (New Brunswick, N.J.: Rutgers Univ. Press, 1952–55), 3: 275–76. Both the entire text of Davis's letter and Lincoln's response are reprinted by Basler.

34.   Ibid., 3: 273; Paludan, *The Presidency of Abraham Lincoln*.

35.   Benjamin P. Thomas, *Abraham Lincoln*, 265–67. Thomas explains Lincoln's view on the Civil War and its "wages."

36.   Lincoln, *Collected Works*, 8: 277–78.

37.   Stephens, *Memoirs*, 2: 613; Campbell memorandum to R. M. T. Hunter included in the Hunter Papers.

38.   Lincoln, *Collected Works*, 8: 260–61; Fitzhugh Lee, "The Failure of the Hampton Roads Conference," *Century Magazine* 52 (July 1896): 478; Campbell, *Remi-*

nisces, 14; Johnson, "Lincoln's Solution," 586. On his return to Washington, Lincoln went so far as to draft a $400 million appropriation measure to be sent to Congress. The Cabinet, remarkably, including Seward, unanimously rejected Lincoln's proposal. In light of this Cabinet opposition, Lincoln never sent the message, which was probably doomed in Congress without the support of a reinstated Southern constituency.

39. Memorandum by Campbell, Hunter Papers. Campbell apparently penned, immediately after the conference, this detailed account of the discussions. It is probably the most accurate available account of the conversations that took place. The participants in the conference agreed from the very beginning that no notes should be taken during the meeting that might later be used to politically embarrass the participants.

40. Lincoln, *Complete Works,* 10: 133.

41. Richard N. Current, *The Lincoln Nobody Knows* (New York: McGraw-Hill, 1958), 243–47; Johnson, "Lincoln's Solution"; Stephens, *Memoirs,* 2: 6, 11–12; Nicolay and Hay, *Lincoln: A History,* 10: 91–129; Campbell memorandum in Hunter Papers.

42. Miers, *John B. Jones,* 411; Nicolay and Hay, *Lincoln: A History,* 10: 130. *The Richmond Dispatch,* Feb. 7, 1865; the entire text of Davis's speech is quoted.

43. William T. Sherman, *Memoirs of General William T. Sherman,* 2 vols. (New York: D. Appleton & Co., 1875), 2: 269–70. Sherman burned Columbia to punish South Carolinians for their active role in the secession movement. The Union General admitted that Columbia had little military or strategic significance by this time.

15. The Legacy of Failure

1. Ferris, *Desperate Diplomacy,* ch. 1; Owsley, *King Cotton Diplomacy,* ch. 1, 2.

2. Crook, *The North, the South,* 71–85; Max Beloff, "Historical Revision No. CXVIII: Great Britain and the American Civil War," *History* 37 (Feb. 1952): 40–48.

3. Van Deusen, *William H. Seward,* 264–68; Case and Spencer, *The United States and France,* 274–77; Blumenthal, *A Reappraisal,* 160–61; Carroll, *Henri Merciér,* 57–63.

4. Jenkins, *Britain and the War,* 2: 70–75; Howard Jones, *Union in Peril,* 135–38.

5. Stephen V. Ash, *When the Yankees Came* (Chapel Hill and London: Univ. of North Carolina Press, 1995). See the prologue for a concise view of the Southern concept of republican values.

6. Beringer, Hattaway, Jones, and Still, *The Elements of Confederate Defeat,* 89–104, 187–205; Paul D. Escott, "Jefferson Davis and the Failure of Confederate Nationalism" (Ph.D. diss., Duke Univ., 1974), 193–203.

Bibliography

Manuscripts and Private Papers

Adams, Charles F. Papers. Massachusetts Historical Society, Boston (microfilm, Emory Univ. Library, Atlanta, Ga.).

Bigelow, John. Papers. New York Public Library.

Bragg, Thomas. Diary. Southern Historical Collection. Library of Congress, Washington, D.C.

Cobb, Howell. Papers. Univ. of Georgia Library, Athens.

Cowley, Henry Richard Charles Wellesley. Papers. British Museum, London.

Davis, Jefferson. Papers. Library of Congress, Washington, D.C.

Dayton, William L. Papers. Firestone Library, Princeton, N.J.

DeLeon, Edouard. Papers. Library of Congress, Washington, D.C.

Erlanger, Baron Emile. Papers. British National Library, London (copy in private collection of Richard I. Lester, Montgomery, Ala.).

Eustis, George. Papers. Library of Congress, Washington, D.C.

Gladstone, William E. Papers and correspondence. British National Library, London.

Gregory, William H. Family Collection. R. W. Woodruff Library, Emory Univ., Atlanta, Ga.

Hotze, Henry. Collection. Library of Congress, Washington, D.C.

———. Papers and correspondence (including complete collection of *Index*). R. W. Woodruff Library, Emory Univ., Atlanta, Ga.

Hunter, R. M. T. Papers. Hunter-Garnett Collection, Univ. of Virginia Library, Charlottesville.

Kenner, Duncan F. Papers. Library of Congress, Washington, D.C.

Lee, Robert E. Papers. Virginia Historical Society, Richmond.

Lincoln, Abraham. Papers. Library of Congress, Washington, D.C.
———. *The Lincoln Papers.* Edited by David C. Mearns. New York: Doubleday & Co., 1948.
Lindsay, William S. *Log of My Leisurely Hours.* 3 vols. London: n.p., 1877.
Mallory, Stephen Russell. Papers. Library of Congress, Washington, D.C.
Maury, Matthew F. Papers. Library of Congress, Washington, D.C.
Mason, James Murray. Papers. Library of Congress, Washington, D.C.
Moran, Benjamin. Papers. Library of Congress, Washington, D.C.
Palmerston, Lord (Henry John Temple). Papers. British Library, London.
Russell, John, First Earl. Papers. British Library, London.
Sanford, Henry S. Papers. General Sanford Memorial Library, Sanford, Fla.
Seward, William H. Papers. Univ. of Rochester Library, Rochester, N.Y. (microfilm, Middle Tennessee State Univ., Murfreesboro).
Stoeckl, Baron Edward de. Papers. Library of Congress, Washington: D.C. (microfilm, Middle Tennessee State Univ., Murfreesboro).
Toombs, Robert. Papers. Univ. of South Carolina Library, Columbia.
Trenholm, George A. Papers. Library of Congress, Washington, D.C.
Trescot, Edward A. Papers. South Carolina Archives, S.C.
Wilkes, Charles. Papers. Library of Congress, Washington, D.C.
Yancey, William Lowndes. Papers. State of Alabama Historical Archives, Montgomery.

U.S. and Confederate Government Publications and Documents

Confederate States. *Journal of the Congress of the Confederate States of America, 1861–1865.* 6 vols. Washington, D.C.: Government Printing Office, 1904–5. Reprint, New York: Kraus, 1968.
———. *The Papers of John Pickett.* Records of the Confederate States of America. Washington, D.C.: Library of Congress.
Congressional Globe. Washington, D.C.: Government Printing Office, 1862–66 (microfilm, Univ. of Tennessee at Chattanooga).
United States. Dept. of the Navy. *Official Records of the Union and Confederate Navies in the War of the Rebellion (ORN).* 30 vols. and index. Series 1, vols. 1–27; Series 2, vols. 1–3. Washington, D.C.: Government Printing Office, 1894–1927.
———. Dept. of the Army. *Official Records of the Union and Confederate Armies in the War of the Rebellion (ORA).* Washington, D.C.: Government Printing Office, 1894–1927.
———. Dept. of State. *Dispatches from United States Ministers to Great Britain, 1792–1870.* Washington, D.C.: National Archives.
———. Dept. of State. *Diplomatic Instructions of the Department of State, 1801–1906.* Washington, D.C.: National Archives.
———. Dept. of State. *Diplomatic Instructions of the Department of State, 1801–1906* (Russia). Washington, D.C.: National Archives.
———. Dept. of State. *Notes from the British Legation in the United States to the Department of State, 1791–1906.* Washington, D.C.: National Archives.
———. Dept. of State. *Notes to Foreign Legations in the United States from the Department of State, 1834–1906.* Washington, D.C.: National Archives.
———. Dept. of State. *Notes to Foreign Legations in the United States from the Department of State, 1834–1906* (France). Washington, D.C.: National Archives.

————. Dept. of State. *Papers Relating to the Foreign Affairs [Relations] of the United States, 1861–1865 (FRUS)*. 15 vols. Washington, D.C.: Government Printing Office, 1862–66. Reprint, New York: Kraus Corp., 1965.

European Public and Government Documents

France. *Expose de la Situation de l'Empire Presente au Senat et au Corps Legislatif.* 10 vols. Paris, 1861–69.

————. Ministere des Affaires Etrangeres. *Documents Diplomatiques (Livres Jaunes)*. Annees, 1861, 1862, 1863, 1866. Paris, 1861–63, 1866.

————. Ministere des Affaires Etrangeres. *Origines, Diplomatiques de la Guerre de 1870–71. Recueil de Documents Publie par le Ministere des Affaires Etrangeres.* 17 vols. Paris, 1910–28.

————. *Archives du Ministere des Affaires Etrangeres.* Correspondence Politique, Etats-Unis. 21 vols. Paris. (Copy at Hayes Library, Univ. of Tennessee, Knoxville.)

Great Britain. *British Parliamentary Papers, 1801–1899.* 1000 vols. Shannon: Irish Univ. Press, date varies by volume.

————. Foreign Office. *British and Foreign State Papers.* 116 vols. Kew, England: Public Records Office, 1812–1925.

————. Foreign Office. *British Foreign Office Dispatches* (American). Kew, England: Public Records Office, 1812–1925.

————. Parliament. *British Sessional Papers* (House of Commons and Lords). 1801–1900 (microfilm, Hayes Library, Univ. of Tennessee, Knoxville).

————. *Hansard's Parliamentary Debates*, 3d ser., 356 vols., 1830–91 (copy, University of Tennessee, Knoxville).

Edited Collections— Public and Government Documents

Bourne, Kenneth, and D. Cameron Watt, eds. *British Documents on Foreign Affairs: Reports and Papers from the Foreign Office Confidential Print.* Pt. 1, ser. C (North America), vols. 5–6, 1837–1914; *The Civil War Years, 1859–1865.* Bethesda, Md.: University Publications of America, 1986.

Case, Lynn M., ed. *French Opinion on the United States and Mexico, 1861–1867. Reports of the Procureurs Generaux.* New York, 1936. Reprint, Archon Books, 1969.

Mallory, William M., ed. *Treaties, Conventions, International Acts, Protocols, and Agreements between the United States of America and the Other Powers, 1776–1923.* 3 vols. Washington, D.C.: Government Printing Office, 1910, 1923.

Manning, William R., ed. *The Diplomatic Correspondence of the United States: Inter-American Affairs, 1831–1860.* 12 vols. Washington, D.C.: Carnegie Endowment for International Peace, 1932–39.

Matthews, James M, ed. *Public Laws of the Confederate States of America.* 1st Cong., sess. 1–4; 2d Cong., 1st sess. Richmond, Va.: R. M. Smith, 1862–64.

————. *The Statutes at Large of the Provisional Government of the Confederate States of America.* 3 vols. Richmond, Va.: R. M. Smith, 1864.

Monroe, Haskell M., Jr., et al., eds. *The Papers of Jefferson Davis.* 8 vols. Baton Rouge: Louisiana State Univ. Press, 1971–85.

Moore, Frank, ed. *The Rebellion Record.* 12 vols. New York: G. P. Putnam, 1861–66. Reprint, Arno Press, 1977.

Morley, John. *Life of William Ewart Gladstone*. 3 vols. London: Macmillan, 1903.

Richardson, James D., ed. *Compilations of Messages and Papers of the Confederacy, Including Diplomatic Correspondence, 1861–1865*. 2 vols. Nashville: U.S. Publishing Co., 1905.

———. *Compilations of Messages and Papers of Jefferson Davis and the Confederacy*. 2 vols. Nashville: U.S. Publishing Co., 1905. Reprint, New York: Chelsea House, 1966.

———. *Compilations of the Messages and Papers of the Presidents, 1789–1897*. 53d Cong., 2d sess. 10 vols. Washington, D.C.: Government Printing Office, 1907.

———. *Messages of the President of the United States to the Two Houses of Congress at the Commencement of the Second Session of the Thirty-Seventh Congress*, accompanied by Papers Relating to Foreign Affairs, 37 Cong., 2d sess. Sen. Ex. Doc. No. 1. 6 vols. Washington, D.C.: Government Printing Office.

Wallace, Sarah A., and Frances E. Gillespie, eds. *The Journal of Benjamin Moran, 1857–1865*. 2 vols. Chicago: Univ. of Chicago Press, 1948.

Yearns, Wilfred Buck, ed. *Proceedings of the Confederate Congress*. Vol. 49. Washington, D.C.: U.S. Government Printing Office.

Autobiographies, Diaries, Letters, and Memoirs

Adams, Charles F., Jr. *Charles Francis Adams 1835–1915: An Autobiography*. Boston and New York: Houghton Mifflin Co., 1916.

Bates, Edward. *The Diary of Edward Bates, 1859–1866*. Edited by Howard K. Beale. Washington, D.C.: U.S. Government Printing Office, 1933.

Bigelow, John. *Retrospections of an Active Life*. 5 vols. New York: The Baker & Taylor Co., 1909.

Bulloch, James Dunwoody. *The Secret Service of the Confederate States in Europe: Or How the Confederate Cruisers Were Equipped*. 2 vols. New York: R. Bentley & Son, 1884; Reprint, Franklin, 1972.

Campbell, John A. *Reminisces and Documents Relating to the Civil War during the Year 1865*. Baltimore: John Murray & Co., 1887.

Charles, Henry Richard, First Earl of Cowley. *Conversations with Napoleon III: A Collection of Documents Mostly Unpublished and Almost Entirely Diplomatic, Selected and Arranged with Introductions*. Edited by Victor Wellesley and Robert Sencourt. London: Longmans, Green & Co., 1934.

———. *Secrets of the Second Empire: Private Letters from the Paris Embassy during the Second Empire; Selections from the Papers of Henry Richard Charles Wellesley, First Earl of Cowley, Ambassador to Paris, 1852–1867*. Edited by F. A. Wellesley. New York: Harper, 1929.

Chase, Salmon P. *Inside Lincoln's Cabinet: The Civil War Diaries of Salmon P. Chase*. Edited by David Donald. New York and London: Longmans, Green & Co., 1954.

Davis, Jefferson. *Jefferson Davis, Constitutionalist, His Letters, Papers, and Speeches*. 10 vols. Edited by Dunbar Rowland. Jackson: Mississippi Dept. of Archives and History, 1923.

———. *Jefferson Davis: Private Letters, 1823–1889*. Edited by Hudson Strode. New York: Harcourt, Brace and World, 1966.

Davis, Varina H. *Jefferson Davis: A Memoir by His Wife*. 2 vols. New York: Bel Ford and Co., 1890.

De Bellet, Pecquet Paul. *The Diplomacy of the Confederate Cabinet of Richmond and Its Agents Abroad: Being Memorandum Notes Taken in Paris during the Rebellion of the Southern States from 1861 to 1865.* Edited by William Stanley Hoole. Tuscaloosa, Ala.: Confederate Publishers, 1963.

DeLeon, Thomas C. *Four Years in Rebel Cities: An Inside View of Life in the Southern Confederacy from Birth.* Reprint, Dayton, Ohio: Morningside Press, 1962.

Dennett, Tyler, ed. *Lincoln and the Civil War in the Diaries and Letters of John Hay.* New York: Dodd, Mead, 1939.

Evans, Thomas W. *Memoirs of Dr. Thomas W. Evans.* 2 vols. Edited by Edward R. Crane, M.D. London: Longmans, Green, 1906.

Ford, Worthington C., ed. *A Cycle of Adams Letters, 1861–1865.* 2 vols. Boston: Houghton Mifflin, 1920.

Frederick, George William. *The Life and Letters of George William Frederick, Fourth Earl of Clarendon.* 2 vols. Edited by Sir Herbert Eustace Maxwell. London: Edward Arnold, 1913.

Gladstone, William Ewart. *The Gladstone Diaries.* 9 vols. Edited by H. C. G. Matthew. Oxford: Clarendon, 1978.

Gorgas, Josiah. *The Civil War Diary of General Josiah Gorgas.* Edited by Frank E. Vandiver. Tuscaloosa: Univ. of Alabama Press, 1947.

Hughes, Archbishop John. *Complete Works of the Most Rev. John Hughes, D.D., Archbishop of New York.* 2d ed. Edited by Lawrence L. Kehoe. New York: American News, 1864.

Jenkins, T. A., ed. *The Parliamentary Diaries of Sir John Trelawny, 1858–1865.* London: Royal Historical Society, 1990.

Leader, Robert E., ed. *Life and Letters of John Arthur Roebuck.* London: Edward Arnold, 1897.

Lincoln, Abraham. *The Complete Works of Abraham Lincoln.* 12 vols. Edited by John G. Nicolay and John Hay. New York: The Lamb Publishing Co., 1894. Reprint, Lincoln Memorial Univ. Press, 1905.

———. *The Collected Works of Abraham Lincoln.* 9 vols. Edited by Roy P. Basler. New Brunswick, N.J.: Rutgers Univ. Press, 1952–55.

———. *The Life and Writings of Abraham Lincoln.* Edited by Philip Van Dorn Stern. New York: Random House, 1940.

Mason, Virginia. *The Public Life and Diplomatic Correspondence of James M. Mason: With Some Personal History by His Daughter.* 2 vols. Roanoke, Va.: Stone Printing, 1903.

Miers, Earl Schenck, ed. *John B. Jones: A Rebel War Clerk's Diary, 1866.* New York: Sagamore Press, 1958. Reprint, Baton Rouge: Louisiana State Univ. Press, 1993.

Motley, John Lothrop. *The Correspondence of John Lothrop Motley.* 2 vols. Edited by G. W. Curtis. New York: Harper Bros., 1889.

Palmer, Beverly W., ed. *The Selected Letters of Charles Sumner.* 2 vols. Boston: Northeastern Univ. Press, 1990.

Palmerston, Lord (Henry John Temple, Viscount). *Gladstone and Palmerston, Being the Correspondence of Lord Palmerston with Mr. Gladstone, 1851–1865.* Edited by Philip Guedalla. Convent Garden, England: Victor Gollancz, 1928.

Russell, Lord John. *The Later Correspondence of Lord John Russell, 1840–1878.* 2 vols. Edited by G. P. Gooch. London: Longmans, Green, 1925.

———. *Recollections and Suggestions, 1813–1873.* Boston: Roberts Brothers, 1875.

Russell, William Howard. *My Diary North and South.* Edited by Eugene H. Berwanger. Philadelphia: Temple Univ. Press, 1988.

————. *William Howard Russell's Civil War Private Diary and Letters, 1861–1862.* Edited by Martin Crawford. Athens: Univ. of Georgia Press, 1990.

Seward, Frederick William. *Reminiscences of a War-Time Statesman and Diplomat, 1830–1915.* New York: Putnam's, 1916.

————. *Seward at Washington as Senator and Secretary of State: A Memoir of His Life with Selections from His Letters, 1861–1862.* 2 vols. New York: Derby & Miller, 1891.

————. *The Works of William H. Seward: The Diplomatic History of the War for the Union.* 5 vols. Edited by George E. Baker. Boston: Houghton Mifflin, 1884.

Sherman, William T. *Memoirs of General William T. Sherman.* 2 vols. New York: D. Appleton & Co., 1875.

Stephens, Alexander Hamilton. *Memoirs: A Constitutional View of the Late War between the States: Its Causes, Character, and Results.* 2 vols. Philadelphia: National Publishing Co., 1868.

Victoria, Queen. *Regina vs. Palmerston: The Correspondence between Queen Victoria and Her Foreign and Prime Minister, 1837–1865.* Edited by Brian Connell. Garden City, N.Y.: Doubleday, 1961.

Weed, Thurlow. *Life of Thurlow Weed.* 2 vols. Edited by Harriet A. Weed and Thurlow Weed Barnes. Boston: Houghton Mifflin, 1883–84.

Welles, Gideon. *Diary of Gideon Welles, Secretary of the Navy under Lincoln and Johnson.* 3 vols. Edited by Howard K. Beale. New York: Norton, 1960.

Other Published Books

Adams, Ephraim Douglass. *Great Britain and the American Civil War.* 2 vols. New York: Russell & Russell, 1924.

Anbinder, Tyler. *Nativism and Slavery: The Northern Know Nothings and the Politics of the 1850s.* New York: Oxford Univ. Press, 1992.

Ash, Stephen V. *When the Yankees Came.* Chapel Hill and London: Univ. of North Carolina Press, 1995.

Auchampaugh, Philip G. *James Buchanan and his Cabinet on the Eve of Secession.* Boston: J. S. Canner & Co., 1926. Reprint, 1960.

Bailey, Thomas A. *A Diplomatic History of the American People.* 10th ed. New York: Prentice Hall, 1980.

Ball, Douglas B. *Financial Failure and Confederate Defeat.* Champaign: Univ. of Illinois Press, 1991.

Bancroft, Frederick. *The Life of William H. Seward.* 2 vols. New York: Harper Bros., 1900.

————. *Slave-Trading in the Old South.* Baltimore: Harper Bros., 1931.

Banning, Lance. *The Jeffersonian Persuasion: Evolution of a Party Ideology.* Ithaca, N.Y.: Cornell Univ. Press, 1978.

Barney, William L. *Battleground for the Union: The Era of the Civil War and Reconstruction, 1848–1877.* Englewood Cliffs, N.J.: Prentice-Hall, 1990.

Bateman, Fred, and Thomas Weiss. *A Deplorable Scarcity: The Failure of Industrialization in the Slave Economy.* Chapel Hill: Univ. of North Carolina Press, 1981.

Bauer, Craig A. *A Leader among Peers: The Life and Times of Duncan Farrar Kenner.* Lafayette: Center for Louisiana Studies, Univ. of Southwestern Louisiana, 1993.

Beringer, Richard E, Herman Hattaway, Archer Jones, and William N. Still Jr. *The*

Elements of Confederate Defeat: Nationalism, War Aims, and Religion. Athens: Univ. of Georgia Press, 1986.

———. *Why the South Lost the Civil War*. Athens: Univ. of Georgia Press, 1986.

Bernard, Montague. *A Historical Account of the Neutrality of Great Britain during the American Civil War*. London: Longmans, Green, 1870.

Bernath, Stuart L. *Squall Across the Atlantic: American Civil War Prize Cases and Diplomacy*. Berkeley: Univ. of California Press, 1970.

Berwanger, Eugene H. *The British Foreign Service and the American Civil War*. Lexington: Univ. Press of Kentucky, 1994.

Bigelow, John. *France and the Confederate Navy, 1862–1865*. New York: Harper, 1888. Reprint, 1968.

———. *Lest We Forget: Gladstone, Morley, and the Confederate Loan of 1863*. New York: Harper Bros., 1905.

Blake, Robert. *Disraeli*. New York and London: St. Martin's Press, 1967.

Blumenthal, Henry. *A Reappraisal of Franco-American Relations, 1830–1871*. Chapel Hill: Univ. of North Carolina Press, 1959.

———. *France and the United States: Their Diplomatic Relations, 1789–1914*. Chapel Hill: Univ. of North Carolina Press, 1970.

Bock, Carl H. *Prelude to Tragedy: The Negotiation and Breakdown of the Tripartite Convention of London, October 31, 1861*. Philadelphia: Univ. of Pennsylvania Press, 1966.

Bonham, Milledge L., Jr. *The British Consuls in the Confederacy*. New York: Longmans, Green & Co., 1911.

———. *The French Consuls in the Confederate States: Studies in Southern History and Politics*. New York: Columbia Univ. Press, 1915.

Bourne, Kenneth. *Britain and the Balance of Power in North America, 1815–1908*. London: Longmans, Green & Co., 1967.

Boykin, Edward. *Ghost Ship of the Confederacy: The Story of the Alabama and Her Captain, Raphael Semmes*. New York: Funk & Wagnalls, 1957.

———. *Sea Devil of the Confederacy: The Story of the Florida and Her Captain, John Newland Maffitt*. New York: Funk & Wagnalls, 1959.

Callahan, James M. *American Foreign Policy in Mexican Relations*. New York: Frederick Ungar, 1932.

———. *Diplomatic History of the Southern Confederacy*. Baltimore: Johns Hopkins Univ. Press, 1901. Reprint, New York: Frederick Ungar, 1964.

Campbell, Charles S. *From Revolution to Rapprochement: The United States and Great Britain, 1783–1900*. New York: John Wiley & Sons, 1974.

Campbell, Mary Emily. *The Attitude of Tennesseans Toward the Union, 1847–1861*. New York: Vantage Press, 1961.

Carman, Harry J., and Reinhard H. Luthin. *Lincoln and the Patronage*. New York: Columbia Univ. Press, 1943. Reprint, Gloucester: Peter Smith, 1964.

Carroll, Daniel B. *Henri Merciér and the American Civil War*. Princeton, N.J.: Princeton Univ. Press, 1971.

Case, Lynn M. *Diplomatic History of the Southern Confederacy*. Baltimore: Johns Hopkins Univ. Press, 1901.

———. *The Evolution of Seward's Mexican Policy*. Morgantown: Univ. of West Virginia Press, 1909.

Case, Lynn M., and Warren F. Spencer. *The United States and France: Civil War Diplomacy*. Philadelphia: Univ. of Pennsylvania Press, 1970.

Channing, Edward. *A History of the United States, The War for Southern Independence.* Vol. 6. New York: Macmillan, 1927.

Chapman, John. *The Cotton and Commerce of India Considered in Relation to the Interests of Great Britain.* London: Farrah, Straus and Cudahy, 1951.

Chesnut, Mary Boykin. *A Diary from Dixie.* Edited by Ben Ames Williams. Cambridge: Harvard Univ. Press, 1949. Reprint, 1980.

Chevalier, Michael. *France, Mexico, and the Confederate States.* Translated by William Henry Hulbert. New York, 1863.

Christy, David. *Cotton Is King: Or Slavery in the Light of the Political Economy.* Cincinnati, 1855.

Clapp, Margaret. *Forgotten First Citizen: John Bigelow.* Boston: Little, Brown, 1947.

Cleveland, Henry. *Alexander H. Stephens, in Public and Private, with Letters and Speeches, Before, During, and Since the War.* Philadelphia, 1866.

Cooper, William J., Jr. *The South and the Politics of Slavery, 1828–1856.* Baton Rouge: Louisiana State Univ. Press, 1978.

Coulter, E. Merton. *The Confederate States of America, 1861–1865.* Baton Rouge: Louisiana State Univ. Press, 1950.

Craven, Avery O. *The Coming of the Civil War.* Chicago: Univ. of Chicago Press, 1942. Reprint, 1957.

Crawford, Martin. *The Anglo-American Crisis of the Mid-Nineteenth Century: The Times and America, 1850–1862.* Athens: Univ. of Georgia Press, 1987.

Crofts, Daniel W. *Reluctant Confederates: Upper South Unionists in the Secession Crisis.* Chapel Hill: Univ. of North Carolina Press, 1989.

Crook, David P. *Diplomacy during the American Civil War.* New York: John Wiley & Sons, 1975.

———. *The North, the South, and the Powers.* New York: John Wiley & Sons, 1974.

Cullop, Charles P. *Confederate Propaganda in Europe, 1861–1865.* Coral Gables, Fla.: Univ. of Miami Press, 1969.

Cunningham, Noble E., Jr. *In Pursuit of Reason: The Life of Thomas Jefferson.* Baton Rouge: Louisiana State Univ. Press, 1987. Reprint, New York: Ballantine Books, 1988.

Current, Richard N. *Lincoln and the First Shot.* Philadelphia and New York: J. B. Lippincott Co., 1963.

———. *The Lincoln Nobody Knows.* New York: McGraw-Hill, 1958.

Daddysman, James W. *The Matamoras Trade.* Newark: Univ. of Delaware Press, 1984.

Dalzell, George W. *The Flight from the Flag.* Chapel Hill: Univ. of North Carolina Press, 1940.

Davis, Burke. *The Long Surrender.* New York: Random House, 1985.

Davis, Charles S. *Colin J. McRae: Confederate Financial Agent.* Tuscaloosa, Ala.: Confederate Publishing Co., 1961.

Davis, Jefferson. *The Rise and Fall of the Confederate Government.* 2 vols. New York: D. Appleton, 1881.

Davis, William C. *Jefferson Davis: The Man and His Hour.* New York: Harper Collins, 1991.

———. *A Government of Our Own: The Making of the Confederacy.* New York: The Free Press, 1994.

Delaney, Norman C. *John McIntosh Kell of the Raider Alabama.* Tuscaloosa: Univ. of Alabama Press, 1973.

Donald, David Herbert. *Lincoln.* New York: Simon & Schuster, 1995.

———. *Charles Sumner and the Coming of the Civil War.* New York: Alfred A. Knopf, 1961.

———. *Charles Sumner and the Rights of Man.* New York: Alfred A. Knopf, 1970.

Dowdey, Clifford. *Experiment in Rebellion.* Garden City, N.Y.: Doubleday & Co., 1946.

———. *The Land They Fought For: The Story of the South as the Confederacy, 1832–1865.* Garden City, N.Y.: Doubleday & Co., 1955.

Duberman, Martin. *Charles Francis Adams, 1807–1886.* Boston: Houghton Mifflin, 1961.

DuBose, John W. *The Life and Times of William Lowndes Yancey.* 2 vols. Reprint, New York: Peter Smith, 1942.

Dumond, Dwight L., ed. *Southern Editorials on Secession.* Gloucester, Mass.: D. Appleton & Company, 1931. Reprint, New York: Peter Smith, 1964.

Durden, Robert F. *The Gray and the Black: The Confederate Debate on Emancipation.* Baton Rouge: Louisiana State Univ. Press, 1972.

Durkin, Joseph T. *Stephen R. Mallory: Confederate Navy Chief.* Chapel Hill: Univ. of North Carolina Press, 1954.

Eaton, Clement. *A History of the Southern Confederacy.* New York: Macmillan, 1954.

———. *Jefferson Davis.* New York: The Free Press, 1977.

———. *The Mind of the Old South.* Baton Rouge: Louisiana State Univ. Press, 1964.

Ellison, Mary. *Support for Secession: Lancashire and the American Civil War.* Chicago: Univ. of Chicago Press, 1972.

Evans, Eli N. *Judah P. Benjamin, the Jewish Confederate.* New York: Free Press, 1988.

Faust, Drew Gilpin. *The Creation of Confederate Nationalism: Ideology and Identity in the Civil War South.* Baton Rouge: Louisiana State Univ. Press, 1988.

Ferris, Norman B. *Desperate Diplomacy: William H. Seward's Foreign Policy, 1861.* Knoxville: Univ. of Tennessee Press, 1976.

———. *The Trent Affair: A Diplomatic Crisis.* Knoxville: Univ. of Tennessee Press, 1977.

Filler, Louis. *The Crusade Against Slavery, 1830–1860.* New York: Harper & Brothers, 1960.

Fogel, Robert W., and Stanley L. Engerman. *Time on the Cross: The Economics of American Negro Slavery.* Boston: Little, Brown, 1974.

Foner, Eric. *Politics and Ideology in the Age of the Civil War.* New York: Oxford Univ. Press, 1980.

———. *Reconstruction: America's Unfinished Revolution (1863–1867).* New York: Harper & Row, 1988.

Ford, Lacey, Jr. *Origins of Southern Radicalism.* New York: Oxford Univ. Press, 1988.

Franklin, John Hope. *The Emancipation Proclamation.* Garden City, N.J.: Doubleday, 1963.

Freehling, Alison G. *Drift Toward Dissolution: The Virginia Slavery Debate of 1831–1832.* Baton Rouge: Louisiana State Univ. Press, 1982.

Freehling, William W. *The Road to Disunion: Secessionists at Bay, 1776–1854.* London: Oxford Univ. Press, 1990.

Fry, Joseph A. *Henry S. Sanford: Diplomacy and Business in Nineteenth-Century America.* Reno: Univ. of Nevada Press, 1982.

Gavronsky, Serge. *The French Liberal Opposition and the American Civil War.* New York: Humanities Press, 1968.

Genovese, Eugene. *Roll, Jordan, Roll: The World the Slaveholders Made.* New York: Patheon Books, 1974.

Goebel, Julius. *The Recognition Policy of the United States*. New York, 1915.

Going, Charles Buxton. *David Wilmot, Free-Soiler: A Biography of the Great Advocate of the Wilmot Proviso*. Gloucester, Mass.: D. Appleton and Company, 1924. Reprint, New York: Peter Smith, 1966.

Guedalla, Phillip, ed. *Gladstone and Palmerston, 1861–1865*. Covenant Garden, England: Victor Gollancy, 1926.

Hammond, Bray. *Banks and Politics in America from the Revolution to the Civil War*. Princeton, N.J.: Princeton Univ. Press, 1957.

Hanna, Alfred J., and Kathryn A. Hanna. *Napoleon III and Mexico: American Triumph over Monarchy*. Chapel Hill: Univ. of North Carolina Press, 1971.

Harris, Thomas L. *The Trent Affair*. Indianapolis: Bobbs-Merrill, 1896.

Henderson, William O. *The Lancashire Cotton Famine, 1861–1865*. 1934. Reprint, Augustus M. Kelley, 1969.

Hendrick, Burton J. *Lincoln's War Cabinet*. Boston: Little, Brown & Co., 1946.

———. *Statesmen of the Lost Cause: Jefferson Davis and His Cabinet*. New York: Literary Guild, 1939.

Hendrickson, Robert. *Sumter: The First Day of the Civil War*. Chelsea, Mich.: Scarborough House Publishers, 1990.

Holt, Michael F. *The Political Crisis of the 1850's*. New York: W. W. Norton & Company, 1983.

Hoole, W. S., ed. *Diplomacy of the Confederate Cabinet at Richmond and Its Agents Abroad*. Tuscaloosa: Univ. of Alabama Press, 1963.

Horner, Harland Holt. *Lincoln and Greeley*. Champaign: Univ. of Illinois Press, 1953.

Horsman, Reginald. *Race and Manifest Destiny: The Origins of American Racial Anglo-Saxonism*. Cambridge: Harvard Univ. Press, 1981.

Huse, Caleb. *The Supplies for the Confederate Army: How They Were Obtained and How Paid For, A Fragment of History*. Boston: Marvin, 1904.

Jahns, Patricia. *Matthew Fontaine Maury and Joseph Henry: Scientists of the Civil War*. New York: Hastings House, 1961.

Jenkins, Brian. *Britain and the War for the Union*. 2 vols. Montreal and London: McGill-Queen's Univ. Press, 1973.

———. *Sir William Gregory of Coole: The Biography of an Anglo-Irishman*. Gerrards Cross, Buckinghamshire: C. Smythe, 1986.

Johnson, Ludwell H., III. *Division and Reunion: America 1848–1877*. New York: John Wiley & Sons, 1978.

Jones, Howard. *Union in Peril: The Crisis over British Intervention in the Civil War*. Chapel Hill and London: Univ. of North Carolina Press, 1992.

Jones, Wilbur Devereux. *The American Problem in British Diplomacy, 1841–1861*. Athens: Univ. of Georgia Press, 1974.

———. *The Confederate Rams at Birkenhead: A Chapter in Anglo-American Relations*. Tuscaloosa, Ala.: Confederate Publishers, 1961.

Jordan, Donaldson, and Edwin J. Pratt. *Europe and the American Civil War*. Boston: Houghton Mifflin, 1931.

Kinchen, Oscar A. *Daredevils of the Confederate Army: The Story of the St. Albans Raiders*. Boston: The Christopher Publishing House, 1959.

King, Spencer B., ed. *The War-Time Journal of a Georgia Girl*. Macon, Ga.: The Ardivan Press, 1960.

King, Willard L. *Lincoln's Manager: David Davis*. Cambridge: Harvard Univ. Press, 1960.

Kirkland, Edward Chase. *The Peacemakers of 1864*. New York: Macmillan, 1927. Reprint, AMS Press, 1969.

Kissinger, Henry. *Diplomacy*. New York: Alfred Knopf, 1993.

Knapp, Charles Merrian. *New Jersey Politics during the Period of the Civil War and Reconstruction*. Geneva, N.Y.: W. F. Humphrey, 1924.

Krein, David F. *The Last Palmerston Government*. Ames: Iowa State Univ. Press, 1978.

Lauterpacht, Hersh. *Recognition in International Law*. Cambridge, England: Cambridge Univ. Press, 1947.

Lester, Richard I. *Confederate Finance and Purchasing in Great Britain*. Charlottesville: Univ. Press of Virginia, 1975.

Lonn, Ella. *Foreigners in the Confederacy*. Chapel Hill: Univ. of North Carolina Press, 1940.

McCardell, John. *The Idea of a Southern Nation: Southern Nationalists and Southern Nationalism, 1830–1860*. New York: W. W. Norton & Company, 1979.

McCash, William B. *Thomas R. R. Cobb: The Making of a Southern Nationalist*. Macon, Ga.: Mercer Univ. Press.

McElroy, Robert. *Jefferson Davis: The Unreal and the Real*. 2 vols. New York: Harper & Brothers Publishers, 1937.

McPherson, James M. *Battle Cry of Freedom: The Civil War Era*. New York: Oxford Univ. Press, 1988.

———. *Abraham Lincoln and the Second American Revolution*. New York: Oxford Univ. Press, 1991.

Meade, Robert Douthat. *Judah P. Benjamin and the American Civil War*. New York: Oxford Univ. Press, 1943.

Melton, Maurice. *The Confederate Ironclads*. New York: 1968.

Meredith, Roy. *The Storm Over Sumter*. New York: Simon & Schuster, 1957.

Merli, Frank J. *Great Britain and the Confederate Navy, 1861–1865*. Bloomington: Indiana Univ. Press, 1970.

Miers, Earl Schenck. *New Jersey and the Civil War*. Princeton, N.Y.: D. Van Nostrand Company, 1964.

Monaghan, Jay. *Diplomat in Carpet Slippers: Abraham Lincoln Deals with Foreign Affairs*. New York: Bobbs-Merrill Co., 1945.

Neiman, S. I. *Judah P. Benjamin*. Champaign: Univ. of Illinois Press, 1963.

Nevins, Allan. *The Ordeal of the Union: The War for the Union*. 8 vols. New York: Charles Scribner's Sons, 1947–72.

Nevins, Allan, and Irving Stone, eds. *Lincoln: A Contemporary Portrait*. Garden City, N.Y.: Doubleday & Company, 1962.

Newton, Thomas Wodehouse Legh. *Lord Lyons: A Record of British Diplomacy*. 2 vols. London: Edward Arnold, 1913.

Nicholas, H. G. *The United States and Britain*. Chicago: Univ. of Chicago Press, 1975.

Nicolay, John G., and John Hay. *Abraham Lincoln: A History*. 10 vols. New York: The Century Company, 1890.

Oakes, James. *Slavery and Freedom: An Interpretation of the Old South*. New York: Alfred Knopf, 1990.

———. *The Ruling Race: A History of American Slaveholders*. New York: Alfred Knopf, 1982.

Owsley, Frank L. *King Cotton Diplomacy: Foreign Relations of the Confederate States of America*. Chicago: Univ. of Chicago Press, 1936. 2d ed., 1959.

———. *States Rights in the Confederacy*. Chicago: Univ. of Chicago Press, 1925.

Paludan, Phillip Shaw. *The Presidency of Abraham Lincoln.* Lawrence: Univ. Press of Kansas, 1994.

Parish, Peter J. *The American Civil War.* New York: Holmes and Meier, 1975.

Patrick, Rembert W. *Jefferson Davis and His Cabinet.* Baton Rouge: Louisiana State Univ. Press, 1944.

Piggot, F. *The Declaration of Paris, 1856.* London, 1919.

Potter, David M. *The Impending Crisis, 1848–1861.* New York: Harper & Row, 1976.

———. *Lincoln and His Party in the Secession Crisis.* New Haven: Yale Univ. Press, 1994.

———. *The South and the Sectional Conflict.* Baton Rouge: Louisiana State Univ. Press, 1968.

Rable, George. *The Confederate Republic: a Revolution Against Politics.* Chapel Hill: Univ. of North Carolina Press, 1994.

Ramsdell, Charles W. *Behind the Lines in the Southern Confederacy.* Baton Rouge: Louisiana State Univ. Press, 1944.

Randall, James G. *Lincoln the President: Springfield to Bull Run.* 4 vols. New York: Dodd, Mead & Co., 1956.

Randall, James G., and Richard N. Current. *Lincoln the President: The Last Full Measure.* New York: Dodd, Mead, 1955.

Randall, James G., and David Donald. *The Civil War and Reconstruction.* 2d ed. Lexington, Mass.: D. C. Heath, 1969.

Raymond, Henry J. *The Life, Public Service, and State Papers of Abraham Lincoln.* New York: J. C. Derby and N. C. Miller, 1863.

Rhodes, James Ford. *History of the Civil War, 1861–1865.* 7 vols. New York: Macmillan, 1917.

Rich, Norman. *Great Power Diplomacy, 1814–1914.* New York: McGraw-Hill, 1995.

Ridley, Jasper L. *Lord Palmerston.* London: E. P. Dutton & Co., 1971.

Roark, James L. *Masters without Slaves: Southern Planters in the Civil War and Reconstruction.* New York: W. W. Norton & Co., 1977.

Roberts, W. Adolphe. *Semmes of the Alabama.* New York: Bobbs-Merrill, 1938.

Roland, Charles P. *The Confederacy: Failure of King Cotton Diplomacy.* Chicago: Univ. of Chicago Press, 1960.

St. Paul, H. *Our Home and Foreign Policy, November 1863.* Mobile: Univ. of Alabama Press, 1863.

Sandburg, Carl. *Abraham Lincoln: The War Years.* 4 vols. New York: Harcourt, Brace & Co., 1939.

Saul, Norman E. *Distant Friends: The United States and Russia, 1763–1867.* Lawrence: Univ. Press of Kansas, 1991.

Scharf, J. Thomas. *History of the Confederate States Navy from Its Organization to the Surrender of Its Last Vessel.* New York, 1887.

Scherer, James. *Cotton As a World Power.* New York: Frederick A. Stokes & Co., 1916.

Schroeder, John H. *Shaping a Maritime Empire: The Commercial and Diplomatic Role of the American Navy, 1829–1862.* Westport, Conn.: Greenwood Press, 1985.

Schurz, Carl. *Charles Sumner.* Edited by A. R. Hogue. Champaign: Univ. of Illinois Press, 1951.

Schwab, John C. *The Confederate States of America, 1861–1865: A Financial and Industrial History of the South during the Civil War.* New York: Charles Scribner's Sons, 1901.

Sears, Louis M. *John Slidell.* Durham, N.C.: Duke Univ. Press, 1925.

Sellers, Charles. *The Market Revolution.* New York: Oxford Univ. Press, 1991.

Semmes, Raphael. *Service Afloat or the Remarkable Career of the Confederate Cruisers Sumter and Alabama during the War between the States.* New York: P. J. Kennedy, 1869.

Sewell, Richard H. *A House Divided: Sectionalism and Civil War, 1848–1865.* Baltimore: Johns Hopkins Univ. Press, 1988.

Shea, William L., and Earl J. Hess. *Pea Ridge: Civil War Campaign in the West.* Chapel Hill: Univ. of North Carolina Press, 1992.

Simms, Henry H. *Life of Robert M. T. Hunter.* Westport, Conn.: Greenwood Press, 1935.

Sitterson, Joseph C. *The Secession Movement in North Carolina.* Chapel Hill: Univ. of North Carolina Press, 1939.

Smith, Ernest. *History of Confederate Treasury.* New York, 1901.

Soley, James R. *The Blockade and the Cruisers.* New York, 1883.

Spencer, Warren F. *The Confederate Navy in Europe.* Tuscaloosa: Univ. of Alabama Press, 1983.

Stampp, Kenneth M. *American in 1857: A Nation on the Brink.* New York: Oxford Univ. Press, 1990.

———. *The Imperiled Union: Essays on the Background of the Civil War.* New York: Oxford Univ. Press, 1980.

Stansky, Peter. *Gladstone: A Progress in Politics.* Boston: Little, Brown, 1979.

Stern, Philip Van Dorn. *When the Guns Roared, World Aspects of the American Civil War.* New York: Doubleday & Co., 1965.

Strode, Hudson. *Jefferson Davis: American Patriot.* New York: Harcourt, Brace & Co., 1955.

———. *Jefferson Davis: Confederate President.* New York: Harcourt, Brace & Co., 1959.

———. *Jefferson Davis: Tragic Hero.* New York: Harcourt, Brace & Co., 1964.

Summersell, Charles G. *The Cruise of C.S.S. Sumter.* Tuscaloosa, Ala.: Confederate Publishing Co., 1965.

Swanberg, W. A. *First Blood: The Story of Fort Sumter.* New York: Charles Scribner's Sons, 1957.

Taylor, Thomas E. *Running the Blockade: A Personal Narrative of Adventures, Risks, and Escapes during the American Civil War.* 2d ed. London: John Murray, 1896.

Thomas, Benjamin P. *Abraham Lincoln.* New York: Alfred A. Knopf, 1952. Reprint, New York: Barnes & Noble, 1993.

Thomas, Emory M. *The Confederacy as a Revolutionary Experience.* Englewood Cliffs, N.J.: Prentice Hall, 1971. Reprint, Columbia: Univ. of South Carolina Press, 1991.

———. *The Confederate Nation.* New York: Harper & Row, 1979.

———. *The Confederate State of Richmond: A Biography of a City.* Athens: Univ. of Georgia Press, 1971.

Thompson, Samuel B. *Confederate Purchasing Operations Abroad.* Chapel Hill: Univ. of North Carolina Press, 1935.

Todd, Richard. *Confederate Finance.* Athens: Univ. of Georgia Press, 1954.

Trevelyan, George Macaulay. *British History in the Nineteenth Century, 1782–1901.* New York: Longmans, Green & Co., 1934.

Tyler, Ronnie C. *Santiago, Vidaurri, and the Southern Confederacy.* Austin: Univ. of Texas Press, 1973.

Tyrner-Tyrnauer, A. R. *Lincoln and the Emperors.* New York: Harcourt, Brace & World, 1962.

Van Deusen, Glyndon G. *Thurlow Weed, Wizard of the Lobby.* Boston: Houghton Mifflin, 1947.

———. *William Henry Seward.* New York: Oxford Univ. Press, 1967.

Vandiver, Frank E., ed. *Confederate Blockade Running through Bermuda, 1861–1865: Letters and Cargo Manifests.* Austin: Univ. of Texas Press, 1947.

———. *Their Tattered Flags: The Epic of the Confederacy.* New York: Harper & Row, 1970.

Wagandt, Charles Lewis. *The Mighty Revolution: Negro Emancipation in Maryland, 1862–1864.* Baltimore: Johns Hopkins Univ. Press, 1964.

Walpole, Spencer. *The Life of Lord John Russell.* 2 vols. London: Longmans, Green & Co., 1889.

Warren, Gordon H. *Fountain of Discontent: The* Trent *Affair and Freedom of the Seas.* Boston: Northeastern Univ. Press, 1981.

Watts, J. *Facts of the Cotton Famine.* London, 1866.

Wells, Tom Henderson. *The Confederate Navy: A Study in Organization.* Tuscaloosa: Univ. of Alabama Press, 1971.

West, W. R. *Contemporary French Opinion of the Civil War.* Baltimore: Johns Hopkins Univ. Press, 1924.

White, Laura A. *Robert Barnwell Rhett: Father of Secession.* New York, Century Co., 1931. Reprint, Gloucester: P. Smith Publishers, 1965.

Wiley, Bell I. *Confederate Women.* Westport, Conn.: Greenwood Press, 1975.

Williams, Frances L. *Matthew Fontaine Maury: Scientist of the Sea.* New Brunswick, N.J.: Rutgers Univ. Press, 1963.

Willson, Beckles. *John Slidell and the Confederates in Paris.* New York: AMS. Press, 1932.

Winks, Robin W. *Canada and the United States: The Civil War Years.* Baltimore: Johns Hopkins Univ. Press, 1960.

Winters, John D. *The Civil War in Louisiana.* Baton Rouge: Louisiana State Univ. Press, 1963.

Wise, Stephen R. *Lifeline of the Confederacy: Blockade Running during the Civil War.* Columbia: Univ. of South Carolina Press, 1988.

Woldman, Albert A. *Lincoln and the Russians.* Cleveland and New York: The World Publishing Co., 1952.

Woodman, Harold D. *King Cotton and His Retainers: Financing and Marketing the Cotton Crop of the South, 1800–1925.* Lexington: Univ. Press of Kentucky, 1968.

Wright, Gavin. *Old South, New South: Revolution in Southern Economy Since the Civil War.* New York: Basic Books, 1986.

———. *The Political Economy of the Cotton South: Households, Markets, and Wealth in the Nineteenth Century.* New York: W. W. Norton & Co., 1978.

Yearns, Wilfred Buck. *The Confederate Congress.* Athens: Univ. of Georgia Press, 1960.

Articles, Essays, and Proceedings

Adamov, E. A., ed. "Documents Relating to Russian Policy during the American Civil War." *Journal of Modern History* 2 (1930): 603–11.

Adams, Brooks. "The Seizure of the Laird Rams." *Proceedings of the Massachusetts Historical Society* 45 (1911–12): 243–333.

Adams, Charles F., Jr. "The British Proclamation of May, 1861." *Proceedings of the Massachusetts Historical Society* 48 (Jan. 1915): 190–241.

———. "Crisis in Downing Street." *Proceedings of the Massachusetts Historical Society* (May 1914): 372–424.

————. "The Crisis of Foreign Intervention in the War of Secession, September–November, 1862." *Proceedings of the Massachusetts Historical Society* 47 (1914): 372–424.

————. "The *Trent* Affair." *Proceedings of the Massachusetts Historical Society* 46 (Nov. 1911): 49.

————. "Queen Victoria and the Civil War." Parts 1–3. *Proceedings of the Massachusetts Historical Society* 17 (1903): 439–48; 18 (1905): 123–54; 20 (1907): 453–74.

Adams, Henry. "Why Did Not England Recognize the Confederacy?" *Proceedings of the Massachusetts Historical Society* 66 (1942): 204–22.

Alvarez, David J. "The Papacy in the Diplomacy of the American Civil War." *Catholic Historical Review* 69, no. 2 (1983): 227–48.

Anderson, Stuart. "1861: Blockade vs. Closing the Confederate Ports." *Military Affairs* 41, no. 4 (1977): 190–94.

Barker, Nancy Nichols. "France, Austria, and the Mexican Venture." *French Historical Studies* 3 (1963): 224–45.

Bauer, Craig A. "The Last Effort: The Secret Mission of the Confederate Diplomat, Duncan F. Kenner." *Louisiana History* 22 (winter 1981): 67–95.

Baxter, James P. "The British Government and Neutral Rights, 1861–1865." *American Historical Review* 34 (Oct. 1928): 9–29.

————, ed. "Papers Relating to Belligerent and Neutral Rights." *American Historical Review* 34 (Oct. 1928): 77–91.

Beloff, Max. "Historical Revision No. CXVIII: Great Britain and the American Civil War." *History* 37 (Feb. 1952): 40–48.

Bernath, Stuart L. "Squall across the Atlantic: The *Peterhoff* Episode." *Journal of Southern History* 34, no. 3 (1968): 382–401.

Bernstein, S. "French Diplomacy and the American Civil War." In *Essays in Political and Intellectual History*. New York: Paine-Whitman, 1955.

Bigelow, John. "The Confederate Diplomats and Their Shirt of Nessus." *The Century Magazine,* May 1891, 113–16.

Bigelow, Poultney. "John Bigelow and Napoleon III." *New York History* 13 (1932): 154–65.

————. "John Bigelow and His Relations with William H. Seward." *Proceedings of the Ulster County Historical Society* (1932): 32–42.

Blumenthal, Henry. "Confederate Diplomacy: Popular Notions and International Realities." *Journal of Southern History* 32 (1966): 151–71.

Bourne, Kenneth. "British Preparations for War with the North, 1861–1862." *English Historical Review* 76 (Oct. 1961): 600–632.

Brady, Eugene A. "A Reconsideration of the Lancashire 'Cotton Famine.'" *Agricultural History* 37 (July 1963): 156–62.

Brauer, Kinley J. "British Mediation and the American Civil War: A Reconsideration." *Journal of Southern History* 38 (Feb. 1972): 49–64.

————. "Seward's 'Foreign War Panacea': An Interpretation." *New York History* 55 (Apr. 1974): 133–57.

————. "The Slavery Problem in the Diplomacy of the American Civil War." *Pacific Historical Review* 46 (Aug. 1977): 439–69.

Brook, Michael. "Confederate Sympathies in North-East Lancashire, 1862–1864." *Lancashire and Cheshire Antiquarian Society* 75–76 (1977): 211–17.

Callahan, James M. "Diplomatic Relations of the Confederate States with England, 1861–1865." *Annual Report of the American Historical Association (Washington)* (1898).

Carroll, Daniel B. "Lincoln and the American Minister of France." *Lincoln Herald* 70 (1968): 142–53.

Carson, Gerald. "God Bless the Russians." *Timeline* 3, no. 4 (1986): 2–17.

Claussen, M. P. "Peace Factors in Anglo-American Relations." *Mississippi Valley Historical Review* 26 (Mar. 1940): 511–22.

Cohen, V. H. "Charles Sumner and the *Trent* Affair." *Journal of Southern History* 22 (1956): 205–19.

Conrad, James L. "Sacrificed to Diplomacy." *Civil War Times Illustrated* 24, no. 6 (1985): 38–42.

Cortada, James W. "Relaciones Diplomaticas Entre los Estados Unidos y España, 1861–65" (Diplomatic Relations between the United States and Spain, 1861–65), *Cuadernos de Hist. Econ. de Cataluna* 4 (1970): 107–23.

Coulter, E. Merton. "The Effects of Secession Upon the Commerce of the Mississippi Valley." *Mississippi Valley Historical Review* 3 (1916–17): 280.

Crawford, Martin. "William Howard Russell and the Confederacy." *Journal of American Studies* 15, no. 2 (1981): 191–210.

Cresap, Bernarr. "Frank L. Owsley and King Cotton Diplomacy." *Alabama Review* 26, no. 4 (1973): 235–51.

Crook, Cauland Elaine. "Benjamin Theron and the French Designs in Texas during the Civil War." *Southwestern Historical Quarterly* 68 (1965): 432–54.

Crook, D. P. "Portents of War: English Opinion on Secession." *Journal of American Studies* 4, no. 2 (1970): 163–79.

Current, Richard N. "God and the Strongest Battalions." In *Why the North Won the Civil War*, edited by David Donald. Baton Rouge: Louisiana State Univ. Press, 1960. Reprint, New York: Collier Books, 1963.

Daddysman, Jim. "British Neutrality and the Matamoros Trade: A Step Toward Anglo-American Rapprochement." *Journal of the West Virginia Historical Association* 9, no. 1 (1985): 1–12.

Dana, Richard Henry. "The *Trent* Affair." *Proceedings of the Massachusetts Historical Society* 45 (1913): 509–22.

Delaney, Norman. "The Strange Occupation of James Bulloch: When Can You Start?" *Civil War Times Illustrated* 21, no. 1 (1982): 18–27.

Delaney, Robert W. "Matamoros, Port for Texas during the Civil War." *Southwestern Historical Quarterly* 58, no. 4 (1955): 473–87.

Diamond, William. "Imports of the Confederate Government from Europe and Mexico." *Journal of Southern History* 6, no. 4 (1940): 470–503.

DuBose, J. W. "Confederate Diplomacy." *Southern Historical Society Papers* 32 (1904).

Dudley, Thomas H. "The Inside Facts on Lincoln's Nomination." *Century Magazine,* July 1890.

Duncan, Bingham. "Franco-American Tobacco Diplomacy." *Maryland Historical Magazine* 51 (Dec. 1956): 273–301.

Dyer, Brainerd. "Thomas H. Dudley." *Civil War History* 1, no. 4 (1955): 401–13.

Ellsworth, Edward W. "America's Gideon in the 'Scepter' D Isle': The British Tour of Henry Ward Beecher." *Lincoln Herald* 73, no. 3 (1971): 138–49.

———. "Anglo-American Affairs in October of 1862." *Lincoln Herald* 66 (summer 1964): 89–96.

Farley, M. Foster. "Confederate Financier George Trenholm: 'The Manners of a Prince.'" *Civil War Times Illustrated* 21, no. 8 (1982): 18–25.

Ferris, Norman B. "Abraham Lincoln and the *Trent* Affair." *Lincoln Herald* 69 (1957): 131–35.

————. "The Prince Consort, the *Times,* and the *Trent* Affair." *Civil War History* 6 (1960): 152–56.

————. "William H. Seward and the Faith of a Nation." In *Traditions and Values: American Diplomacy, 1790–1863,* edited by Norman A. Graebner. Lanham, Md.: Univ. Press of America, 1985.

————. "Transatlantic Misconception: William H. Seward and the Declaration of Paris Negotiations of 1861." In *Rank and File: Civil War Essays in Honor of Bell I. Wiley,* edited by James I. Robertson Jr. and Richard M. McMurry. San Rafael, Ca.: Presidio Press, 1976.

Fisher, LeRoy H., and B. J. Chandler. "United States–Spanish Relations during the American Civil War." *Lincoln Herald* 75, no. 4 (1973): 134–47.

Foner, Eric. "Politics, Ideology, and the Origins of the American Civil War." In *Politics and Ideology in the Age of the Civil War.* New York: Oxford Univ. Press, 1980.

Foreman, Allan. "A Bit of Secret Service History." *The Magazine of American History* 12 (1884): 223–31.

Franks, Kenny A. "The Implementation of the Confederate Treaties with the Five Civilized Tribes: A Breakdown of Relations." *Journal of the West* (1973): 439–54.

Gaddy, David W. "Secret Communications of a Confederate Navy Agent." *Manuscripts* 30, no. 1 (1978): 49–55.

Gavronsky, Serge. "American Slavery and the French Liberals: An Interpretation of the Role of Slavery in French Politics during the Second Empire." *Journal of Negro History* 51 (1966): 36–52.

Genovese, Eugene. "The Slave South: An Interpretation." In *The Political Economy of Slavery.* New York: Pantheon, 1965.

Gentry, Judith F. "A Confederate Success in Europe: The Erlanger Loan." *Journal of Southern History* 36, no. 2 (May 1970): 157–88.

Ginzberg, Eli. "The Economics of British Neutrality during the American Civil War." *Agricultural History* 10 (Oct. 1936): 147–56.

Gipson, Lawrence H. "The Collapse of the Confederacy." *Mississippi Valley Historical Review* 4 (1917–18): 437–58.

Golder, Frank A. "The American Civil War through the Eyes of a Russian Diplomat [Baron Edouard de Stoeckl]." *American Historical Review* 26 (Apr. 1921): 454–63.

————. "The Russian Fleet and the Civil War." *American Historical Review* 20 (1915): 801–12.

Graebner, Norman. "European Intervention and the Crisis of 1862." *Journal of Illinois State Historical Society* 69 (Feb. 1976): 35–45.

————. "Northern Diplomacy and European Neutrality." In *Why the North Won the Civil War,* edited by David Donald. Baton Rouge: Louisiana State Univ. Press, 1960. Reprint, New York: Collier, 1963.

Gwin, Stanford P. "Slavery and English Polarity: The Persuasive Campaign of John Bright Against English Recognition of the Confederate States of America." *Southern Speech Communication Journal* 49, no. 4 (1984): 406–19.

Hammond, Bray. "The North's Empty Purse, 1861–1862." *American Historical Review* 67, no. 1 (1961): 1–18.

Hanna, Kathryn A. "Incidents of the Confederate Blockade." *Journal of Southern History* 11, no. 2 (1945): 253–75.

————. "The Role of the South in the French Intervention in Mexico." *Journal of Southern History* 20 (1954): 3–21.

Harrington, Fred H. "A Peace Mission of 1863." *American Historical Review* 66 (1940): 76–86.

Harrison, Royden. "British Labor and the Confederacy." *International Review of Social History* 2, no. 1 (1957): 78–105.

———. "British Labor and American Slavery." *Science and Society* 25 (Dec. 1962): 291–319.

Hatton, Roy O. "The Prince and the Confederates." *Civil War Times Illustrated* 19, no. 5 (1980): 8–13.

Heckman, Richard A. "British Press Reaction to the Emancipation Proclamation." *Lincoln Herald* 71 (winter 1969): 150–53.

Hefferman, John B. "The Blockade of the Southern Confederacy, 1861–1865." *Smithsonian Journal of History* 2, no. 4 (1967–68): 24–44.

Henderson, Conway W. "The Anglo-American Treaty of 1862 in Civil War Diplomacy." *Civil War History* 15 (winter 1969): 150–53.

Henderson, William O. "The Cotton Famine on the Continent, 1861–1865." *Economic Historical Review* 4 (1933): 195–207.

Henry, William W. "Kenner's Mission to Europe." *William and Mary Quarterly* 25 (July 1916): 9–12.

Hernon, Joseph M., Jr. "British Sympathies in the American Civil War: A Reconsideration." *Journal of Southern History* 33 (Aug. 1967): 356–67.

Higham, Robin. "When the Russians Conquered New York." *Mankind* 3, no. 8 (1972): 10–17.

Hitchcock, William S. "Southern Moderates and Secession: Senator Robert M. T. Hunter's Call for Union." *Journal of American History* 59, no. 4 (1973): 871–84.

Holt, Michael F. "James Buchanan, 1857–1861." In *Responses of the Presidents to Charges of Misconduct,* edited by C. Vann Woodward. New York: Delacorte Press, 1974.

Holt, Robert H. "Long Live the King?" *Agricultural History* 37 (July 1963): 166–69.

Hoole, W. Stanley, ed. "Notes and Documents: William L. Yancey's European Diary, March–June, 1861." *Alabama Review* 25 (Apr. 1972): 134–42.

Hunt, Gillard. "April 1908." *American Historical Review* (Oct. 1918).

Hunter, R. M. T. "The Peace Commission of 1865." *Southern Historical Society Papers* 3 (Apr. 1877): 168–76.

Jenkins, Brian. "Frank Lawley and the Confederacy." *Civil War History* 23 (June 1977): 144–60.

———. "William Gregory: Champion of the Confederacy." *History Today* 28, no. 5 (1978): 322–30.

Johnson, Ludwell H., III. "Abraham Lincoln and the Development of Presidential War-Making Powers: Prize Cases (1863) Revisited." *Civil War History* 35, no. 3 (1989): 208–24.

———. "Blockade or Trade Monopoly? John A. Dix and the Union Occupation of Norfolk." *Virginia Magazine of History and Biography* 93, no. 1 (1985): 54–78.

———. "Contraband Trade during the Last Year of the Civil War." *Mississippi Valley Historical Review* 49, no. 4 (1963): 635–52.

———. "Lincoln's Solution to the Problem of Peace Terms, 1864–1865." *Journal of Southern History* 34 (1968): 581–86.

———. "Trading with the Union: The Evolution of Confederate Policy." *Virginia Magazine of History and Biography* 78, no. 3 (1970): 308–25.

Johnson, Robert E. "Investment by Sea: The Civil War Blockade." *American Neptune* 32 (Jan. 1972): 45–57.

Jones, Robert H. "Anglo-American Relations, 1861–1865, Reconsidered." *Mid-America* 45 (Jan. 1963): 38–49.

———. "Long Live the King?" *Agricultural History* 37 (July 1963): 166–71.

Jones, Wilbur Devereux. "The British Conservatives and the American Civil War." *American Historical Review* 58 (Apr. 1953): 527–43.

Kenneth, Rick, B. L. Fuqua, and C. S. Fuqua. "Australia's Stake in America's Civil War." *Naval History* 3, no. 2 (1989): 50–54.

Kennett, Lee. "The Strange Career of the 'Stonewall.'" *United States Naval Institute Proceedings* 94 (Feb. 1968): 74–85.

Khasigian, Amos. "Economic Factors and British Neutrality, 1861–1865." *Historian* 25 (Aug. 1963): 451–65.

Kiger, J. J. "Federal Government Propaganda in Great Britain during the American Civil War." *Historical Outlook* 19 (1928): 204–9.

Kirke, Edmund. "Our Visit to Richmond." *Atlantic Monthly*, Sept. 1864.

Krause, Allen. "The Enigmatic Judah Benjamin." *Midstream* 24, no. 8 (1978): 17–20.

Krein, David F. "Russell's Decision to Detain the Laird Rams." *Civil War History* 22, no. 2 (1976): 158–63.

Kushner, Howard J. "The Russian Fleet and the American Civil War: Another View." *Historian* 34, no. 4 (1972): 633–49.

Landry, Harral E. "Slavery and the Slave Trade in Atlantic Diplomacy, 1850–1861." *Journal of Southern History* 27 (1961): 184–207.

Lankiewicz, Donald. "Journey to Asylum" *Civil War Times Illustrated* 26, no. 8 (1987): 16–21, 44–45.

Leary, William M., Jr. "*Alabama* versus *Kearsarge:* A Diplomatic View." *American Neptune* 29, no. 3 (1969): 167–73.

Lebergott, Stanley. "Through the Blockade: The Profitability and Extent of Cotton Smuggling, 1861–1865." *Journal of Economic History* 41, no. 4 (1981): 867–88.

Lee, Fitzhugh. "The Failure of the Hampton Roads Conference." *Century Magazine* 52 (July 1896): 478.

Leemhuis, Robert P. "William W. Boyce: A Leader of the Southern Peace Movement." *Proceedings of the South Carolina Historical Association* (1978): 21–30.

Leibiger, Stuart. "Lincoln's 'White Elephants': The *Trent* Affair." *Lincoln Herald* 84, no. 2 (1982): 84–92.

Lester, Richard I. "An Aspect of Confederate Finance during the American Civil War: The Erlanger Loan and the Plan of 1864." *Business History* 16, no. 2 (1974): 130–44.

———. "Confederate Fiscal and Procurement Activity in Great Britain during the Civil War." *Military Collector and History* 27, no. 4 (1975): 163–65.

———. "The Procurement of Confederate Blockade Runners and Other Vessels in Great Britain during the American Civil War." *Mariner's Mirror* 61, no. 3 (1975): 255–70.

Logan, Kevin J. "The *Bee-Hive* Newspaper and British Working Class Attitudes toward the American Civil War." *Civil War History* 22 (Dec. 1976): 337–48.

Long, John S. "Glory-Hunting off Havana: Wilkes and the *Trent* Affair." *Civil War History* 9 (June 1963): 133–44.

Lorimer, Douglas A. "The Role of Anti-Slavery Sentiment in English Reactions to the American Civil War." *Historical Journal* 19 (June 1976): 405–20.

Mallison, Sally V., and Thomas W. Mallison Jr. "A Survey of the International Law of Naval Blockade [1776–1976]." *U.S. Naval Institute Proceedings* 102, no. 2 (1976): 44–53.

Marini, A. J. "The Rams That Never Were." *Nautical Res. Journal* 20, no. 3 (1974): 129–33.

Maurer, Oscar. "'Punch' on Slavery and Civil War in America, 1841–1865." *Victorian Studies* 1 (Sept. 1957): 5–28.

Maynard, Douglas H. "The Confederacy's Super-*Alabama*." *Civil War History* 5, no. 1 (1959): 80–95.

———. "The Forbes-Aspinwall Mission." *Mississippi Valley Historical Review* 45, no. 1 (1958): 67–89.

McCormick, Richard P. "New Jersey: An Historical Overview." In *Politics in New Jersey: A Collection of Essays,* edited by Alan Rosenthal and John Blydenburgh. Newark: Rutgers Univ. Press, 1975.

McKitrick, Eric. "Party Politics and the Union and Confederate War Efforts." In *The American Party Systems: Stages of Political Development,* edited by William N. Chambers and Walter Dean Burnham. New York: Oxford Univ. Press, 1967.

McVeigh, Donald R. "Charles James Faulkner in the Civil War." *West Virginia History* 12 (Jan. 1951): 129–41.

McWhiney, Grady. "Jefferson Davis and the Art of War." *Civil War History* 21, no. 2 (1975): 101–12.

Meade, Robert D. "The Relations between Judah P. Benjamin and Jefferson Davis." *Journal of Southern History* 5 (1939): 468–78.

Melvin, Philip. "Steven Russell Mallory: Southern Naval Statesman." *Journal of Southern History* 10, no. 2 (1944): 137–60.

Melton, Maurice. "Bringing in the *Fingal*." *Civil War Times Illustrated* 11, no. 5 (1972): 16–25.

Merli, Frank J. "Crown versus Cruiser: The Curious Case of the *Alexandra*." *Civil War History* 9, no. 2 (1963): 167–77.

Merli, Frank J., and Theodore A. Wilson. "The British Cabinet and the Confederacy." *Maryland Historical Magazine* 65 (fall 1970): 239–62.

Michalek, Krzysztof. "Teoria 'King Cotton' A Polityka Zagraniczna Konfederacji W Okresie Amerykanskiej Wojny Domowe" (The King Cotton Theory and Confederate Foreign Policy during the Civil War), *Przeglad History* 72, no. 4 (1981): 683–95.

Milne, A. Taylor. "The Lyons-Seward Treaty of 1862." *American Historical Review* 38 (Apr. 1933): 511–25.

Moore, J. Preston. "Lincoln and the Escape of the Confederate Commissioner." *Illinois State Historical Journal* 57: 23–27.

Moore, Richard. "A Smuggler's Exile: S. M. Swenson Flees Texas." *East Texas Historical Journal* 25, no. 2 (1987): 23–29.

Nelson, Larry E. "Independence or Fight." *Civil War Times Illustrated* 15, no. 3 (1976): 10–14.

Oates, Stephen B. "Henry Hotze: Confederate Agent Abroad." *Historian* 27 (Feb. 1965): 131–54.

O'Connor, Thomas H. "Lincoln and the Cotton Trade." *Civil War History* 7 (1961): 20–35.

O'Daniel, Victor F. "Archbishop John Hughes-American Envoy to France, 1861." *Catholic Historical Review* 3 (1917): 336–39.

O'Rourke, Alice. "The Law Officers of the Crown and the *Trent* Affair." *Mid-America* 54, no. 3 (1972): 157–71.

Orzell, Laurence J. "A 'Favorable Interval': The Polish Insurrection in the United States and France, 1863." *Civil War History* 24, no. 4 (1978): 332–50.

Owsley, Frank L. "America and the Freedom of the Seas, 1861–65." In *Essays in Honor of William E. Dodd,* edited by Avery Craven. Chicago: Univ. of Chicago Press, 1935.

———. "Defeatism in the Confederacy." *North Carolina Historical Review* 3 (July 1926): 446–56.

Owsley, Harriet Chappell. "Henry Shelton Sanford and Federal Surveillance Abroad, 1861–1865." *Mississippi Valley Historical Review* 48, no. 2 (1961–62), 211–28.

Pelzer, John D. "'Cotton, Cotton, Everywhere!': Running the Blockade through Nassau." *Civil War Times Illustrated* 19, no. 9 (1981): 10–17.

———. "Liverpool and the American Civil War." *History Today* 40 (Mar. 1990): 46–52.

Pierce, Edward L., ed. "Letters of Richard Cobden to Charles Sumner, 1861–1865." *American Historical Review* 2 (1897): 306–19.

Plowman, Robert J. "An Untapped Source: Civil War Prize Case Files, 1861–65." *Prologue* 21, no. 3 (1989): 197–206.

Polignac, Camille A. J. M. de. "Polignac's Diary." Parts 1 and 2. *Civil War Times Illustrated* 19, no. 5 (1980): 14–18; no. 6: 34–39, 41.

Pomeroy, Earl S. "French Substitutes for American Cotton, 1861–1865." *Journal of Southern History* 9 (1943): 555–60.

Pratt, Julius W. "The British Blockade and American Precedent." *U.S. Naval Institute Proceedings* 46, no. 11 (1920): 1789–1802.

Price, Marcus W. "Masters and Pilots Who Tested the Blockade of the Confederate Ports, 1861–1865." *American Neptune* 21, no. 2 (1961): 81–106.

Reid, Robert L., ed. "William E. Gladstone's 'Insincere Neutrality' during the Civil War." *Civil War History* 15, no. 4 (1969): 293–307.

Reuter, Paul H. "United States–French Relations Regarding French Intervention in Mexico: From the Tripartite Treaty to Queretaro." *Southern Quarterly* 6, no. 4 (1968): 469–89.

Rice, Allen T. "A Famous Diplomatic Dispatch." *North American Review* 142 (1886): 402–10.

Robbins, Peggy. "Caleb Huse, Confederate Agent." *Civil War Times Illustrated* 17, no. 5 (1978): 30–40.

Roberts, William P. "James Dunwoody Bulloch and the Confederate Navy." *North Carolina Historical Review* 24, no. 3 (1947): 315–66.

Russia. E. A. Adamov, ed. "Documents Relating to Russian Policy during the American Civil War." *Journal of Modern History* 2 (1930): 603–11.

St. Clair, Sadie D. "Slavery as a Diplomatic Factor in Anglo-American Relations during the Civil War." *Journal of Negro History* 30 (July 1945): 260–75.

Sanders, Neill F. "Cotton, Lard, and Rebels: James Osborn Putnam as Lincoln's Le Havre Consul." *Lincoln Herald* 88, no. 4 (1986): 157–69.

———. "'Even the Less Important Consular Posts': The English Consulates and Lincoln's Patronage Policy." *Lincoln Herald* 85, no. 2 (1983): 61–79.

———. "Freeman Harlow Morse and the Forbes-Aspinwall Mission: An Aberration in Union Foreign Policy." *Lincoln Herald* 80, no. 1 (1978): 15–25.

———. "'When a House Is on Fire': The English Consulates and Lincoln's Patronage Policy." *Lincoln Herald* 83, no. 4 (1981): 579–91.

Scherer, Paul H. "Partner or Puppet? Lord John Russell at the Foreign Office, 1859–1862." *Albion* 19 (fall 1987): 347–71.

Schmidt, Louis B. "The Influence of Wheat and Cotton on Anglo-American Relations during the Civil War." *Iowa Journal of History and Politics* 16 (July 1918): 400–439.

Schoonover, Thomas. "El Algodon Mexicano y la Guerra Civil Norteamericana" (Mexican Cotton and the U.S. Civil War). *Hist. Mexicana* 23, no. 91 (1974): 483–506.
———. "Mexican Cotton and the American Civil War." *Americas* 30, no. 4 (1974): 429–47.
Sears, Louis M. "A Confederate Diplomat at the Court of Napoleon III." *American Historical Review* 26, no. 2 (Jan. 1921): 255–81.
———, ed. "*The London Times*' American Correspondent in 1861: Unpublished Letters of W. H. Russell." *Historical Outlook* 16 (1925): 251–57.
Silverman, Jason H. "Confederate Ambitions for the Southwest: A New Perspective." *Red River Valley Historical Review* 4, no. 1 (1979): 62–71.
Smith, Geoffrey S. "Charles Wilkes and the Growth of American Naval Diplomacy." In *Makers of American Diplomacy from Benjamin Franklin to Henry Kissinger* (vol. 1), edited by Frank J. Merli and Theodore A. Wilson. New York: Charles Scribner's Sons, 1974.
Somerville, Mollie. "The Confederacy's Special Commissioner to Great Britain." *Virginia Record* 90 (Sept. 1968): 24–29.
Sowle, Patrick. "A Reappraisal of Seward's Memorandum of April 1, 1861 to Lincoln." *Journal of Southern History* 33 (1967): 234–39.
Spencer, Warren F. "French Tobacco in Richmond." *Virginia Magazine of History and Biography* 7 (1963): 187–92.
———. "The Jewett-Greeley Affair: A Private Scheme for French Mediation in the American Civil War." *New York History* 51 (Apr. 1970): 238–68.
Stock, Leo F. "American Consuls to the Papal States." *Catholic Historical Review* 9 (1929): 233–51.
———. "Catholic Participation in the Diplomacy of the Southern Confederacy." *Catholic Historical Review* 16 (1930): 1–18.
Strong, Edwin, Thomas Buckley, and Annetta St. Clair. "The Odyssey of the *C.S.S. Stonewall*." *Civil War History* 30, no. 4 (1984): 306–23.
Thomas, Mary Elizabeth. "The *C.S.S. Tallahassee:* A Factor in Anglo-American Relations, 1864–1866." *Civil War History* 21, no. 2 (1975): 148–59.
Tissier, Andre. "Ces Couples Qui Traversent L'Histoire" (These Couples Who Traverse History), *Ecrits de Paris* 391 (1979): 83–88.
Trescot, Edward A. "The Confederacy and the Declaration of Paris." *American Historical Review* 23 (July 18, 1918): 826–35.
Venable, Austin L. "The Public Career of William Lowndes Yancey." *Alabama Review* 16 (1963): 200–12.
Warren, Gordon H. "The King Cotton Theory." In *Encyclopedia of American Foreign Policy,* edited by Alexander DeConde. New York: Charles Scribner's Sons, 1978.
Washington, L. Q. "The Confederate State Department." *The Independent,* Sept. 1901.
Weeks, William. "The Directions of Early American Foreign Relations." *Diplomatic History* (1993).
Welborn, Robert H. "The British Consulate in Georgia, 1824–1981." *Proceedings and Papers of the Georgia Association of History* (1982): 105–11.
Welles, Gideon. "The Capture and Release of Mason and Slidell." *Galaxy* 15 (1873): 640–51.
Wheeler-Bennett, Sir John. "The *Trent* Affair: How the Prince Consort Saved the United States." *History Today* 11 (1961): 805–16.
Whitridge, Arnold. "British Liberals and the American Civil War." *History Today* 12 (Oct. 1962): 688–95.

———. "Jefferson Davis and the Collapse of the Confederacy." *History Today* 11 (1961): 79–89.

Whittlesey, W. L. "William Dayton, 1825, Senator, Presidential Candidate, Civil War Minister to France, A Forgotten Princetonian Who Served His Country Well." *Princeton Alumni Weekly* 30 (May 9, 1930): 797.

Wilk, Richard. "United States–Belize Relations in a Time of Tension: 1861–62." *Belizean Studies* 17, no. 2 (1989): 16–22.

Willis, Virginia Bullock. "James Dunwoody Bulloch." *Sewanee Review* 34, no. 4 (1926): 386–401.

Woodworth, Celia. "The Confederate Raider *Shenandoah* at Melbourne." *U.S. Naval Institute Proceedings* 99, no. 6 (1973): 66–75.

Wright, D. G. "Bradford and the American Civil War." *Journal of British Studies* 8 (May 1969): 69–85.

Wright, Gordon. "Economic Conditions in the Confederacy as Seen by the French Consuls." *Journal of Southern History* 7 (May 1941): 195–214.

Zingg, Paul J. "John Archibald Campbell and the Hampton Roads Conference— Quixote Diplomacy, 1865." *Alabama Historical Quarterly* (spring 1974): 27.

Zorn, Roman J. "John Bright and the British Attitude to the American Civil War." *Mid-American* 38 (July 1956): 131–45.

Dissertations, Theses, and Unpublished Manuscripts

Ballard, Michael B. "A Long Shadow: Jefferson Davis and the Final Days of the Confederacy." Ph.D. diss., Mississippi State Univ., 1983.

Bauer, Craig A. "Life and Times of Duncan Farrar Kenner." Ph.D. diss., Univ. of Southern Mississippi, 1989.

Blume, Kenneth J. "The Mid-Atlantic Arena: The United States, the Confederacy, and the British West Indies, 1861–1865." Ph.D. diss., State Univ. of New York at Binghamton, 1984.

Brumgardt, John R. "Alexander H. Stephens and the Peace Issue in the Confederacy, 1863–1865." Ph.D. diss., Univ. of California (Riverside), 1974.

Bugg, James L., Jr. "The Political Career of James Murray Mason: The Legislative Phase." Ph.D. diss., Univ. of Virginia, 1950.

Clines, Virginia T. "The Role of Charles Francis Adams as American Minister of Great Britain during the Civil War." Ph.D. diss., St. John's Univ., 1964.

Cullop, Charles P. "Confederate Propaganda in Europe, 1861–1865." Ph.D. diss., Univ. of Virginia, 1962.

Edwards, Frank T. "The United States Consular Service in the Bahamas during the American Civil War: A Study of Its Function within a Naval and Diplomatic Context." Ph.D. diss., The Catholic Univ. of America, 1968.

Escott, Paul D. "Jefferson Davis and the Failure of Confederate Nationalism." Ph.D. diss., Duke Univ., 1974.

Evans, Elliot A. P. "Napoleon III and the American Civil War." Ph.D. diss., Stanford Univ., 1940.

Fenner, Judith. "Confederate Finances Abroad." Ph.D. diss., Rice Univ., 1969.

Ferris, Norman B. "Tempestuous Mission, 1861–1862, the Early Diplomatic Career of Charles Francis Adams." Ph.D. diss., Emory Univ., 1962.

Gallas, Stanley. "Lord Lyons and the Civil War, 1859–1864: A British Perspective."
    Ph.D. diss., Univ. of Illinois at Chicago, 1982.
Graf, LeRoy P. "The Economic History of the Lower Rio Grande Valley, 1820–1875."
    Ph.D. diss., Harvard Univ., 1972.
Husley, Fabian Val. "Napoleon III and the Confederacy: A Reappraisal." Ph.D. diss.,
    Mississippi State Univ., 1970.
Maynard, Douglas H. "Thomas H. Dudley and Union Efforts to Thwart Confederate
    Activities in Great Britain." Ph.D. diss., Univ. of California (Los Angeles), 1951.
Merli, Frank J. "Great Britain and the Confederate Navy, 1861–1865." Ph.D. diss.,
    Indiana Univ., 1964.
———. "The American Way with Blockades: Reflections on the Union Blockade of
    the South." Paper delivered before the Tenth Naval History Symposium, U.S.
    Naval Academy, Annapolis, Md., Sept. 1991.
Muldowny, John. "The Administration of Jefferson Davis as Secretary of War." Ph.D.
    diss., Yale Univ., 1959.
O'Rourke, Mary M. "The Diplomacy of William H. Seward during the Civil War: His
    Policies as Related to International Law." Ph.D. diss., Univ. of California, Berke-
    ley, 1963.
Raney, William F. "The Diplomatic and Military Activities of Canada, 1861–1865, as
    Affected by the American Civil War." Ph.D. diss., Univ. of Wisconsin (Madison),
    1919.
Sanders, Neill Fred. "Lincoln's Consuls in the British Isles, 1861–1865." Ph.D. diss.,
    Univ. of Missouri, 1971.
Sanders, Phyllis M. "Jefferson Davis: Reactionary Rebel, 1808–1861." Ph.D. diss.,
    Univ. of California (Los Angeles), 1976.
Smith, Van M., Jr. "British Business Relations with the Confederacy, 1861–1865."
    Ph.D. diss., The Univ. of Texas at Austin, 1949.
Spencer, Warren F. "Edouard Drouyn de Lhuys and the Foreign Policy of the Second
    French Empire." Ph.D. diss., Univ. of Pennsylvania, 1955.
Todd, H. H. "The Building of the Confederate States Navy in Europe." Ph.D. diss.,
    Vanderbilt Univ., 1941.
Wise, Stephen R. "Lifeline of the Confederacy: Blockade Running during the Ameri-
    can Civil War." Ph.D. diss., Univ. of South Carolina, 1983.
Young, Robert W. "Jefferson Davis and Confederate Foreign Policy." M.A. thesis,
    Univ. of Maryland, 1987.

Newspapers and Periodicals

Atlanta Southern Confederacy.
Charleston Mercury.
The *Constitutionnel.*
DeBow's Review.
The *Index.*
London *Economist.*
London *Gazette.*
London *Times.*
Lynchburg Virginian.
The *Moniteur.*
Montgomery Advertiser.
Morning Herald.
Morning Star.

National Intelligencia.
New York Herald.
New York Times.
New York Tribune.
Punch.
Raleigh Standard.
Richmond Dispatch.
Richmond Inquirer.
Richmond Whig.
St. Louis Democrat.
Southern Confederacy.
Toronto Leader.

Index

The Burden of Confederate Diplomacy was designed and typeset on a Macintosh computer system using PageMaker software. The text and titles are set in Galliard. This book was designed and composed by Kimberly Scarbrough and manufactured by Thomson-Shore, Inc. The recycled paper used in this book is designed for an effective life of at least three hundred years.